A Way Beyond Religion

To Our Inner Spirit

By

Raja Bhat, MD

authorHOUSE™

1663 LIBERTY DRIVE, SUITE 200
BLOOMINGTON, INDIANA 47403
(800) 839-8640
WWW.AUTHORHOUSE.COM

First published by AuthorHouse 09/15/04

ISBN: 1-4184-6057-5 (e)
ISBN: 1-4184-3470-1 (sc)
ISBN: 1-4184-3469-8 (dj)

Library of Congress Control Number: 2004105291

Printed in the United States of America
Bloomington, Indiana

This book is printed on acid-free paper.

TABLE OF CONTENTS

ACKNOWLEDGMENTS

My family has been very patient with me during the countless hours I have been at the computer writing, and for that I am infinitely grateful. My wife Vidya hardly ever reads books on religion, and yet she is so naturally spiritual that she has been a source of inspiration; she is vibrant with goddess-like beauty and energy and is a yogi without ever having tried to be one! She just lives in the moment the way an accomplished Zen practitioner does, yet makes no pretence of practicing anything.

However, goddess energy can be just a little exasperating at times; it is quite a challenge to maintain composure and not get upset while married and living the life of a *grihastha,* a householder. It is probably much easier to be a *sādhu,* an ascetic, perhaps living in the serene beauty of the Himalayas, *alone*; who knows, perhaps some of those "sages" just could not cope with being householders! Still, marriage is a bed of roses, and it is the thorns which are the true test of one's state of spiritual achievement. It is easy to break down in anger, but it takes great strength and inner wisdom to forgive. Recovering from anger in seconds or minutes rather than in hours or days is crucial to health and spirituality, and is perhaps an excellent index of one's level of spiritual achievement. Sometimes I've failed the test, only to rise to the challenge again…and again, until I achieve near-perfection. I doubt I'll get perfect, but then many great sages of the past weren't perfect at controlling anger, either!

I am very appreciative of the time and effort made by Marjorie Megivern proof-reading the text. Timothy Freke, a most prolific writer of books on spirituality and religion, whose work I admire enormously, most graciously agreed to review the manuscript. It was with delight that I read his email after he went through the book, in which he said: "Raja, I love your book; in fact, once I got started, I could not put it down!" My work is not even a fraction as scholarly as his, and I have learned much from his books, particularly *The Jesus Mysteries* and *Jesus and the Lost Goddess* among others. To have him say that I have written something worth putting into print is truly heartening.

Great care has been taken with copyright material taken from books and other sources, and proper credit has been given, limiting quotations as much as possible to what is generally considered to be fair use. I have used several excerpts from *The Jesus Mysteries* by Timothy Freke and

Peter Gandy, and permission has been obtained from Random House. Extracts from other books have been limited to one or two paragraphs, and giving proper credit to the sources. I have used five passages from the book *The Buddha His Life Retold* by Robert Allen Mitchell to acknowledge the beauty of the Buddha's words, but permission could not be obtained, as it is out of print, and the publisher no longer has contact with the estate of the late author. It is of interest that the manuscript of that book was found in the author's attic after his death; I encourage the reader to find and read a used copy of this excellent book if possible. I also acknowledge the use of a few paragraphs from *The Christ Conspiracy* by Acharya S., which according to the book allows free use of quotations without permission. In any case, I have kept all quotations to a minimum. I sincerely believe that giving due credit and respect to the original text will enhance the value of those books by bringing attention to them. The more people take from books, the more their value is enhanced; in this way, books are unique treasures, never to be exhausted.

PREFACE

When I was at a restaurant one day, I found my waiter to be a somewhat unpleasant fellow; curt though not outright rude. And I thought to myself: if only the man would correct his manner, he would not only become very successful in what he did, but would make the world around him a much more pleasant place. His religion was totally irrelevant to me, but his demeanor was. Whatever his religion, spiritually he was in a shoddy state: our demeanor is controlled much more by our spiritual state rather than our religious one. There is indeed a big difference between the two. In every walk of life we meet people who claim something, but reveal the opposite in their actions. They claim to be very religious, yet they make us uneasy. Therefore, it is the spirituality in us that must be understood, and improved upon, and not our religious conviction. Whether we are waiters or executives, we have great impact on those around us. Our spiritual state of development has great impact on our manner, behavior, and attitude; our belief system is not anywhere as likely to have an impact; indeed, it may be of a negative nature.

This book will explore the difference between the two, and explore a simple method of improving our spirituality, regardless of our religion. The book will also reveal the inadequacies of many religions as regards practicing a way of spirituality that could be used by anyone, whatever their beliefs. The book will hopefully be a source of inspiration for those of us who seek a simple, yet effective way of being, synthesizing wisdom from various religions and wisdom paths, particularly from the mystics within them. There have been attempts to tear down each other's religions, but and not enough done to bring them together. You will find in these pages, an attempt to extract the best from the major religions. Early in my spiritual path, I was told by many that one cannot and should not mix practices from different religions, but I have found that it is possible to extract pieces of wisdom from different spiritual traditions and blend them into one practice. It is neither my interest nor my purpose to do a scholarly review of different religions, as I am not much of a scholar. Indeed, most scholarly books avoid comparing religious and spiritual traditions. The book is going to find inadequacies in virtually all of the established religions. It is my prayer that I offend no one in this work; I beg forgiveness if any part of it does. But I am tired of the killing, the pain, and the hate that has resulted from people trying to make false claims about their religions, which very often their founder-teachers did not make.

It is easy to acquire approval from people who profess a certain religious faith; you simple claim to accept their religion and you have become approved; indeed, you have become "saved." At which time you have become "lost" in the eyes of a competing religious tradition. However, it takes what could be called "persistent spiritual awakening" to be approved by humanity in general. The characteristics and behavior of a person who will likely be universally accepted involve friendliness, warmth, truth, compassion, kindness, equanimity, helpfulness, and again, friendliness. What about love, you say? Love radiates outward with these characteristics I have just mentioned. Love is a primordial state beyond definition. In the great spiritual and mystical traditions of the world that I have come to know and appreciate, the ability to abandon hostility and radiate friendliness seems to rank the highest.

This quest has taken over thirty years. It has been a quest for the ultimate truth. When the truth exploded from within me, I realized that the answers had already been there within me, echoed in various scriptures, some dating back thousands of years. Yet these are revelations that have been disputed and battled over, for many millennia. There are scriptures that seem to please some and accepted as holy truth, but not by others. One person's religion is another's heresy. There are answers that seem adequate for a while and then no longer fit our overall scheme of things. Above all, this is a quest for one way of thinking and being that every human being can find acceptable, indeed desirable. Needless to say, founders of religions have tried to do just that. But even the best of teachings get either misinterpreted or corrupted, and people have a way of making deities out of their own teachers, and demons out of the teachers of others.

In India, a spiritual teacher is called a guru, someone divinely inspired and able to radiate the inner light, though the definition has broadened to include learned persons who teach various arts, not just religious ideas. The greatest gurus in history have clearly stated their limitations, and encouraged students to move on when they have learned all that the guru could teach. But the human ego is such that some gurus like to claim that they have all the answers. It is up to the student to beware of such claims and ponder over everything that has been taught to see if the teaching makes sense. A noteworthy aspect of Zen is that a student is taught to carefully observe a teacher before accepting the teacher. One of the themes of this book is that each of us is endowed with an inner guru who can teach us all that we need to know; it is just a matter of learning the right technique to be able to listen. The Buddha said, as quoted from the book *The Buddha-His Life Retold* by Robert Allen Mitchell: "A being, student, is the master of his destiny. Oneself is lord of oneself-who else could be the lord? By oneself is the evil done, by oneself one suffers. By oneself is the evil left undone, by oneself is one purified. The pure and impure stand and fall by themselves: no one can purify another."

To change or eliminate ideas and teachings that we grow up with is the most difficult. We humans are much more conditioned by our upbringing than we realize. Beliefs and attitudes become deeply ingrained into our consciousness. It must be so easy for someone who has no need to question the teachings they grew up with, as they have no burden to bear. Children are so blessed, until they grow up and become caught up in ideology and hold up ideological flags. They must then suffer through the tribulations of the learning process. There is much that I have learned, but there is much to be learned yet. On the other hand, the way toward spirituality is the process of *unlearning.*

This book is meant to be a kind of legacy, something to leave for my family and friends, to help save them many years of searching for answers, or at least some insight that I have obtained after all these years of searching. I do hope and trust they will treasure what I have written. Yet, I advise my children to question what I have told them or taught them. They must rediscover the truth for themselves; such a discovery is not only possible, it would be the greatest achievement of a lifetime. In this sense the teachings of Buddhism and Gnostic Christianity, as well as the mystical traditions in Hinduism and Taoism are very helpful, telling us to discover the truth for ourselves, *within ourselves.* Otherwise, trying to combine wisdom from different religions is rather like taking pieces from different jigsaw puzzles and trying to fit them in together!

After reading this book, dear reader, tear it to shreds, at least in your mind. Neither this book, nor any "holy" book, has the ultimate answer. Deep in your consciousness, in your center, are all the answers. Revelation will frequently flow forth, as have my poems; from where, I do not know…well, actually I do, and perhaps you'll find it hiding in the book! All I know is that each and every one of us is a veritable wellspring of knowledge, and joy. I have found the truth. And the truth, dear reader, is that the truth is in you, around you, and *is* you. You may wonder what I mean by stating that the truth is you. Over the course of reading this book, you will find out that we search everywhere, and wind up coming back in peace to our own inner selves, where all the answers were to begin with, waiting to be discovered. The truth is that you are a prophet, a son of God, an avatär (a manifestation of God), and the embodiment of truth. If you have personally discovered this truth, then you have no need for the rest of this book!

I have realized that it would be quite egotistical on my part to state that "I" wrote this book. Well, in a way, yes, I wrote this book. But the process of exploration that has led to this book has also revealed that each one of us needs to question ourselves as to who is the "I" that has done what it has done. This is the teaching of one of the greatest sages who lived in India in the recent past, Ramana Maharshi. I might say that it is my mind that directed the writing of this book. Ideas obtained from countless authors and teachers have been invaluable. But upon deeper exploration, I have found that my mind is really very vast, much more so than I had ever realized, and the same is true of your mind as well. Sometimes ideas pour out from this inner Mind-with-a-capital-M, particularly in the early hours of the morning. In India this time of day is called Brahma Mühürtha, or the time of/for God. It is difficult to fathom the depths of this inner greater Mind. This Great Mind is within us all. Which must make us realize one thing: our minds are like overlapping spheres, in a space full of such spheres. There are many occasions in which I come up with an idea, for instance the idea that our very beings are just like waves of an ocean of a Greater Being, and then upon reading, I find that many authors have used this as an analogy as well. Wherever I have used someone's idea or ideas, I have most certainly given credit. However, this phenomenon, call it telepathy, psychic connection or what you will, is very real. Explorers once discovered that monkeys on an island had learned to wash fruit in water before eating it, and soon after, monkeys on a neighboring island discovered the same thing themselves. Cultures across the globe have discovered similar values, traditions and myths, independent of each other. Have you not been in a group of people, come up with an idea, and within minutes, someone stands up and says just what you were about to say?

You can read, in a lifetime,
A thousand books;
It takes a thousand lifetimes,
To write just one.

By "a thousand lifetimes," I mean that it takes collective wisdom of numerous people to collectively come up with ideas that work, and are tested by time. Perhaps indeed our minds, in the process of evolving over several lifetimes, progressively achieves deeper and deeper levels of understanding, until it achieves true gnosis, or Jnäna as it is called in the Hindu tradition.

What is just as fascinating, is the concept that, given the same wells of paint, and the same general theme, a hundred different artists will create their own vision on canvas, each so very different. The "exposition of the truth" over the thousands of years of known human civilization, has been the same. Rather than enjoy all these various expositions, or revelations, we have, as groups of people, clung to them and claimed that each one is the ultimate truth. The ultimate truth has never been adequately expressed by the human mind. As Lao-Tzu said in so sublime a manner twenty five hundred years ago in his book *Tao Te Ching*, (translated by Jonathan Star): "A way that can be walked is not The Way. A name that can be named is not The Name. Tao is both named and nameless. As nameless, it is the origin of all things. As named, it is the mother of all things. A mind free of thought, merged within itself, beholds the essence of Tao. A mind filled with thought, identified with its own perceptions, beholds the mere forms of the world." Lao-Tzu called the Way the Tao. He said: "for lack of a better name, I call it the Tao." One of the end results of the inner search, as I see it, is the understanding that people are capable of an infinite play of ideas, and concepts, "revelations" and such. Mystic understanding is one, but stating it in words is something altogether a different story; stories which are the essence of myth.

So let us stop naming that which cannot be named, but let us find ways to become "aware" of That which has no name. Guru Nanak, the founder of the Sikh religion, must have had this insight when he stated that Sat Näm, or the "True Name," his phrase for God, is the only truth. However, even the words of the greatest mystics are like the expressions of the artists on canvas that I mention above. Even their words only point to the truth. Even the phrase "True Name" is just a phrase: in many religions, God is expressed by many names, and "True Name" is yet another!

Besides, are there "false names" for God? I think not. We can only find the truth within ourselves, all around ourselves. We float in it, yet desperately swim to what we think is a distant shore of safety, when all along we really have no need to swim to a goal, we are already in it, the ultimate haven of safety. The best part is to just paddle along and stop by at one shore after another!

There are several poems I have written that seem to fit in nicely in some sections, which turned out to be a delightful merger. The appearance of poetry within the mind is one of the most fascinating things I have ever experienced. The words and concepts seem to materialize out of nowhere, and sometimes a whole poem appears and when written, seems not to need a single correction! One is reminded of the music of Mozart, which was often written down without a single correction or modification. But having discovered the incredible depth of human consciousness in meditation, I find this not to be surprising. While paddling along a waterway one day, this poem came to my mind, a poem that expresses the utter simplicity yet boundless joy of obtaining spiritual insight:

Blessed indeed is the state of being,
A state of such utter simplicity,
Of innocent play, laughter, and lightness.
It is to take a million volumes of wisdom
And roll them all into one,
Then allow that one to disperse, vaporize,
Across all barriers that the mind creates.

A state so vivid, heartfelt and joyful,
Yet near impossible to describe.
Never was such wisdom, yet utterly absurd.
Call it the knowledge of no-mind, but best
Call it not anything at all.
Once found, all else is play.

Hold up a fistful of sand on the beach,
Feel and caress it, play with it, then throw it away,
For whether in the hand or on the dune,
The sand and you are one;
Your laughter and the sounds of the surf
Are but one symphony of the ocean.

Written April 1998

Regarding pronunciation, I have chosen the following:
ä is pronounced as in 'father.' ā is pronounced as in ate.
ĕ is pronounced with an 'ay' sound as in hay.
ē is pronounced as in easy
ü is pronounced as in book   ũ is pronounced as in fool
u is pronounced as in mud
ĭ is pronounced as in sin   ī is pronounced as in pie
î is pronounced as in sleet
t is pronounced with a 'th' sound is in thin.
ś is pronounced 'sh' as in shame.

The consonant d is pronounced in Sanskrit in a different way than in the west, with a sound as in the word thus or there. There is also a d pronounced with a retroflexed position of the tongue.

CHAPTER ONE:
THE SOURCE OF RELIGIOUS CONFLICTS

Our religions are as carousel horses
That we children of God ride on,
On the carousel of the universe.
Dancing, prancing, we ride in joy,
Each on his or her own steed,
We feel uplifted, invincible, we fly.

Let us share the joy of others,
Also on their horses, also in rapture.
For we are all on the same carousel.
Painted, pretty, and proud,
Is each of our horses,
Gilded in gold, plumed in color.

Let us enjoy our carousel forever,
And never ride the pretty horses
Into a battlefield of hate and intolerance,
Or the carousel will stop,
The music silenced, and the children will
Play no more.

Poem: Carousel Horses
Raja Bhat, May 21, 1994

Dear reader, I don't know what your religion is. I respect whatever it is, but what I really respect and care about, is that you are a human being, just like me. Any differences are created in our minds. The divine truth is that we are both human, and subject to the same divine laws. There really are not different laws for people of different religions. If there seems to be, that is entirely man-made. The truth is one. People speak, for instance, of "Buddha-Dharma," or the "truth of the Buddha." But there is no separate truth for Buddhists as compared to others; true Buddhas would call it a dharma or set of laws governing all people. For instance, the Buddha once said: "In this world, hate never yet dispelled hate. This is the law, ancient and eternal." I am certain that this statement would be accepted by all as a "law" applicable to all people. My purpose is to help you discover real freedom, something taught by mystics time and time again. That real freedom is to go above and beyond the religion that you have been taught or brought up in. There is no need to abandon it; there is a way to enjoy the trimmings of your faith without the trappings: that way is to transcend religion. You must rise above it to know that there are others who have the same spells of happiness or sadness that you have, the same hopes and aspirations, the same fears; they are people of different religions. And they are all human like you. Consider them your equals and you will have started transcending your own religion, and yet be within it. Ecumenism is the shallow and limited process of trying to agree, whereas with transcendence you will find you really do not disagree!

The Tao Te Ching says: "The great Way is easy, yet people prefer the side paths." The side paths are—religions. The followers of each religion consider their scripture to be uniquely revealed by God. The fact is, religions are collections of thought, belief and practice devised by man and attributed to God. This includes the major religions of the world, as well as numerous "breakaway" religions whose founders also claimed to have obtained divine revelation. As Joseph Campbell has shown throughout his life and career, virtually all religions have arisen from myth.

One wonders how the one God of the Universe could reveal so many varying doctrines, often in severe conflict with others. The answer to me is fairly simple. When you ignite various materials, each material displays a flame that is unique. Fire is the same, but it manifests so many different ways with so many different materials. In the same way, when divinely inspired, people have the incredible ability to come forth with different forms of "revelation." Very often, the mystic who conceives these ideas create a myth with a god-like being created to express those ideas; after all, if you say that "God said so" people are likely to believe it. Such revelation is usually very poetic, very deep, expressive and profound; over many years, a great many people accept such "revelation", and a religion is born. Using the analogy above, the "revelation" is often reflective of the culture existing among the people and the personal views and attitudes of the sage who reveals or expresses it. Myth starts with a search for meaning, and then comes up with answers which suit the mind and seem to explain the nature of the world around. Myth, from which religion arises, is conditioned by culture. Myth tries to solve the unsolvable, tries to explore what cannot be explored, and seemingly explains what cannot be explained.

I submit, therefore, that there never has been what can be said to be "exclusive, pure, absolute and infallible" revelation that is the *entire truth,* in any one religion or system of thought. Pure and absolute truth, when translated into words, by humans, for humans, often gets "colored," as colorless light is changed by colored glass, by the personality of the sage, his or her attitudes, and above all, the need and relevance for that particular revelation in space and time.

The origin of religions that started within the past two thousand years, particularly Christianity and Islam, is attributed to what the early followers regarded as "the word of God" as revealed to their founders. Indeed, Judaism is founded upon what "God spoke and revealed" to its prophets. Therefore we have multiple religions each claiming that God spoke to their founders. Yet the "word" is dramatically different in each. So who are we to believe, and whose "revelation" is to be considered *the* Word? The answer, in my view, is that no so-called revelation to date was, or perhaps ever in the future will be, the "actual words of God." It is all inspired prose and poetry. God is an infinite power dwelling equally within each one of us, whether a "prophet" or an "ordinary" person. Each one of us is equally capable of "revelation." When inspired, countless people have come up with incredible mystical understanding which has created the most beautiful poems and prose.

Caesar E. Farah, in his book *Islam,* states that Islam considers the Qur'an to be revealed by none other than God, whereas poetry and other inspired literature is that inspired by and revealed by Jinns, or Spirits. This is a very devout and reverent Islamic attitude, no doubt; but one that emphasizes the conflict between Islam and the rest of the world. This is the way I see it:

Never in the history of humanity,
Has God spoken even once;
Rather every word from every human,
Is in truth, yet another word of God.

God resides in each one of us, and therefore every one of these inspired pieces of literature is, in a way, a "word of God." And yet none of them are actual "words of God." Perhaps someday God will decide to address

3

THE SOURCE OF RELIGIOUS CONFLICTS

all of humanity in one voice, at one instant, but in hundreds of thousands of years of human existence this has not happened; it likely never will, since each one of us is equally endowed with divine energy. It will always be one's word against another until we realize our essential unity and divinity, and stop claiming that any one "revelation" is the final word of God. We have to make good sense, good understanding, of all that has been "revealed" to date, and try to synthesize their uniformity and not emphasize their diversity. Many people wait impatiently for a Messiah to give them everlasting relief from suffering, and yet others claim that the Messiah has come and gone, and whatever was recorded as the "Messiah's" words are to be taken at face value as the Truth for all time. The truth is that there never was a moment that the "Messiah" was not here with us, in and around us, and there never will be a moment that S/he will not be with us, in and around us. There is no one section of humanity which will be "delivered" from its enemies. Not one.

All these conflicts have been created by myths. A myth, as mentioned above, is a story not so much contrived as inspired, in order to impart spiritual truths, and characters of such myths, therefore, are imaginary. Merriam-Webster's dictionary says this of a myth: "a usually traditional story of ostensibly historical events that serves to unfold part of the world view of a people or explain a practice, belief, or natural phenomenon." "Ostensibly historical" means "supposedly historical." However, over the centuries, the characters of myths, often called "gods," become real enough to live for, and worse still, to die for.

It is my deep conviction that the character of a myth does not necessarily have to be the story of a God/Man who lived on earth, it could be a godly being who claims never to incarnate on earth, such as the gods Yahweh and Allah. *In other words, the conceptual gods Yahweh and Allah are mythical gods as well.* It must be so, because if either Yahweh or Allah were, or are, 'the only true God', then by the tradition attributed to those religions, any other gods are "false." Also, Jewish sages created their mythical yet personal deity, YHVH, or Yahweh. Yahweh equates to what is called a "küla-dĕvata" or deity of the tribe, in Hinduism; deities can be at the personal level, the level of the tribe, or could be village deity. The myth of one despotic deity, initially created in the Jewish tradition and then sustained by Muhammad using an alternative word Allah for the same Jewish god Elohim, and then modified by Christianity adding an "only true Son," is the reason we have religious wars today. Jewish myth is full of stories of the destruction of Pagans because of

4

their beliefs, though it is not likely that such an extent of destruction ever took place. The seeming destruction of people, who have beliefs different from those dictated by the deity, becomes part of myth as well, in order to show the supposed power of the deity characterized by the myth. Historically, as far as I have understood it, the Jewish people have been persecuted, but have never actually persecuted others. They have taken the attitude of "leave us alone to practice our religion and spiritual practices." Whereas for Muhammad, even though his revelations had the same origins as other myths, the need to destroy or overcome Pagans (and Jews, particularly) became real, and he not only perpetrated such activity, but was the founder of an entire tradition to maintain this activity which is historically verifiable. The third chapter in this tragic trilogy of the superiority of gods is that of Christianity, with the myth that the God-Man Christ is supreme, the one who must be believed in to obtain salvation (to the exclusion of all other gods, even his "Father", the Jewish Yahweh, who can only be accessed through him).

Hindu/Pagan gods, in contrast, usually co-existed in relative harmony. I say relative because, interestingly enough, Vishnu the god of Vaishnavite Hindus, is thought to be the Supreme One, whereas for Shaivites, the God Shiva was able to transform himself into a pillar of light that no other god could challenge or overcome. Happily, because of benign Hindu diplomacy, these conflicting views of the relative power of the gods were resolved by creating a concept of the tri-moorty, or three supreme gods- Brahma the creator, Vishnu the preserver, and Shiva the destroyer. There is perhaps some uneasiness about which God really is more powerful, but Hindus usually worship both Vishnu and Shiva, the latter being considered by his devotees to be both the origin and the destruction of life. There is a myth that the God Brahma was cursed by the God Shiva, so Brahma, a God of great veneration at the time of the Buddha, except for at one solitary temple dedicated to him, is not worshiped by Hindus in temples anymore.

It is essential for humanity to understand the nature of these myths. Joseph Campbell, the greatest expert on myths of all time, made it his life's mission to understand myths. He believed that if we don't understand the nature of myths, there will be no peace for humanity. For centuries to come, we will be at war with one another based on beliefs created by—myth. In the outstanding video series "Joseph Campbell and the Power of Myth with Bill Moyers," Moyers said to Campbell: "The interesting thing to me is, far from undermining my

5

faith, your work in mythology has liberated my faith from the cultural prisons to which it had been sentenced. Campbell responded: "It has liberated my own. I know its going to do it with everyone that gets the message. Every mythology, every religion, is true in this sense: it is true as metaphorical of the human and cosmic mystery. But when it gets stuck to the metaphor, then you're in trouble." He explained that, for example, the Christian faith accepts literally that Jesus ascended to heaven, whereas the real metaphorical meaning is that Jesus "ascended" to his inner Spirit, guiding us to do the same. He also quoted a logion from the Gospel of Thomas, which reads: (logion 108) "He who drinks from my mouth will become like me; I will become that person, to whom obscure things will be revealed." This is a metaphor, explained Campbell: we need to become Buddha or Christ ourselves. The spiritual activities of a cult using a particular myth are called mysteries. The mysteries are known to have two layers: outer mysteries which the majority of participants are introduced to, and the inner mysteries, into which some of the participants graduate into. Many, perhaps most, of these mysteries, involve deities who die and then resurrect. Such a deity could be worshiped by participants in the outer mysteries, but those who use the myth to enlighten themselves, realize that the myth represents the death of their own ego, resurrecting to the Spirit within: they become the participants and teachers of the inner mysteries. These mysteries were never ever meant to be enforced on the public in the form of mass religion. They were private, open to anyone who wanted to participate in the outer mysteries while people were chosen to participate in the inner mysteries; but they were never ever enforced. The greatest tragedy which has afflicted humanity is how people in power have enforced any one mystery cult on the rest of the people under either threat of death in this life or the threat of hell in the next, as the only religious practice allowed. Christianity and Islam, the two religions with the largest numbers of adherents, are the ones guiltiest of this tragic imposition. It is my prayer that the Christian world will eventually realize the mythical nature of the Christ, and awaken itself in the manner of the original mystery myth. It is also my prayer that the Islamic world will realize that much of the "revelation from God" in the Qur'an is mystical material similar to that of earlier myths, meant to awaken its readers and listeners, and not to be enforced in its literal form on the rest of the world. Just as a brutal Church in Christian Europe imploded on itself, I believe that fundamentalist Islam will also eventually settle into a gentler secular Islam.

I believe that these mythical messages were meant to awaken us. It would ordinarily be heresy to claim that we become Jesus or Buddha, but that was exactly the intent of the mystics who created the myths, to begin with. A Hindu mystic once exclaimed that unless we become Vishnu, there is no point worshiping Vishnu. All these mystics speak the same language: these deities are projections, expansions, of our consciousness. In the outer mystery/myth, we create mythical images of the ideal being, and then in the inner mystery/myth, allow that being to merge back into us. Very few people realize that there is no point in worshiping these gods unless we learn to become those gods ourselves. A "god" becomes known to humanity in this way: A mystic envisions a deity in a certain form with certain attributes. The deity becomes not only an object of devotion, but his or her energy focus; a lofty concept of what his or her real nature is like. The mystic then proceeds to identify with, and merge with, that deity which all the while is simply an expansion of the mystic's mind. Having effectively used the deity to achieve a state of higher consciousness, the mystic then teaches others to do the same. Unfortunately many of the students get stuck with the deity as a being apart, and never learn to do exactly as the mystic did. As an end result, we have all these "gods," leaving our minds in no higher a state of awareness and consciousness. Not knowing this is perhaps the real heresy.

There is a philosophy called Euhēmerism, also referred to as Evēmerism, founded by the philosopher Euhēmerus who lived in the fourth century BCE. This philosophy says that all gods were once mortal human beings who either taught or performed in such a great manner that they were later deified and all their deeds so embellished that they became gods. There probably are a great number of people who believe that this is what applies to Jesus and the Buddha. I have thought much about this. It is much easier to simply just say that Jesus or Buddha said something, rather than keep reiterating that a sage so taught something, using the character of Jesus or Buddha to speak the words. Besides, *somebody* did come up with those wonderful teachings; it does not matter as to what the name of the person who revealed them really was. Sages of the past just loved to have the gods speak their words…only then did people listen! Countless books have been written about the details of a "historical" Jesus, each conflicting with another one, to the point that it becomes a futile quest and a monumental waste of time. Myth gave a community identity, but communities have got into such conflict based on myth that perhaps it is time we realized the true mythical nature of virtually all

7

our religions. Just as patients obtain relief with a placebo drug, realizing the mythical nature of a god is not going to belittle the comfort obtained from prayer to that god. Most of us will probably use the Euhemerist approach because it gives a glimmer of hope that indeed the deity we worship was a reality sometime in the past. I have learned, however, that such clinging hinders personal spiritual awakening. It stops us from progressing to the inner mysteries from the outer mysteries. We need get these "gods" off their pedestals, and elevate all of life to that exalted state while at the same time degrading people like suicide bombers who take innocent lives to the state of demons.

So there we have it: humanity has created a variety of gods, and the gods have "spoken" to humanity with a variety of ideas, messages and commandments. The gods created to represent the "One" such as Allah have been the gods with the most demanding, vindictive, wrathful, jealous and unforgiving nature. Such a god is like a spoiled only-child: completely intolerant of others, wanting complete and total attention and dedication from its believers. The creators of those mythical gods helped create a tribal identity, focus and purpose for their people; those gods dictated the "covenant," or two-way agreement. For adhering to the rules, the people are offered the protection of the deity. There is a strong tendency to consider monotheism to be something superior, but in reality, creators of these monotheistic gods have wreaked havoc on the peace of humanity. Unless and until we human realize the nature of all these gods, all man-made, there will never be peace on earth. The one infinite mind-energy of the universe lies silent and luminous within us and within all beings and things, whereas we have created a variety of gods supposed to represent that One. In the greatest irony, the gods created to represent "the One" have been the least luminous, the least enlightening, of them all.

Hinduism has been the religion most maligned by Christians and Muslims, largely because Paganism, a European version of Hinduism, has already been wiped out by brute force, but Hinduism, which really is Paganism as practiced in India, continues to be practiced by more than a billion people. Starting with the Vĕdas, consisting of devotional hymns to the infinite One who manifests as various gods with rites of offering and sacrifice (now limited to flowers, butter and grain), Hindu scripture then evolved into the Üpanishads, called Vedänta or the culmination of the Vĕda, and subsequently added various other scriptures. Even Hinduism, among the oldest of all religions, probably the most ancient of all, has evolved over thousands of years, and its practice now is very different than it was three thousand years ago. Hindus believe that the Vĕdas (sacred knowledge) to be Shrüthi, or "that which was heard by the sages" as pure revelation. However, Shrüthi includes the Üpanishads, also called footnotes to the Vĕdas. These latter often advise the reader to transcend above and beyond the Vĕdas! The Bhagavad-Gîta, containing the essential teachings of the Üpanishads, exclaims: "to an enlightened mind, all of the Vĕdas are just about as useful as water in a well when everywhere there is a flood." So the goal is to have direct knowledge of God; everything else is just religion and scripture. Hindus revere the "Sapta (pronounced suptha, meaning seven) Rishi," or the seven mythical sages, from whom the divinely revealed scripture was obtained. Indeed, it is considered by many of great understanding that the "gods," rather than being distinct entities floating around in space, are simply "visions" of the powers of the Infinite One focused or limited to certain forms to allow ordinary people to understand or communicate with the One. Some scholars therefore have considered Hinduism to be neither polytheistic nor monotheistic, rather a "henotheism," defined by the Merriam-Webster Dictionary as "the worship of one god without denying the existence of other gods." Hindus believe in only one supreme power in the Universe and pervading the Universe while yet transcending it—while believing in a variety of worship forms to reach that one God. In the chapter on Hinduism, the nature of the various "gods" is explored further.

In this book I use the word Pāganism with a capital P giving it the respect it deserves. The word Pāgan is a derogatory word, and it is most unfortunate that the word Pāganism is the only word that seems to remain for the variety of religious practices followed prior to the "monotheistic" religions mentioned above. The ideas of great "Pāgan" philosophers such as Plato, Aristotle, Pythagoras, Socrates and others, constitute just a fragment of the collective wisdom of the ages, all once part of a vast collection of teachings and practices included in all-encompassing "Pāganism." As Timothy Freke and Peter Gandy write in their book *The Jesus Mysteries,* "Paganism was the spirituality which inspired the unequaled magnificence of the Giza pyramids, the exquisite architecture of the Parthenon, the legendary sculptures of Phideas, the powerful plays of Euripides and Sophocles, and the sublime philosophy of Socrates and Plato."

Careful reading of the various scriptures from the different religions that have appeared over the past several hundreds of years reveals literature that is not only magnificent, but also absolutely unique and impressive. It is no wonder at all that millions of people have been enchanted by them and become followers of that particular doctrine. Sadly, however, numerous such "revelations" have appeared over the millennia, causing enormous confusion and conflict. It is common knowledge that the biggest cause of war in the past couple of thousand years has been conflict in ideology. Once absolutely convinced of the "divine exclusive truth" of their particular scripture, adherents of religion become champions of its cause, and feel compelled to spread the word and bring in more converts. The original aim of such conversion was probably altruistic, but later on the realization comes, that in greater numbers of adherents, comes greater mutual strength. There are many Churches today that proselytize very aggressively. There is one church that has been banned from the city of Moscow.

Interestingly, the followers of Judaism and Hinduism, probably the oldest of the world's major religions today, are the least likely to indulge in proselytism. Judaism, as mentioned above, has mythical stories of the destruction of people practicing polytheistic religions, we must doubt as to whether such great wars really took place; killing is anathema to the Jewish faith. Hindus have their history of the subjugation of the *däsyus,* the 'dark people,' as servants and untouchables in the guise of the caste system. Yet for them, their religion consists of a diverse and rich source of scripture, revelation and wisdom. The Jewish people have absorbed the teachings of their faith taught by mystics using stories of various prophets, as well as rabbinic wisdom over thousands of years. Indeed, even the Qur'an has always spoken very highly of the Jewish prophets, and Christianity draws heavily upon Jewish wisdom.

The followers of each religion usually obtain enormous mental and emotional satisfaction from the practice of that particular religion. They may just have been brought up in that tradition, or they just found the ideology of that particular religion very appropriate. In the Hinduism section, I will discuss Sri Ramakrishna's wonderful teaching on the validity of each religion's practice. He was convinced that true devotion to one's own path can always lead not just to satisfaction in that practice but to an exalted state of being that is the common goal of all mankind.

One of the most important teachings of the Baha'i religion is that each religion is to be respected and revered, and that there is wisdom to be found in them all. However, myth has not escaped the Baha'i faith, which believes that Baha'u'llah was a manifestation of God. For them, a prophet was a manifestation of God, and Baha'u'llah was a prophet also. Baha'u'llah said, according to the website www.bahai.org: "These sanctified mirrors, these day springs of ancient glory are, one and all, the exponents on earth of Him who is the central Orb of the universe, its Essence and ultimate Purpose. From Him proceed their knowledge and power; from Him is derived their sovereignty...." In other words, the prophets are much more than ordinary humans. Further, said Baha'u'llah, "By the revelation of these Gems of Divine virtue all the names and attributes of God, such as knowledge and power, sovereignty and dominion, mercy and wisdom, glory, bounty, and grace, are made manifest." In other words, prophets are to be revered because they helped radiate the light and power of God.

Baha'u'llah advised people that all the prophets known to man have been equally endowed with spiritual power. Eventually, whether he made the claim or his followers did, he became considered a prophet by his followers, and this caused severe conflict with Islam, which believes that Muhammad was the seal, or the last, of the prophets. There are Baha'i who are part-Hindu, who believe that the God Vishnu became incarnated as Baha'u'llah. The greatest thing about Baha'i, however, is their equanimity and attitude of non-violence. However, if a religion teaches dependence on a prophet or prophets and their teachings alone, that religion has not conducted the greatest exploration of all, that of our own mind.

Hatred and intolerance develop when a group of people becomes indoctrinated by a certain teaching. Islam is a religion in which severe intolerance is practiced, and the religion was indeed spread by the sword to quite an extent. Consider this section of the *Qur'an*, Surah 5 "The Table," verse 69 translated by Thomas Cleary: "Indeed, be they Muslims, Jews, Sabîans or Christians, those who believe in God and the final day and who do good have nothing to fear, and they will not grieve." It is to be noted that Pagans and Hindus are not on the list of people who "will not grieve." And indeed, Muslims have subjected Hindus to grievous and terrible persecution ever since the days of Muhammad.

The aggression and radical violence of some Muslims is contrary to the divine advice of at least some verses of the Qur'an, which teaches that the spilling of blood is against the will of God; however, the fanatical killing of non-Muslims is not contrary to the directives in some parts of the Qur'an. Therefore it is seems that people can pick whatever they choose; the way its practitioners use particular sections of the Qur'an to oppress "the unbelievers" is entirely up to them. It is impossible and indeed unacceptable to judge someone to be an "unbeliever," which really is something that ought to be left to God, but many Muslims over the years have taken it upon themselves to so judge, and destroy whoever they want, whenever they want. Muslims have developed all kind of Hadith, or tradition, which gives them the privilege of such destruction. Fortunately, Muslims have come to understand the difference between ignorant idolatry practiced at the time of Muhammad, and the incredibly deep philosophical considerations of the devotion to consecrated images as practiced by Hindus. Hatred between Hindus and Muslims has gone on long enough. Over a million people died in the clashes between the communities during the partition Pakistan from India, which was one of the greatest tragedies humanity has witnessed. The followers of each of the two religions are largely ignorant of the beauty of the others' faiths, and hate simply comes from the ignorant influencing the ignorant.

Fundamentalism in Christianity is significantly on the rise in America today and appears to be worsening. A recent misguided attempt at a Constitutional amendment that would have undone the great blessing of the separation of Church and State, fortunately, was defeated. On the surface, very little religion is discussed in everyday life, but the undercurrent of religious bigotry quickly shows itself given the right circumstances. The descendents of the pilgrims, who came to America to escape religious persecution, have often practiced the same persecution from which their forefathers came to escape.

As I have discussed in much more detail in the chapter on Christianity, the essential belief of literalist Christianity is that Jesus is the only son of God, and the only one through whom all salvation can be obtained. The Qur'an denounces the concept of God having a son, and Hinduism teaches that the divine light of the One has radiated through numerous sages and prophets throughout human history and radiates through each one of us. Until people accept and realize the joy of others in their own respective religions, there never will be "peace on earth and goodwill to men."

This book plans to explore a few religions, and reveal what is unacceptable in each of those as regards the needs of world peace and unity. Each of these religions has hundreds of millions of adherents; it is particularly for that reason that I have discussed them; the combined strength of hundreds of millions of people can easily destroy the Earth. It is my prayer that followers of each religion not only appreciate the greatness within it, but also realize its shortcomings. It is only then that we will truly open our hearts to the rest of humanity.

We could perhaps use as a guide the words of the South Indian sage Thirümülar, quoted from his monumental work *Thirumandiram,* (which translates as "The Great Mantra") from the third or fourth century, translated by the late Satguru Śiväya Subramuniyaswami. It can be found on-line at the Himalayan Academy web site: http:// www.himalayanacademy.com/books

I have chosen to use my own words to convey the meaning. The Thirumandiram refers to "the six faiths," which actually refers to the six systems of Hindu philosophy that were in use in ancient India. Thirümülar, the author, refers to God as Shiva, which means "the auspicious One." Shiva could be meant to refer to one of the deities of Hinduism, but for such sages, there are not multiple deities, just one Supreme Lord.

1530: The six faiths come to no avail,
The six faiths all try together,
Yet, not one knows the God within.
Their adherents drop deep into the pit of illusion
And tied down by traditions of bondage,
They shake and tremble, in vain accomplishment.

1531: Formal faiths do not know God within
He hides in your heart, yet He pervades all.
He is the generous One, the Lord Supreme;
In a state of penance, He seats himself in your heart;
As a cunning thief, he enters the hollow shell of the body
And then leaves it; no one knows His plans.

1532: The Existence of God is in our minds and faith:
Say that the Lord is within you and around you,

Then surely the Lord is within you and around you.
To those that that say He is neither within nor without,
Surely he is non-existent for them.

1533: God transcends all the faiths of man.
Men founded the six faiths,
Yet they found Him not;
What the six faiths speak of is not He.
So in great faith do seek Him,
And be resolved of all your doubts,
And then surely you will enter your Father's mansion.

The chapters to follow include those that discuss the major religions of the world. My focus has been to show that none of the major religions have adequate expression of a universal truth that is comfortably accepted by all. Christianity separates those that have apparently been "saved" from those who have not, and Islam claims to be the only true religion and ridicules Christianity and the Jews, and positively denounces Pagan religious practice. The chapters on religions to follow reveal a glimmer of truth within them, but assert that none of them has the final answer. The book then explores a simple way of meditation that takes for its support the teachings obtained from various religions, and shows that anyone, no matter what their religion, can obtain inner peace and enlightenment. They can then continue to enjoy their own religion, *but what is more important, allow others to enjoy theirs without interference.*

We must *tear out of religion whatever is tearing humanity apart.* We need to explore our religions honestly and with open hearts, and try and separate out whatever appears to be universally applicable, and applaud it; we also need to find whatever is unacceptable to the rest of humanity, and declare that it is not worth clinging to. It is quite likely that we will find that every religion has elements of belief that are either unfair to, or inappropriate for, the rest of humanity. We then need to have the heart to graciously drop the clinging to those elements of belief. From that kindness and compassion, world peace will arise. If not, we will continue to have wars, hatred and strife. If large numbers of people peacefully demand a change, then such change will happen.

I can only hope that the words of Ibn Arabi, who lived 1165-1240 CE, will resonate in the hearts of all people (From the superb book *God's Breath: Sacred Scriptures of the World* by John Miller—I left a copy of the book in my office waiting room for patients to read, but someone stole it):

"My heart holds within it every form;
It contains a pasture for gazelles,
A monastery for Christian monks,
There is a temple for Idol Worshipers,
A holy shrine for pilgrims,
There is the table of the Torah,
And the book of the Koran.
I follow the religion of love,
And go whichever way his camel leads me.
This is the true faith,
This is the true religion."

CHAPTER TWO:
THE SEARCH FOR MEANING

My spiritual awakenings have led me to tears at times. The first time
I cried, in the last few decades anyhow, was on seeing the statue of
Liberty. I had seen the statue before, but after having been in the United
States for several years, the statue has come to symbolize real freedom,
the ability to think clearly for oneself, and express oneself freely. Liberty
also symbolizes the ability to practice one's preferred religion in peace
without persecution, *and the ability to expose the harm that religion has
done to humanity*. The intense gratitude to my adopted country, without
which I could never have spiritually matured to the extent I have, often is
expressed in my tears. Teardrops sometimes come too, when I remember
the kind immigration official who, as I was returning from a trip to
India, said: "Welcome home." This, sadly, was in sharp contrast to the
behavior of an Indian Immigration Officer who mindlessly stamped my
passport and muttered "jao" which means, "go." It is often claimed that
America is a Christian country, but the truth is that it is a truly secular
nation, yet guided by Christian spiritual traditions of love, hospitality
and consideration; the immigration officer, to me, represented the best of
America. Congress tacked on the statement "One Nation under God" to
the original pledge of allegiance to try and make people realize the Spirit
in their daily lives. Though a Judge recently struck down this pledge, he
then withdrew his decision the next day. I hope that the pledge will stay
as it is. The word God simply denotes a spiritual basis for American life,
and is not limited to any one religion in particular.

While it is true that the first Colonists were Christians, the first American
statesmen and leaders were Deists. According to the Merriam-Webster's
Dictionary of World Religions, the first three Presidents, Washington,
Adams and Jefferson, subscribed to Deist beliefs. Part of the movement
of the Enlightenment, Deists believed that religious knowledge is either
inborn or acquired by reason, as opposed to knowledge acquired during
revelation or the teaching of any church. They had distrust in religious
claims of revelation that they felt led to dogmatism and intolerance.
Bruce Kuklick writes in his book *A History of Philosophy in America
1720-2000*: "Some of these colonial statesmen explicitly rejected
Protestant Christianity because it offended this idea of reason. The virgin
birth, the miracles of Jesus, the tale of redemption, the notion of a Trinity,
and the resurrection of Christ were dismissed as unworthy of critical

THE SEARCH FOR MEANING

inspection. The many inconsistencies in the Bible itself underscored these shortcomings for the Founders. Instead, the perusal of the harmonies of the natural world led them to conclude that a benevolent and orderly deity had created the cosmos. There had to be a first cause of nature, and it was only reasonable to assume that this cause—God— reflected the same law like principles inherent in the organization of the world."

America, my adopted homeland, is the land the great Founders planned to offer as home to people of any religious belief whatsoever, and yet a place of orderliness not unlike the orderliness of nature. Nature nurtures, and so does America. God bless America and its great people. The greatest treasures that I have found in American cities are the libraries. It would have been quite difficult to have access to such a wealth of literature in India. As a teenager growing up in Madras, India, I recall bicycling down to the library of the British Council and that of the United States Embassy, but even County Libraries in the United States are often just as well stocked with books covering a wide range of subjects. I hope that charitable institutions will stock India's community libraries with such wealth as well.

The search for understanding started in childhood. Call it the influence of my prior birth or whatever, but I have had a preoccupation with religion and philosophy for as long as I can remember. Most children happily practice whatever religion is taught them, but I somehow had this great apprehension about religious practices. I still recall sitting in the family Pooja (prayer) room, and staring at all the pictures of the Hindu Gods and wondering how real they were. I would stare at the faces trying to see if they would smile at me!

My parents are deeply religious people. Father was well versed in Sanskrit, and would read stories from the Mahabhäratha or Ramayana, the most famous of the Puränas, or mythological stories. I imagine he did not feel that we boys could understand the philosophy of the Bhagavad-Gîta or other important texts. I had heard of the Üpanishads, Hinduism's most profound philosophical texts at high school, but never did see even a chapter until several years later while living in the United States. Hinduism slowly grows on you. Interestingly, I read and learned about the Bible long before I learned any Hindu holy books. The Bible was a most fascinating book to me, and there was many a lunch hour at high school that I would sit in the library reading it. The Old Testament was far more interesting to me as a teenager, what with all its stories of the Garden of Eden, the flood, the Tower of Babel, the stories of Moses and the prophets, and so on. All of my schooling was at parochial schools, so I was steeped in Christianity all of my growing life. My ancestors were part of a community of Brahmins called Havyakas who live on the west coast of Southern India, in the lush green fertile strip of land between the Western Ghats (mountains) and the Arabian Sea. My parents, however, moved to the city of Madras (called Chennai now) in the 1940s. My father decided not to run the family plantation, but studied medicine instead, and then dentistry. He has practiced dentistry at the city of Chennai ever since, and has been a past president of the Indian Dental Association. He continues to be actively involved in Indian dentistry on a national level. Chennai in the 1950s was a very gentle city, and violence was very limited partly because of the gentle nature of Tamil people, and also due to the fact that the police department was known to be very strict and incorrupt. I consider myself very fortunate to have been able to learn the Tamil language and culture. The Tirükküral, written about twenty two hundred years ago, is a masterpiece of ethics, culture, behavior and devotion to God. The scripture consists of 133 chapters with each chapter elucidating a different aspect of human virtue or human fault. There are ten couplets per chapter, making a total of 1,330 couplets. There is probably no book like it in the world, and it has yet to be discovered in the West. Each couplet verse is a gem of wisdom. Just as the Tao Te Ching has become widely read and appreciated in the past two decades, I believe that the Tirukkural will become widely known in the years to come. It can be found online at the web site of the Himalayan Academy monastery in Kauai, Hawaii, (see below), as well as published in a book called *Weaver's Wisdom* by Satguru Sivaya Subramuniyaswami, though one section called the section on romantic love has not been included in this translation because it is considered by some to be a later addition. *Weaver's Wisdom* is a superb translation of the Tirukkural. It is published in India simply as *Tirukural* with the original Tamil text translated into a simpler Tamil as well as English. *Weaver's Wisdom* does not have the Tamil text as hardly anyone in America knows Tamil. No English translation or even a Tamil translation, for that matter, can begin to approach the magnificence and beauty of the original Tamil poetry. The academy is in the process of construction of a granite Shaivite temple at their Kauai monastery, and publishes a superb magazine called *Hinduism Today.* Go to http://www.himalayanacademy.com, click on *books*, and then click on *Weaver's Wisdom*. This book, which could easily be ordered through any bookstore, will always be a part of my home library, and I recommend it highly.

The first chapter is called "In Praise of God." God is referred to with various words or phrases in Tamil, including Kadavül and Iraivan. Yet another phrase used to describe God is Ädi Bhagavan. Ädi is simply an extension of the letter A, revealing the simple beauty of the first verse (I have attempted my own translation of the first chapter from Tamil):

1. With the letter A begins the entire alphabet; similarly, with the primordial God begins the entire world.

2. There is no academic knowledge that could help a man who does not worship God who is pure knowledge Himself.

3. God dwells in the lotus flower of the heart and those who attain Him dwell on earth with long lives.

4. God is free of the extremes of desire and aversion. To be devoted to Him is to be free of suffering forever.

5-6. God transcends the duality of good and bad. A man who controls his five senses will be rewarded with a long and happy life.

7-8. Having taken refuge in the Lord who is an ocean of virtue, you will swim across the oceans of life free of distress in the mind.

9. A head which will not bow before God's feet is blinded by senses which do not perceive.

10. The endless oceans of birth and death cannot be crossed by those who have not attained to the feet of God.

Though I was richly blessed growing up in the heart of Tamil culture at Madras, during the summer holidays I would stay in what seemed to be a world apart: the community around my grandparents' ancestral home on the west coast of India four hundred miles to the west. My grandparents and the rest of our community are Brahmins called Havyaka Brähmanas whose ancestors moved south about eight hundred years earlier, at the invitation of a local King who wanted some northern Brahmins to be part of the community. Our ancestors managed to carry out their duties, but acquired property, partly from grants and largely from loans, and flourished as plantation owners. The workers on the plantation are beautiful and gentle people, dark complexioned from thousands of years in the tropical sun, and with beautiful features. The plantations were created from previously untilled land, employing workers who lived nearby. The workers are supposedly of 'Dravidian' origin, based on their complexion, as compared to the more fair-skinned plantation owners, who are supposedly of 'Aryan' descent. However, are there really two races, Aryan and Dravidian? Southern Indians, except perhaps for the aboriginal tribes, while being somewhat more dark complexioned, still have the same nicely chiseled out features of the more light skinned northerners, the so-called Aryans, and have very similar cultural patterns. The so-called Dravidian languages, Tamil and Malayalam, have a great deal of Sanskrit and Sanskrit-derived words. I see both these groups as just subsets of one race, the southerners relatively more dark because of millennia of living in the hot tropical sun. The 'Aryan invasion India' theory has been thrown out by modern scholars, and there is no doubt whatsoever that all these people, the 'Aryans' and 'Dravidians,' have been indigenous to India for thousands of years. It could simply be that the southern 'Dravidians' came to the area in waves long before the light skinned northerners (who moved from Africa to eastern Europe and the middle East first), long enough to turn darker in the hot tropical sun than the newcomer "Aryans." In the December 2003 issue of *Scientific American* magazine, authors Michael J. Bamshad and Steve E. Olson write: "When Bamshad and his co-workers used their 100 Alu polymorphisms to try to classify a sample of individuals from southern India into a separate group, the Indians instead had more in common with either Europeans or Asians. In other words, because India has been subject to many genetic influences from Europe and Asia, people on the subcontinent did not group into a unique cluster." Therefore, there is no Aryan superiority for anyone to boast about. However, it is a fact that the lowest caste in the Hindu hierarchy is largely, if not entirely, composed of dark skinned people. I can't help but wonder whether fair complexioned people are inherently more domineering and aggressive when among darker people. On the other hand, just as the South American Mayans and Aztecs accepted the white Spaniards as gods, perhaps in the old days there was a tendency for human beings to consider those lighter skinned than themselves to be superior in some way. Besides, it is quite possible that the lighter skinned northerners had better weapons including horse-drawn chariots. The Aryans had a hierarchy of three castes: Brahmins or priests, Kshathriyas or warriors, and Vaishyas or traders/craftsmen. They dominated over the (not too much more) dark skinned people whom they designated to be the fourth, the working caste. However, there appears to have been no need for any violence to maintain order once the social hierarchy was established, which likely occurred over thousands of years. In the years following the independence of India, there came a movement in the State of Tamil Nadu for the liberation and promotion of the Dravidians in the form of a powerful political party, the DMK. A majority of positions in the government, schools and colleges, as well as admissions to university, were, and still are, reserved for people from backward classes and castes. India's aim at independence was to rid itself of the caste system, but designating certain people as belonging to backward castes has effectively ruined any chance of eliminating the caste system. The constitution of India was written with the aim of helping the long-oppressed and suffering backward castes, but has, in my view, perpetuated the caste system in an even more virulent form. I was denied a medical school admission at Madras because I am a Brahmin. It became the Orwellian situation of "all people are equal but some people are more equal than others." The Indian equivalent, which was unfortunately written in the constitution itself, is: 'there is no caste system, but the lower castes will be promoted over the higher castes.' Unless the constitution is changed, and the quota system removed forever, there will be no true equality among the people of India, and the caste system will be perpetuated. However, since the majority of the people of India belong to the "backward castes and classes," it is unlikely that this privilege will be rescinded.

Brahmins have practiced ritual purity from time immemorial. They meticulously avoid a state of being ritually impure, a state they call *ashüddha*. What is ritually pure is *shüddha*. For instance, a menstruating woman is impure. This practice is not different from the directive in the Bible, Leviticus 15:19: "When a woman has her menstrual flow, the impurity of her monthly state will last seven days, and anyone who touches her will be unclean till evening." In the same way, in our community anyone who touched a menstruating woman or even her clothes, became ritually impure and had to have a bath to be cleansed. Menstruating women, therefore, were very careful to avoid contact with others. This was a strict practice when I was growing up, but people do not adhere to it much these days. My mother did follow the custom while at the ancestral home but not at our city home. It was a superstition likely created to allow a menstruating woman to have complete rest for a week. The community seldom follows the practice now.

Hebrews were directed in the Bible, in Numbers 19:11-15: "Whoever touches a corpse will be unclean for seven days; if someone dies in a tent, anyone who enters the tent will be unclean for seven days, and any open container without a lid fastened will become unclean." Brahmins similarly consider themselves to be ritually impure if they touch a corpse; therefore those who work in cremation grounds are always ritually impure. People in a variety of occupations are considered to be in a state of ritual impurity, such as those cleaning toilets, working with leather, barbers, and so on. This is what led to a state of those people becoming "untouchables." This is indeed an ancient superstition, which as I said above must have been practiced across the world as evidenced by the ritual impurity obsessed about in the Bible; this is a practice which must be abandoned for all time. Our community was quite fastidious about ritual purity in the old days, but they are less prone to follow it now. The concept of ritual impurity fascinated me even in childhood, and I would secretly touch someone untouchable to see if I felt different in any way! I rejected the practice very early in my life.

What stays in my mind is the fact that the workers on our family's plantation were treated with gentleness and respect. In turn, the workers revealed great love and respect for the landowners. They were not bonded or indentured workers in any way; they were entirely free, right from the beginnings of the plantations, and were paid proper wages. It is likely the workers were tribals who happened to live nearby, and chose to work on the plantations and live in them. Never did I hear any of my relatives utter harsh words against the workers. Another amusing fact is that in those days both the landlords and the servants wore just loincloths, and aside from the fact that they actually owned the land, the landlords were not too much better off. The landlords ate simple, healthy meals, and worked hard from dawn to dusk. They were extremely pious people, always prayed twice a day at *sandhya,* the twilight. The essential religious practice of my ancestors was *japa,* or the recitation of mantras, during the sandhya. At times, especially during community events, *hōma,* or the practice of burnt offerings in Vedic ritual, was performed. Just as in the old biblical days, it is possible that meat was involved in burnt offerings a very long time ago, but Brahmins are strict vegetarians, and the offerings included clarified butter, grain, flowers and fruit. They would visit temples on occasion, but that was not an important aspect of their lives. They knew quite a bit of the Vĕdas, and either conducted rituals themselves or had priests come in periodically to carry out Vedic ritual. What is noticeable about the Havyakas is their gentle dignity and warm hospitality. Arrogance is looked down upon, and proper courteous behavior extolled.

My grandfather's home altar had no *moorthis,* or images of the Divine. He had a simple altar made of sandalwood, on which were placed lots of flowers, and two sacred stones. He would sit in front of the altar as he recited the Vĕdas and other prayers. I was given the sacred thread in a ceremony called *üpanayana,* which included a ritual immersion, baptism so to speak, in water to denote becoming *dvĭja* or twice-born, as is the custom among Brahmins. However, I soon cut the thread away as I would not accept a mark of caste superiority. Indeed, in the cities anti-Brahminism had already started, that being the second decade of Indian independence. I therefore wished to conform, and not be apart from my friends, many of whom were not Brahmin. Ironically, I was taught a few mantras, particularly the *Gäyathri,* during the Upanayana, but not their meaning, so they were soon forgotten. The Gäyathri is one of the most revered of all Hindu mantras. The meaning of the mantra (which I only learned decades after I learned the mantra) is:

O God who is the syllable Aum, You are the giver of life, remover of pain and sorrow, and the One who bestows happiness. O Creator of the universe, may we receive your supreme sin-destroying light. May only You guide our intellect in the right direction.

Overall, however, I think back with great pride at being part of such a friendly, gentle and unassuming Brahmin community. I seldom saw arrogance in those who eventually became wealthy landowners, partly because they had struggled hard to pay back loans with which they acquired their land but largely because that was their nature and cultural norm. Violence within the community was very rare indeed, though some of my relatives did have a bad temper. However, anger was frowned upon, and the entire family would get involved to resolve a dispute.

Curiously, despite being a Brahmin household, the ancestral home had a cottage adjacent to the main home, which housed a brass mask and sword of a *bhootha,* or demon spirit. The spirit was never worshiped, but once a year the family hosted a *bhootha kōla,* or demon dance, to allow the spirit to express itself. A man would come down from the hills, don the mask, hold the brass sword, and become possessed by the spirit. The possession lasted all day, and the spirit would answer questions, make predictions, resolve disputes, and so on. The man, once possessed developed a tremor in his sword bearing hand the entire time. The sword had chains of metal beads which jangled constantly. In the evening the function would end with the man walking on red hot coals, after which he gave up the spirit and became his normal self again. This ritual is performed faithfully every year. One year one of my neighbors at Madras, who also had an ancestral property four hundred miles away, failed to perform the ritual. Within a few weeks, stones suddenly started being hurled at their home. The police were called, but they could not find anyone on the street when the stones would fly into the home. The police were actually frightened, and said there was nothing they could do. The family then performed the required ritual, and the stone throwing stopped the same day.

There were a couple of shotguns and an old First World War musket in my grandfather's home. The musket was a muzzle loader, a real antique. However, it worked quite well. We would pour in gunpowder, then ram in coconut fiber, pour in steel pellets, ram in more coconut fiber, cap the tip of the muzzle, and the gun was ready! An uncle and I once loaded up the musket and went up into the hills around us. I shot a bird, and when I saw the poor thing lying lifeless on the ground, it grieved me so much that I put the musket back and never touched it again. Adding to my own personal pain after the episode was my relatives' scolding at killing a harmless bird. I was firmly told that I had committed a sin, and instructed not to use guns to shoot innocent creatures ever again. The guns were there for protection against wild animals, such as tigers in the old days, and also to deal with wild boars and monkeys that came to the plantation and wreaked havoc on the crops. Cartridges for the shotguns were never kept near the guns themselves, and indeed one relative kept his handgun carefully locked and would not show it to anyone. Here at home in America I see no reason to own a gun. In the event of a robbery, assault or whatever, it is likely that my weapon will be useless against a determined desperate thug; it is more than likely my own weapon could be used against me. It is my sincere belief that the orderliness of society and freedom from corruption are what constitute the best defense. Yes, America has an enormous amount of violent crime, far worse than in the South Indian cities that I grew up in, but I still refuse to carry a weapon. Those who live by the sword, die by the sword.

The Havyaka Brahmin community isn't necessarily entirely wealthy. There are many poor Havyakas, partly due to plantations being broken up into pieces by partition based on inheritance. In the old tradition, when the father dies, his property is divided into equal portions for himself and his sons. From his portion, the daughters get their shares. It is this system which led to the dowry system in India, as the daughters don't normally inherit much. However, the Havyakas have never allowed or maintained a dowry system. Today large numbers of them have left the ancestral plantation for careers in medicine, law, engineering and computer science. The poor Brahmins of India are now in a most sad situation. They are discriminated against by the majority population of lower castes, who now run the governments. At the same time, poverty does not allow them the luxury of private college. Therefore, they are in a sad predicament. They are not allowed equal opportunity. Well, at least the situation in India is nowhere as bad as it was in Cambodia where millions of intellectuals were murdered in order to make the country composed of only two classes: peasants and the ruling Junta. It was so ironically the exact reverse of the French revolution.

In 1965 I was accepted for admission to the Christian Medical College in Vellore, South India. CMC, as it is called, is considered to be the finest Medical School in India. Little did I realize how profoundly it would widen my horizons. CMC was founded by an American missionary called Ida Scudder. While growing up as a girl with her parents who were missionaries, Ida was distressed to see men who would rather allow their wives to die than be attended to by male physicians, so she resolved to study medicine in America and return to India to be a physician and train women physicians, who were desperately needed. Now the college admits both men and women students. Vellore is a small town eighty miles from Chennai (formerly called Madras), and the world would be oblivious to the town if it were not for the medical school and hospital. CMC Vellore is the stronghold of Christendom in South India, largely of the Thomas Christians of Kerala, who are neither Catholics nor Protestants. Transplanted from the orthodox Brahmin society of Madras, I was now plunged into a deeply Christian yet cosmopolitan culture. Having attended Christian elementary and high schools, however, I felt quite at home. I joined in chapel services, attended Bible classes, sang Christmas carols as a tenor, and munched "hot cross Easter buns" on Easter Sundays. On one occasion, however, I asked a friend how he could munch on a bun, imagining it was the flesh of Jesus, and my friend just shrugged it away. The practice puzzled me deeply, and I found it incomprehensible. It was only decades later that I learned how the "body of Christ" is a metaphor for the Deity whose very being constitutes the earth, so the consumption of a consecrated offering signifies blending with God. This is very much the same practice as consuming *prasäd* after pooja, a prayer ceremony, in Hinduism, but I did not realize it at the time. Sometimes I would argue with ultra-conservative members of what was called the EU, or Evangelical Union, following which I would have piles of Christian literature slid under my dorm room door in the middle of the night. However, despite being part of a Hindu minority in the college, I never felt either out of place or alienated. I recall Bible classes conducted by the college chaplain, a delightful gentleman called Reverend Oommen, (the eastern accented version of Amen) specifically for Hindu students. He did not really quite feel at ease with conducting the classes for Hindus. On one occasion, when questioned about what happens to non-Christians, he generously replied: "Christ died for your salvation; whether you accept that or not, it is already done, and your salvation is assured!"

One of the most memorable experiences of medical training in India was my one-month internship assignment to the Schieffelin leprosy center in Karigiri, near Vellore. This was the place made famous by Dr. Paul Brand, whose biography is captured in the book *Ten Fingers for God*. Philip Yancey has devoted an entire chapter (which is wonderful reading) to Dr. Brand in his superb book *Soul Survivor: How my faith survived the Church*. Dr. Brand had devoted his entire life to the care of Leprosy, particularly in surgical interventions to restore the lost function of crippled hands. The word leprosy was forbidden at Karigiri, and we had to use the proper medical term, Hansen's disease. And use of the word *leper* was considered to be a gross insult to the unfortunate human being who suffered from the disease, and banned from usage at the center. Nowhere in the world, particularly in India where patients with Hansen's disease used to be treated with derision and cruelty, have I seen such patients given so much love and care. It was Christianity at its finest. In one month I had learned all I could about the dreaded disease and learned much about its pathology. There were visitors from Europe and America there just about every week, and the guesthouse where I stayed served Continental breakfast every day, and the rest of the meals were a mixture of Indian and European food. CMC Vellore is probably among the most cosmopolitan of medical colleges in India. The training at CMC was modeled after the best of American medical institutions such as the Mayo Clinic, and I feel truly fortunate at having had CMC as my Alma Mater. Thousands of students apply for admission every year, but only sixty students are selected, of whom 80% are Christians. It continues to be among the very best of medical training facilities in Southern Asia.

Readers are encouraged to visit **http://www.cmch-vellore.edu/** on the Internet to learn more about CMC, and possibly support the wonderful work being done there.

A sweet Havyaka lady came to CMC for treatment. I did not see her again for about four years, at which time I was introduced to the family specifically to meet her oldest daughter. An "arranged marriage" is really not anywhere the imposition it appears to be. Vidya, my prospective bride-to-be, was only seventeen, quiet and shy, but seemed sweet and gentle. Aside from that I could not gather much during a conversation of about twenty minutes: I really did not know much about her. Still, a marriage in our way is determined by initial good impression and mutual attraction, intuition, family guidance, and "the way things are done." I was taught that Havyakas have similar goals, morals and standards, and that with adjustment and consideration, things would "work out." And so they have. Neither of us had to say yes, but we did. We have been happily married for over thirty years now. Truthfully, things were more thorny than rosy during the first few years as we really had grown up in two different cultures: I grew up in a city and she in a village. Still, the strength of our culture has kept the marriage together and aside from brief periods of friction from time to me, we have been happy together. We have been blessed with two beautiful and loving daughters.

The next five years involved medical postgraduate training in England and the USA, and there was hardly any time to explore religion. Medicine and religion were considered to be like oil and water, something you just did not mix. Advising patients' relatives to pray was considered to be a signal that you had given up any hope. Thank goodness the medical community in the United States is opening up to spirituality, with research studies on the value of prayer in healing and similar work. Medicine is also opening itself up to working with alternative health approaches, something that would have been absolutely forbidden just two decades ago. Doctors pray with patients and their families, something not considered acceptable a couple of decades ago. From its very symbol, the wand of Aesculepius, to its declaration of the Hippocratic Oath, Medicine is derived from a variety of Pagan healing systems, and indeed was in conflict with the Church for hundreds of years. The Church in those days believed only in prayer for divine healing, and not in scientific medicine. There still are churches, thankfully only a handful, which instruct their members to seek only God's mercy and not scientific medicine. However, mainstream American society and American medicine have learned to blend spirituality and medicine in most satisfactory ways. Physicians such as Larry Dossey, Herbert Benson, Harold Koenig, Jon Kabat-Zinn, Deepak Chopra and others, have taught ways of merging medicine and spirituality. A variety of healing arts are now part of medicine, and not just "alternative medicine."

I somehow got into the study of Yoga, Buddhism, and the mystical aspects of various religions. I took Yoga classes from various teachers, and attended seminars and conferences on the subject. The chapter on Yoga has more details of this exploration, the various injuries that I suffered from Yoga practice, and the process by which I learned "safe yoga." Several years of Yoga exploration did not bring true mental peace, and I then explored Buddhist meditation practices. Eventually I learned to combine the two great paths, Zen Buddhist meditation and Hindu Yoga practice, to which I later added Taoist practices of letting go, and that is when I really found a combined practice that I have felt at home with ever since. Indeed, the theme of this book is that despite the admonition of various teachers to "stick to one path," I have found that if you extract teachings and truths from different traditions, and blend them all into your life, that seems to yield the greatest results.

Along with personal study, I then found a wonderful place to exchange information: the CompuServe Information Service, particularly the Religion and New Age Forums. I recall the time long before Windows computing, being on CompuServe and connecting at a 2400 bps speed, snail-like compared to today's high speed broadband connections. But the plain DOS programs of those days did very well at slow communication speeds, and you could often finish reading a page as it was loading on to the screen one line at a time! Modem speeds got higher and higher, and eventually CompuServe joined the Windows format. CompuServe has always had wonderful people online, courteous, polite, and many extremely knowledgeable. Unlike some other computer services and the Internet, people maintain decorum, and Forum posts that are abusive, or those that contain expletives, are removed from public display. There is virtually no better place in cyberspace to exchange ideas, meet and talk than on CompuServe; there is probably a Forum for just about any subject you could think of. I would recommend a free trial membership with CompuServe. Go to www.compuserve.com.

I have been section leader of Yoga and Meditation on CompuServe's New Age Spirituality Forum for several years. I have also been an active participant in the Religion Forum, and currently am the section leader for the Hinduism section. Those Forums are where I have come to know so many wonderful people, and where I have grown up along with many of them. At any one time you see messages from novices in any particular discipline, getting replies from those who know a lot. And colleagues promptly jump in to add their ideas. There is so much fun and friendship. At times, however, things turn ugly with one or more individuals attacking someone else, but the Sysops and section leaders usually moderate discussions well and remove offensive messages. I wish I had kept a copy of just about every message that I had read and replied to over the years, but that may well have amounted to volumes! It is interesting to look back and see exactly where I was in terms of knowledge and understanding when I started on CompuServe, and compare that to where I am now; the difference is very significant. I hope to continue serving as one of the section leaders in the Religion and New Age Spirituality Forums on CompuServe. All CompuServe Forums have just been completely redesigned and upgraded and are excellent. The Forums can be accessed at these URLs:

http://community.compuserve.com/newagespirit
http://community.compuserve.com/newageliving
http://community.compuserve.com/religion

Access to the Forum is free; you just have to either create a screen name or use yours from AOL, CompuServe, or AOL Instant Messenger (I have been glad to have been a member of CompuServe; you might really appreciate being a member too). Since CompuServe does not advertise, these Forums are not well known. They are a great place to exchange ideas in the field of spirituality and religion, and the only places on the Internet where discussions are moderated and free of abusive language, and where messages to you are easily and quickly accessed by clicking on "messages to you."

It is impossible to practice medicine without becoming steeped in religion. One sees disease, suffering and death just about every day. While most patients do not inquire about my religious conviction, some

29

do. Many just assume that I am Christian; others probably wonder. I recall the lovely eighty-year-old lady who asked me if I went to church. When I said that I did not, she said I must. "Why?" I inquired. "Well, *I* go to church, so *I* am sure to go to heaven. If *you* go to church, then *you* will go to heaven too. And then you could be my doctor in heaven!" Some have looked me sternly in the eye and said that there is to be no salvation without Christ. Even after completing this book, I still find it difficult to find a proper reply to such a statement, a reply that does anything either useful or constructive. There can be no reply whatsoever to dogma. It is somewhat painful whenever that happens. I just remind myself that the day one truly has Christ in the heart is the day s/he stops questioning someone else's religious practice and just radiates love and goodwill. I have written a great deal more about this in the chapter on Christianity. Still, it is a situation that always keeps me troubled, and in a way a problem without which this book would never have been written.

CHAPTER THREE:
THE HIDDEN TRUTH OF THE
CHRIST

The Jesus Fixation Syndrome

I once spent an hour teaching a young lady some methods of relaxation and meditation. She had been very troubled and restless, and was suffering various constitutional symptoms and ill health. After lying back on the examination table, relaxed, she suddenly sat up and exclaimed that it was too bad I had come that far in spirituality and yet not gone 'all the way.' I was puzzled, and asked her what she meant. "Oh, Jesus," she said, "you have not accepted Jesus. If only you did, your spiritual process would be complete." I was stunned, indeed very upset, that a person who had not yet found her own peace, was accusing me of not finding the "right source of peace;' still, I was not surprised. It was a typical example of how indoctrination into a way of thought could prevent acceptance of any other way of thinking. "Indoctrination" is not too harsh a word: one other lady told me that the peace that one could obtain through meditation is a trick that Satan plays on such practitioners; she stated that only Jesus could give us true inner peace! Such people refuse to find the inner peace within them that they could so easily find; instead, their minds are fixed on the concept of a deity without whom they seemingly have no peace and indeed a concept with which they destroy the peace in others as well.

I call this phenomenon the "Jesus fixation syndrome." It could also be stated to be 'Jesus on the head, anguish in the heart.' It is not what Christianity ought to be all about. I see Christians as belonging to three levels of practice. At the first level, fundamentalism prevails. The person takes the Bible to be the absolute truth, the one and only revelation from God. No other scripture is acceptable; everything and everyone else belongs to Paganism--to the heathens. At the second level, the person goes a little deeper into spirituality. S/he sees a glimmer of light from within, and while still enjoying the Bible, starts seeing the beauty of God in nature and in others. At the third level, they become real Christians: radiant human beings radiating love, compassion, and forgiveness. Such a person has Christ and compassion in the 'heart and head.' Such a Christian has adopted Jesus as a role model, has been inspired by his teachings, and even more important, has had his or her inner spiritual nature transformed by a deeper understanding obtained from the gospels. Such a person has been energized by their inner Spirit: God's power. A person so energized simply radiates the same loving energy, and has no need for dogma which states that Jesus is the only way.

Around two hundred years before Jesus, a sage in India called Pathanjali taught that by meditation on the mind of an illumined soul, one could attain a godly state. But this sage also taught that we could meditate on the light in our own souls and attain the same result. Therefore the essential point is that the goal is God-- Jesus was, and is, a way to God. Yet, because of several intolerant statements made in the gospels, (carefully inserted there by the early church) Christianity has always been a religion of exclusivity, professing a dogma that God can only be attained through Jesus. This is not only an extremely unfortunate situation that has caused countless wars and suffering; it is a serious distortion of the truth.

Obsession with dogma has led Christians to carry out atrocities which are inhuman and barbaric. Paul William Roberts, in his excellent travelogue about India called *Empire of the Soul* describes the horrors of the Spanish Inquisition in Goa, India, carried by the Portuguese rulers during the sixteenth century. Francis Xavier, who later was to achieve sainthood, was one of those who requested the Inquisition. Xavier's body is still enshrined in Goa, missing the right forearm which was removed and sent to Rome in the seventeenth century, and one toe which was bitten off by a devotee. The horrors of the Inquisition were inflicted on Hindus, particularly those who had seemingly converted to Catholicism but still performed Hindu rites and rituals in secret. He writes:

"The palace in which these holy terrorists ensconced themselves was known locally as Vodlem Gor—the Big House. It became a symbol of fear. Recondite ceremonies were conducted in there behind closed shutters, locked doors. People in the street often heard screams of agony piercing the night. All the Inquisition's activities were conducted in strict secrecy, replete with impenetrably arcane terminology, fiendishly discrepant logic, and antonymous questioning. Children were flogged and slowly dismembered in front of their parents, whose eyelids had been sliced off to make sure they missed nothing. Extremities were amputated carefully, so that a person could remain conscious even when all that remained was a torso and head. Male genitals were removed and burned in front of wives, breasts hacked off and vaginas penetrated with swords while husbands were forced to watch. So notorious was the Inquisition in Portuguese India that word of its horrors even reached home. The archbishop of Evora, in Portugal, eventually wrote, "If everywhere the Inquisition was an infamous court, the infamy, however base, however vile, however corrupt and determined by worldly interests, it was never more so than in Goa."" Fortunately, the British ended the Portuguese version of the Spanish Inquisition in India. It is such a relief to live in the twenty-first century and see the horrors of fundamentalist Christianity gone forever; now it is the turn of Islam to deal with its fanatics.

When I think of my twenty-five years in the United States and the thousands of wonderful Christian people whom I have known, and the great orderliness of society in America, I cannot help but feel that Christianity has had a powerfully positive impact on the people. Bruce Bawer in his book *Stealing Jesus* explains: "Conservative Christianity understands a Christian to be someone who subscribes to a specific set of theological propositions about God and the afterlife, and who professes to believe that by subscribing to those propositions, accepting Jesus Christ as savior, and (except in the case of the most extreme separatist fundamentalists) evangelizing, he or she evades God's wrath and wins salvation (for Roman Catholics, good works also count); liberal Christianity, meanwhile, tends to identify Christianity with the experience of God's abundant love and with the commandment to love God and one's neighbor. If, for conservative Christians, outreach generally means zealous proselytizing of the "unsaved," for liberal Christians it tends to mean social programs directed at those in need." That explains very succinctly why so many Americans have been friendly and hospitable. I have, on several occasions, been invited to Church, simply for fellowship and friendship, not for the purpose of conversion.

However, Neale Donald Walsch writes in his new book *The New Revelations—A Conversation with God,* about a newspaper article that appeared in the *Arizona Republic.* The article was titled *Lutheran Pastor Assailed—Joining Interfaith Event called Heresy.* Apparently a Reverend David Benke had joined other religious and civic leaders after the World Trade Center attack. They sang patriotic songs and prayed. However, fellow clergymen saw the participation in the interfaith event as heresy. Six pastors filed charges to have the Pastor expelled from the church, and others even petitioned to oust church president Gerald Kieschnick for condoning Rev. Benke's participation in the event.

Walsch states: "Most people to whom I've shown this story are aghast. Their mouths drop." He wrote: "That story shocked me. I was shocked and saddened and sick at heart when I first read it. I just had no idea…I thought that I had to look elsewhere in the world to find that level of hysterical, radical religious intolerance." He also reports the same degree of intolerance and bigotry in Baptist churches. However, we need to remind ourselves that it is the clergy that is often responsible for such outrageous behavior, and not necessarily everyday Americans. Priesthood within every religion tends to promote exclusivity; it is the way attempts to maintain its status. Unlike Walsch, I was neither shocked nor surprised to read the article.

In the past few years, many scholars have discarded their reluctance to delve deep into the very heart of Christianity and question whether Jesus of Nazareth really was a historical figure. Until the past decade or so, scholars have relied heavily on the gospels and the other writings of the New Testament to validate the nature of Jesus. It has been the equivalent of saying that the proof a book is true is that it says so. Recently, however, scholars have been changing things. They have shown, quite clearly, that Christianity is a religion fashioned after Pagan religions involving dying-resurrecting god-men. They include the gods Mithras of Persia, Dionysus of Greece, and Osiris of Egypt. All these gods die and are then resurrected, bringing hope to their devotees. These authors reveal that Jesus as a man never existed, but rather his entire story was a carefully created myth similar to those above. These are not just simple stories, but mystery myths, used by followers to attain greater spiritual states. This essay, however, discusses how we can understand Christianity to be a valid religious practice even though there likely never was a historical Jesus. Scholars have shown that Christianity was originally a mystery myth cult, with "historical" elements carefully woven into the myth subsequently. Many mystery myths have known historical figures, events and locations blended in to give them an element of validity.

Did Jesus ever exist?

Numerous volumes have been written to show, quite convincingly, that there never was a Jesus of Nazareth, a real, living, god-like man, who was crucified, lay in a grave, and then rose on the third day. Like the citizens of the emperor with his new clothes, even "scholars" have been traditionalists and have based their "scholarship" on the gospels. This is rapidly changing. Timothy Freke and Peter Gandy stunned the world with their book *The Jesus Mysteries—Was the 'Original Jesus' a Pagan God?* Other books on this subject are:

The Christ Conspiracy by Acharya S.;
The Jesus Puzzle by Earl Doherty;
The Christ Myth (Westminster College-Oxford Classics in the Study of Religion) by Arthur Drews, C. Deslisle Burns;
The Jesus Myth by G.A. Wells;
The Myth of the Historical Jesus and the Evolution of Consciousness (Dissertation Series—Society of Biblical Literature) by Hal Childs;
Jesus: God, Man or Myth? An Examination of the Evidence by Herbert Cutner;
Deconstructing Jesus by Robert M. Price;
The Christian Myth: Origins, Logic, and Legacy by Burton L. Mack;
and many others.

Indeed, the first time I read *The Jesus Mysteries* was during vacation in Hawaii where I happened to find it at a book store. It so captivated me that I could not put it down; my family was enjoying the beach at Hanauma Bay while I sat under a palm tree glued to the book! These authors only have one goal in mind: to expose the truth. They do not have an "anti-Christian" agenda. This essay is to show that the worship of Jesus can be as valid a religious and spiritual practice as any that humanity has created, even though it has been shown quite convincingly that there never was a Jesus of history. Now Christianity is on an equal footing with the Pagan religions of old. And indeed, the essential teachings of older religions have been preserved and presented in a different form in the gospels: it is possible to study the various teachings of the gospels and learn from them, and allow them to enrich our lives. The Jesus story must be very carefully analyzed as a mystery myth, and it must be used to help us develop spiritually. Acharya S. feels that the Sadducees of Israel, along with other mystical groups such as the Therapeutae of Egypt, helped develop the Jesus myth. Once we understand the origins of the Jesus myth, we will no longer spend all our time obsessing about how it must have been absolutely and historically true, but rather use it to deepen our spiritual attainment. To insist on historical validity would be to miss the point entirely. We would not only waste our own time but also endanger our peace of mind, not to mention the peace of the world.

In books that try to establish the historicity of Jesus, authors usually take for granted that Jesus was indeed historical, and then try and find bits and pieces of "evidence" that seems to substantiate the fact. Regrettably, they do not start with a clean slate, and never a genuinely questioning or exploratory attitude. Scholars who have questioned the very historicity of Jesus have found that they either lose their academic positions, or are denied promotion: Ian Wilson, writing in his book *Jesus-the Evidence*, reminds us that David Friedrich Strauss, a German tutor at the University of Tubingen, lost his status as tutor as well as his promotion to professor, for such honest questioning.

In their book *Excavating Jesus* John Dominic Crossan and Jonathan L. Reed try and document various archeological finds that they feel substantiate the fact that Jesus did live in the first Century CE, though their stated intention was "digging down archeologically amidst the stones to reconstruct his world and digging down exegetically amidst the texts to reconstruct his life." In other words, they start with the premise that Jesus was indeed a historical person; they are not really out to prove whether Jesus did or did not exist, but to try and reveal various findings that seem to be of value in revealing the nature of his life.

Regarding the apparent birthplace of Jesus, Nazareth, they write: "Outside the gospels and the early Christian texts that rely on them, there are no pre-Constantinian citations referring to Nazareth. It is never mentioned by any of the Jewish Rabbis whose pronouncements are in the Mishnah or whose discussions are in the Talmud, even though they cite sixty-three other Galilean towns. Josephus, the Jewish historian and general over Galilee during the first Jewish revolt in 66-67 C.E., refers to forty-five named sites there, but never to Nazareth. It is unknown in the Christian Old Testament. Even though Zebulun's tribal allotment in the Bible catalogues some fifteen Lower Galilean sites in Nazareth's vicinity, it is not counted among them. It was absolutely insignificant." Yet these authors try to explain this away saying: "It's no surprise that Nazareth is never mentioned. Writing in antiquity was an upper-class activity, so that references to Nazareth increase dramatically after Christianity rose to political power in the fourth century C.E."

The authors try to explain that there was indeed a Nazareth, despite it being unheard of till over three hundred years after the supposed advent of Jesus, and don't seem to realize how weak their argument for the existence of the town really is. In fact the authors seem to provide clear evidence that there never was a town called Nazareth until the gospels containing the story of Jesus were established by the Church in the fourth century as "historical truth," after which people "discovered" (created) the town of Nazareth.

Crossan and Reed also explore other artifacts they feel are of value in establishing the credibility of the fact that Jesus was a historical character. They speak of the discovery of a boat dating back to the first century, and of course jump to conclusions that it could well have been the one that Jesus was on in the Sea of Galilee. I have heard of 'clutching at straws,' but 'clutching at boats' is something new! Other finds that really reveal nothing whatsoever about the historicity of Jesus, include the tomb of Caiaphas, who is well known to have been a High Priest in those days, and inscriptions revealing that Pontius Pilate was indeed a Prefect at the time. These two were historical characters, but the character of Jesus was interposed "historically" with these and others. The New Testament states that Annas and Caiaphas were joint high priests, but scholars have pointed out that there were never two joint high priests; in particular, Annas was not a joint high priest with Caiaphas. Annas was removed from the office of high priest in 15 CE after holding office for some nine years. Caiaphas only became high priest in c. 18 CE, about three years after Annas.

Just as the character of Dr. Zhivago was created by Boris Pasternak, and a realistic "history" of such a character was created amidst known historical characters such as Lenin, and amidst the well-known Bolshevik revolution, the fact is that there never was a real-live Dr. Zhivago. In the same way, the character of Jesus was carefully constructed amidst the lives of known historical characters such as Pontius Pilate, Caiaphas, Herod Antipas, and so on. Some degree of "authenticity" is all that is needed in the creation: the rest is carried on by faith.

Among other books that try desperately to assert a historical Jesus, is Ian Wilson's book *Jesus-The Evidence*. This author admits that German scholars such as Rudolf Bultmann and his predecessors made important points questioning that Jesus ever existed, and quotes Albert Schweitzer as making a similar statement. Yet he continues to make extremely weak and untenable arguments that the gospel stories are truly historical. The historical validity of the gospel stories has never ever stood up to honest criticism, yet faith and tradition firmly stand in support of such validity. Certain things appear to be too precious and valuable to Western tradition and civilization.

The early Church established a doctrine, and made sure that no other viewpoint about Jesus was allowed to prevail. Anything other than Orthodox Church doctrine was, and is, considered heresy. Scholars have shown that the Church, over hundreds of years, resorted to enormous amounts of violence, arson, torture and murder, to ensure that the Jesus story was accepted as literally true. Surely, the truth does not need violence to establish itself?

It is likely that there are tens of millions of people who are perfectly content with Christianity as presented in the gospels, and they are not looking for any other way of looking at their religion. On the other hand, there are an equal number of Christians who have not found solace in the religion they have been taught, and they may find comfort in what is the real nature of Christianity: attitudes and ways of achieving direct communion with God. For indeed, there is much comfort to be obtained in the teachings of the Bible, particularly to learn the meaning of the esoteric, or secretive, teachings of the gospels. If the ideas revealed in the gospels could be considered to be a bright new sun that rose over the ancient land, literalist Christianity constitutes a dark brooding cloud that obscured this radiance, leaving only a 'silver lining.' The teachings of 'Jesus,' are the silver lining; they are extracts of human wisdom both from the Hebrew Bible, and other ancient sources. They are the wisdom of the Gnostics written into a quasi-historical drama.

The story of Jesus is likely to be, simply put, a story; though in truth the story was really a mystery myth. Even so, such a statement would be unacceptable for millions of people, but more and more research is revealing this to be a fact. Flavius Josephus, a Jewish historian, is said to have written this paragraph in the third chapter of the eighteenth book of *Antiquities of the Jews* translated by William Whiston, called the 'Testimonium Flavianum,', and is widely quoted by Christian writers as historical evidence for Jesus.

"Now, there was about this time Jesus, a wise man, if it be lawful to call him a man, for he was a doer of wonderful works- a teacher of such men as receive the truth with pleasure. He drew over to him both many of the Jews, and many of the Gentiles. He was (the) Christ; and when Pilate, at the suggestion of the principal men amongst us, had condemned him to the Cross, those that loved him at the first did not forsake him, for he appeared to them alive again the third day, as the divine prophets had foretold these and ten thousand other wonderful things concerning him; and the tribe of Christians, so named from him, are not extinct at this day."

The words "for he appeared to them alive again the third day" are presented so casually as though it is just another routine event. This would have been a once-in-a-lifetime event, to which a historian would surely devote entire volumes! The "Christ" gets a measly little paragraph? No, this entire paragraph most certainly is to be disregarded and rejected as an interpolation, a forgery. We might as well call this the "Testimonium Fakianum." It is just conditioning and faith that has made even great scholars accept the statement as true. Other scholars feel that parts of the paragraph involving Jesus rising on the third day are Christian interpolations, in order to confirm that at least there was a historical Jesus, but this appears to me to be a very weak argument. They have been arguing quite desperately that some sentences were interpolations and some were not, in order to assert that there at least was a reference to a Jesus of history by Josephus; alas, this pious hope is probably in vain because it is likely that the entire paragraph was a forgery.

In the book *The Jesus Mysteries*, the authors also explore Roman historians as possible sources of the evidence of Jesus as being historically valid; they write that almost thirty historians of the time had nothing to say about Jesus. They state that the Roman historian Suetonius, in a list of miscellaneous notes on legislative matters relates that in 64 CE, punishment was inflicted on the Christians, a class of men given to a new and wicked superstition. But as the authors conclude, all these sources really tell us is that a few Christians existed in the Roman world. They give no information on Jesus himself. The historian Tacitus is quoted by many as providing reliable evidence of a historical Jesus. However, Freke and Gandy state that the evidence of Tacitus, governor of Asia around 112 CE, was not contemporary, and dating to about 50 years after the event. Tacitus called Pilate the 'Procurator' of Judea when he was in fact a 'Prefect,' so Tacitus was quoting hearsay information.

Romans were said to keep meticulous records of the actions of their leaders, and there certainly are no reliable records pertaining to Jesus.

Are the gospels the 'gospel truth?'

Freke and Gandy show that the genealogies of Jesus as revealed in the two gospels, Mathew and Luke, are dramatically different. In any case, they comment about how the genealogy on Joseph's side as laboriously drawn out was quite irrelevant, as Jesus was not really the son of Joseph, but miraculously fathered by God and conceived by Mary.

These authors remind us that according to the gospel of Luke, Jesus was born at the time of the census of Quirinius which took place in 6 CE. The gospel of Mathew tells us that Jesus was born during the reign of King Herod who died in 4 BCE which Luke also states, yet the gospel still reveals Mary with child at the time of the census of 6 CE, which leads to two dates of her pregnancy, ten years apart. They provide further conflicting detail: "John places the cleansing of the temple at the beginning of his narrative, Mathew at the end. Mark has Jesus teaching only in the area of Galilee, and not in Judea, and only traveling the 70 miles to Jerusalem once, at the end of his life. Luke, however, portrays Jesus as teaching equally in Galilee and Judea. John's Jesus, on the other hand, preaches mainly in Jerusalem and makes only occasional visits to Galilee."

Freke and Gandy then speak about the events related to Jesus' crucifixion as being inconsistent in the gospels. They write: "According to Mathew and Mark, Jesus was both tried and sentenced by the Jewish priests of the Sanhedrin. Luke has it that Jesus was tried by the Sanhedrin, but not sentenced by them. Yet, according to John, Jesus does not appear before the Sanhedrin at all. Jesus then goes to his death by crucifixion. Or is it, as Paul says, to be "hanged on a gibbet?" Or, as Peter has it in the Acts of the Apostles, that he was "hung on a tree?""

Freke and Gandy, as well as other scholars, have noticed glaring discrepancies in the Bible. Regarding the fate of the disciple Judas, for instance, the gospel of Mathew states that he hanged himself, but according to the Acts of the Apostles, he died from an accidental fall.

Jesus had predicted that he would be buried in the earth for three days and three nights, but it is recorded that he did on Friday and rose on

Sunday, thus spending only two nights in the earth. Following that, there are conflicting reports of story. The gospel of Mark says that women disciples saw a young man in a white robe, but Luke reported two men in brilliant clothes. The gospel of Mathew reported yet another version, of an angel descending from heaven, and rolling away the stone of the burial chamber. Jesus promised to return within the lifetimes of his followers, but never did. The gospels of Luke and Mathew both assert that there are "some among those standing here will never taste death before they see the Son of Man coming;" however, over two millennia later, Jesus has not returned.

The variations on the gospel story are considered by such scholars to be a hidden sign from the Gnostics who created them, that the quasi-historical story is not to be taken literally, but as part of the myth.

The Hebrew Bible

The Old Testament, as it is called, is not "old" for the Jewish people. It is the Hebrew Bible, their most precious resource. Indeed, most of the Bible consists of Jewish wisdom, Jewish folklore and legend, Jewish Law, and the teachings of Jewish prophets. Justin O'Brien, author of *A Meeting of Mystic Paths: Christianity and Yoga* states: "As a compilation of legends, parables, aphorisms, songs, sagas, poetry, sermons, legislation, historical decrees, epics, liturgical rules, quotations, and myths, these writings offer a wide mixture of literary genre to say the least." I would modify the last part of the sentence to read "Jewish literary genre," because indeed, that is truly what it is. Indeed, there are subtle alterations in the Old Testament to make it appear as though the entire document leads towards Jesus as the Messiah prophesied by the earlier Jewish prophets. To someone accustomed to reading the Bible from childhood, as I have, the entire Old Testament appears to be a saga of Christianity, from the time of creation until the time of Jesus, and the teachings of his apostles afterward. The Bible is a collection of just the right gospels to achieve the purpose of a unified doctrine. It is thought by some to have taken almost four hundred years to establish what is considered 'canon' today. Early church leaders had enormous conflict as to what was appropriate for acceptance as canonical. For instance, Marcion wanted to exclude the entire Old Testament! Freke and Gandy write in their book *The Jesus Mysteries*: "The influential Gnostic teacher Marcion argued for the complete separation of Christianity from Judaism. He produced a text called *The Antithesis,* which juxtaposed quotes from the Old and New

Testaments to demonstrate how they contradict each other. For Marcion, Jehovah was a "committed barbarian" and the Old Testament merely a catalog of his crimes against humanity."

In his most interesting new book, *The New Revelations: A Conversation with God* Neale Donald Walsch writes: "….there have been many books written about the history of massacre and slaughter in God's Holy Name as extensively recorded in many places in the Bible. In these books, we are told how the Bible relates that 12,000 men, women and children of Ai were killed in an ambush that God Himself inspired and supervised (Joshua: 8:1-30), and that the armies of the Amorites were destroyed when "the Lord slew them with a great slaughter" (Joshua 10:10-11). These Bible critiques tell us that a reading of the books of Exodus, Leviticus, Deuteronomy, Joshua, Judges, Samuel, Numbers, Amos, Kings, Chronicles, Esther, and Job, no name a few, will produce a toll of no less than one million people in Old Testament history alone who were smote by God's hand…."

In other words, according to the Bible, God was directly responsible for the killing of about a million people. Or was He? Such "killing" ordered by God was all myth. There is no other way to interpret it. God does not personally order the killing of anyone, be they of another religion, or "sinners." God does not kill. All these stories were created by Jewish writers to establish a national identity, and to try and create the impression that "God is on our side—God helps those who help his cause and destroys those who don't." There are countless groups of people who have myths about the glorious successes of their ancestors against their enemies, either imaginary or real. Unless we realize or accept this fact, we will commit the grave error of believing that God really does kill people who don't believe in the Judeo-Christian way of thought and worship.

The Jewish Tradition

I have known many wonderful Jewish people, and Jews are among the most accomplished and successful people on Earth. Christians and Muslims have revered Jewish scripture but eschewed the Jewish people; this is so sadly ironic. I not only admire the Jewish people as among the greatest of achievers, I consider Jewish scripture and spirituality to be on par with that of any world religion. The Jewish tradition is proud of its most profound achievement, not of buildings and palaces that eventually crumble, but "the Book." Jewish thought and understanding is so vast, it cannot be limited just to the Hebrew Bible, the Old Testament. The Talmud, which is a commentary on the Torah, is considered to have very valuable insight into the teachings of the Torah; the Mishnah is also part of Jewish writing that is considered authoritative. There are meditative and other spiritual practices, particularly the Kabala, making Judaism extremely rich, varied, and vast. Recent books devoted to "Jewish Meditation," however, seem to plagiarize meditation methods from Buddhism and other sources, adding Jewish terms, thereby creating a seemingly new dimension to Jewish spirituality.

One would feel that the Hebrews were quite presumptuous to think that there is only one God, and that one God was the God of the Hebrews, a stern God who destroys the enemies of his chosen people. I believe it would be a great misunderstanding to look at it that way. I see it this way: Hebrew sages had a vision of the Law. The Ten Commandments were just a part of the Law. The Law consisted of Mitzvoth, or commandments. There were 613 Mitzvoth, consisting of 248 affirmative commandments and 365 prohibitions. To the Jews, the Law was inviolable, fair, decent, proper, and was eternally viable and valuable. Anyone who chooses and accepts the Law becomes the chosen, because they have chosen it. Their sages taught such people that they had become the favorites, the supported, of God. It was also the vision of those prophets that God would support all their endeavors, as long as the Law was followed. So the Law comes first, the Lord makes the Law, and the land, Israel, is given to the keepers of the Law. Borrowing from the book *Why the Jews?* by Dennis Prager and Joseph Telushskin, who speak of God, Law and Land, we could say that these are the three precious "L's" of Judaism: their Law, their Lord and their Land. But did God "hand down" these commandments? The theme my book is that all words spoken by human beings are "words of God." There is just too much variation between the "words of God" as revealed in various religions, to reconcile us to the idea that God actually spoke to anyone. Sages come up with very profound ideas and concepts, and then give them a seal of holiness by declaring that they were the "commandments of God." So, rather than the Law being the actual, direct communication of God, I see the Law as a vision conceived by sages, also known as the prophets.

The ancient Hindus, living around the same time as the ancient Hebrews, also believed in a world order, which they called "Rta," or cosmic order, called "Dharma" in later Hinduism and Buddhism. The Dharma is also loosely translated as Law, but refers more to truth itself, which just cannot be listed in a set of ten, or a thousand, commandments. I see the Mitzvoth to be facets of a large diamond, which is the nature of truth itself. Various sages or prophets, over time, have tried to summarize truth into this or that collection of "commandments," but such collections can only cover a fragment of the truth. Jews and Christians hold the Ten Commandments precious, but the fact is that many of the Commandments were had already been taught in earlier cultures. Of the Ten Commandments, the following make excellent sense: "Do not kill. Do not commit adultery. Do not steal. Do not covet what is not yours. Do not give false testimony against anyone." These directives are not unique from a world view point; in Buddhism, for example, practitioners and laypersons take the five precepts: 'I will refrain from taking life, from stealing, from sexual misconduct, from telling lies, and from using intoxicating liquor or drugs.'

The Hebrew concept, or revelation, of the nature of God, is unique. God tells Moses "I am that I am." Told in Hebrew as "Ehyeh Asher Ehyeh," this has been translated into other phrases by various scholars. However, the essential meaning is that God's presence is essentially here and now, moment to moment, for eternity. Hebrew Law includes commandments on monotheism that were seemingly unique in what is commonly known as the Pagan world: "You shall have no other gods before me. You shall not make for yourself an idol in the form of anything in heaven above or earth below, and you shall not bow down to them or worship them; for I am a jealous God. You shall not misuse the name of the Lord your God." Deuteronomy Chapter 17 also prescribes severe punishment for anyone committing idolatry or even worshipping the sun or moon or stars: death by stoning. Pagan idolatry was to be eliminated at all costs. However, one wonders what then happened to the commandment, "Do not kill," as stoning to death is a particularly horrible and brutal way of execution. The commandment "do not kill" is not followed by God in the creation of the Nation of Israel, as he constantly directs "his people" to destroy the nations of their enemies. "Do not covet" is also a directive that is dropped by the wayside on the way to Canaan, as God directs the Israelites to take the land of Canaanites. We must realize that these directives are mythical ones created by prophets to emphasize the concept of monotheism. In America, early colonists created laws that reflect Biblical despotism. In 1641, Massachusetts adopted a law that stated: "If any man after legal conviction shall have or worship any other god but the Lord God, he shall be put to death." In 1680 the

New Hampshire colony enacted an idolatry law that states: "Idolatry. It is enacted by ye assembly and ye authority thereof, yet if any person having had the knowledge of the true God openly and manifestly have or worship any other god but the Lord God, he shall be put to death." We must indeed be thankful to the founding fathers of the American republic for eliminating the evil power of such religion.

Finkelstein and Silberman in their book *The Bible Unearthed* have shown that the Israelites were native people of Canaan, and not "invaders from the desert." Therefore the seeming violations of the commandments above were just myth created in order to establish a national identity. We cannot accept a parochial God such as the one described in the Hebrew Bible as displaying characteristics of being the God of all people, not if he takes sides and directs the killing of entire communities. Revealing the myth of "liberation from the bondage of Egypt" is a very important thing. However, that myth is what gives the Jewish people a unique identity, one of being "chosen by God for liberation" in order to follow all the directives that go with being the chosen.

Circumcision

Though circumcision is an ancient practice, and was practiced in Egypt, among other places, the Jews appear to have been perhaps the first to declare the practice of circumcision to be a part of their religious tradition. The Bible says that God instructed Abraham and his progeny to be circumcised as part of the covenant, or agreement with God. The story of Abraham is, as discussed elsewhere, a myth, but an important one, a meaningful myth relating to the apparent origin of the Jewish people. It appears to me that inspired Jewish mystics created the myth of Abraham. These authors had a vision of what ought to be a unique relationship with God. To them, being circumcised was part of such a relationship.

I was uncircumcised until the age of forty, a period I call BCE, (before circumcision era!) and the period after that, I call CE (circumcised era). I had the procedure done for reasons of personal hygiene. I am so glad I had it done, and having been able to compare my life BCE and CE, I recommend the procedure highly. It is well known that men circumcised at a young age seldom suffer cancer of the penis, and the wives of circumcised men have dramatically less cancer of the cervix. Also, it has been shown that the inner part of the foreskin harbors and breeds the HIV virus. Jeff Levin, Ph.D., writes in his excellent book

45

God, Faith, and Health, page 28: "Scholarly articles published early in the twentieth century noted especially lower rates of uterine and cervical cancer in Jewish women. This was attributed to the hygienic benefit of circumcision in their partners. The assumption was made that Jewish women were more likely to engage Jewish (circumcised) men as sexual partners, which would lower their risk for cancers that were more likely, on average, to be found in uncircumcised men. Lending credence to this assumption is research showing an enormously higher incidence of penile cancer in Hindus, who are not typically circumcised, relative to Muslims, who are, and in whom such cancers are very rare."

The founders of Judaism, as I see it, went through such a process and felt that circumcision was a very important part of life for a man. So the patriarch, or primordial Jew, had to be circumcised. Creating for Abraham a "covenant with God" would ensure that circumcision was divinely ordained. I agree so whole-heartedly that I will teach my children and the generations to follow to make sure that their male offspring are circumcised soon after birth as is widely practiced in the United States today. St. Paul was against circumcision. Elsewhere in the chapter I have discussed how Paul was really a Gnostic, and for the Gnostics the ritual of circumcision was not an important part of relationship with God. The Old Testament seems to have prevailed for many American Christians, fortunately, for whom circumcision of their sons is desirable. Having realized the origin of the story of Abraham allows me to enjoy and appreciate the story all the more. I can see why the covenant and the commandments have always been a guiding light for Jews.

The myth of monotheism

The Semitic, as well as the western world, seems to accept monotheism as a unique and supremely superior concept. Hindus, on the other hand, who are considered to be polytheistic with many gods, have maintained for millennia that there is but one supreme power of the Universe. Pagan philosophers also taught the same thing. However, in the practice of Hinduism and Paganism, myths evolved about various "gods," or heavenly beings. These "gods" had various purposes and functions, but never to be confused with the One Supreme power. The Hindu Kĕna Üpanishad (as translated by Alistair Shearer) has a most charming story of how these "gods" challenged the Supreme Being. The god of fire could not burn straw placed by the Supreme, and neither could the god of wind blow it away. The Goddess then tells the "gods": "That was Brahman, the Supreme God; through Him it was, not of yourselves, that you attained your victory and your glory." The Üpanishad continues: "This is the truth of Brahman in religion to nature: whether in the flash of lightning, or in the wink of the eyes, the power that is shown is the power of Brahman. This is the truth of Brahman in relation to man: in the motions of the mind, the power that is shown is the power of Brahman. For this reason a man should meditate upon Brahman by day and by night. Brahman is the adorable being in all beings. Meditate upon him as such. He who meditates upon him as such is honored by all other beings." The author of the Üpanishad concludes: "I have told you the secret knowledge. Austerity, self-control, performance of duty without attachment-these constitute the body of that knowledge. The Vĕdas (Sacred Hindu scripture) are its limbs. Truth is its very soul. He who attains to knowledge of Brahman, being freed from all evil, finds the eternal, the supreme."

The religion and culture of the Hebrews is fairly ancient, starting around 2000 BCE. This time frame corresponds to the late Vedic Age of ancient India. I believe that Judaism and Brahmanical Hinduism were two profound schools of thought, possibly with considerable exchange and similar cultural patterns such as baptism and anointing. Many scholars think that the ancient Aryans who settled in India, probably over thousands of years rather than in one large "invasion," were nomadic people whose greatest contribution to humanity was the Vĕdas, their sacred scripture. The similarity to the Jews as a nomadic people, who settle in their Promised Land, and claim the Hebrew Bible to be their greatest achievement, is remarkable. Later, the marvelous philosophical expositions called the Üpanishads were added as appendages to the Vĕdas. The Vedic Hindu view of worship involves awareness of One Supreme Being who transcends all "gods." There is a hymn in the *Rig-Vĕda* describing creation in a most profound way (translated by Jonathan Star):

In the beginning there was neither existence nor nonexistence.
Neither sky nor heaven beyond...
That One breathed, without breath, by its own power.
Nothing else was there...
The first born was the Creative Will,
The primordial seed of the mind.
The sages, searching for the truth within their own hearts,

Realized the eternal bond between the seen and the unseen.

This bond was an endless line stretched across the heavens.
What was above? What was below?
Primal seeds were sprouting, mighty forces moving.
Pulsation below, pure energy above.

Who here knows? Who can say for sure,
When it began, and from where it came-this creation?
The gods came afterward,
So who really knows?
From where this creation came,
Whether He formed it or not,
He who watches everything from the highest heaven,
Only He knows --or perhaps even he does not know!

The important message was that "the gods" came afterward. Hindu thinking, therefore, is monotheistic in essence; the "gods" can be considered to be the equals of the angels in the Semitic religions. The *Rig-Věda* is now considered to be thousands of years old. It clearly displays a profound sense of monotheism, and considers the "gods" to be manifestations of the power of the Supreme One. The *Kěna Ūpanishad* teaches what God is: "That which cannot be expressed by speech, but by which speech is expressed; that which cannot be conceived by the mind, but by which the mind is conceived, that alone, know as Brahman, the Supreme, not that which people here worship." Over the years, Hinduism evolved to include worship of the One in myriad forms. The *Rig-Věda* firmly states "Truth is one; sages call it by different names."

The Hebrews had a clear directive in their Bible to destroy idolaters, though it is likely that the real directive was to stop the practice of idolatry among themselves. It is the very thesis of Hinduism, in contrast, that the Supreme accepts any worship whatsoever, because all such worship eventually goes to the One Source. Idols are not just idols, but focuses of God's energy lovingly invited into the image as a means of communication.

The formless "One God" of the Judaic Law has various attributes described in the Hebrew Bible, including those of being jealous and possessive. From the Vedic viewpoint, it is not appropriate to limit the One God in any manner; indeed, descriptions of God include not only

admiration, but also expressions of helplessness in describing Him.
The *Îsha Üpanishad* describes the Supreme as "He who pervades all, is
radiant, bodiless, unbounded and untainted, invulnerable and pure. He is
the Seer, the one Mind, all-pervading and self-sufficient." The Supreme
Lord of the Üpanishads is beyond description, He is the nirgüna (free of
attributes or form) Brahman, or "That from which all originates."

Ibn Warraq, in his book *Why I am not a Muslim* states: "Historically
speaking, monotheism has often shown itself to be ferociously intolerant,
in contrast to polytheism on behalf of which religious wars have never
been waged. This intolerance follows logically from monotheistic
ideology." He quotes Gore Vidal: "The great unmentionable evil at the
centre of our culture is monotheism. From a barbaric Bronze Age text
known as the Old Testament, three anti-human religions have evolved--
Judaism, Christianity, and Islam. These are sky-god religions. They are
patriarchal--God is the omnipotent father--hence the loathing of women
for 2000 years in those countries afflicted by the sky-god and his male
delegates. The sky-god is jealous. He requires total obedience. Those
who would reject him must be converted or killed. Totalitarianism is the
only politics that can truly serve the sky-god's purpose. Any movement
of a liberal nature endangers his authority. One God, one King, one Pope,
one master in the factory, one father-leader in the family."

Warraq also quotes Schopenhauer: "Indeed, intolerance is essential only
to monotheism; an only God is by nature a jealous God who will not
allow another to live. On the other hand, polytheistic gods are naturally
tolerant; they live and let live. In the first place, they gladly tolerate their
colleagues, the gods of the same religion, and this tolerance is afterwards
extended even to foreign gods who are accordingly, hospitably received
and later admitted, in some cases, even to an equality of rights. An
instance of this is seen in the Romans who willingly admitted and
respected Phrygian, Egyptian and other foreign gods. Thus it is only
the monotheistic religions that furnish us with the spectacle of religious
wars, religious persecutions, courts for trying heretics, and also with
that of iconoclasm, the destruction of the images of foreign gods, the
demolition of Indian temples and Egyptian colossi that had looked at the
sun for three thousand years; all this because their jealous God had said:
'Thou shalt make no graven image,' and so on."

I therefore submit that the commandments "You shall have no other
gods before me"; and "You shall not make for yourself an idol" are the

views and visions of the prophets of the Hebrews. Though written as a directive to Jews and adopted by Christians, they must not be taken as commandments for the world. This directive of destroying anyone not of "The Book" was also actively taken up by Muhammad, the founder of Islam. Followers of these Semitic religions have slaughtered millions of people in that cause, and the slaughter must end. The not-so-well known holocaust was the massacre of Hindus in India by various Muslim conquerors and their armies. It is now known that the conquistadors killed millions of Mayans, Aztecs and other South American natives. We must now realize and accept the fact that there are religions which believe in approaching God in stages, simple forms of worship to start, towards the sun and nature, and various image forms, for instance, and later graduating to deep meditative practices that transcend image worship. The Îsha Üpanishad provides an incredibly advanced understanding of the very nature of Hindu worship of the sun:

O Lord of Light, the One that knows, the golden guardian, the giver of life, spread apart your rays, minimize your brilliance, so that I may perceive your truly finest and most splendid nature, that cosmic spirit which permeates your heart. In other words, the sun is only an energy form that radiates the power and light of the One Supreme. Worship of the sun is to acknowledge the life- giving nature of God, who provides our energy through the sun. Over three thousand years ago, then, the sages were able to teach that we need to look beyond the forces of nature for the ultimate truth and power: that this power is manifest in all of nature.

The Genesis Story

The story of creation in Genesis falls severely short of any degree of credibility as historical fact, but it is a great myth, as discussed below. God created the heavens and the earth a few thousand years ago, taking six days to accomplish all of creation including man and woman. He rested on the seventh day. This was the primordial work-week, of a six-day week followed by a day of rest and contemplation. It is a metaphor for what ought to be a work-week for us, requiring six days of work followed by a day of rest and God-awareness. The seven days of a week were devised by Pagans, however, with days of the week assigned to the planets, Sunday representing the solar deity. However, I am not aware of a "day of rest and holiness" being practiced prior to the Hebrew myth regarding Sabbath, the day of rest. Perhaps humanity did not want the auspicious day to be the day of Saturn, (Saturday) rather that of the sun. God creates Adam by breathing his Spirit into "dust," meaning the earth, causing a blend of matter and divine energy. This is an important part of the myth, reminding us of our true nature: a blend of Spirit and matter. Adam is said to be male, with Eve taken from a rib, but mythically Adam represents the primordial androgynous human who splits down the middle to create male and female. The myth could easily have made man and woman created separately, but it did not: its hidden meaning, as I see it, is that the primordial creatures created were neither male nor female.

According to the Bible, when Adam and Eve were created, there were no other people on earth. To them were born Cain and Abel. But Cain killed Abel out of great jealousy. Seth was born later. The Bible does not say how Cain or Seth found wives; one is left to imagine that God created wives for them. And when Cain is banished, he is fearful that someone might kill him and indeed God gives him a mark of safety. One wonders: safety from whom? No one else had yet been created, let alone to be a threat. There is a charming parallel in the Hindu scriptures, described in the Brihadāranyaka Üpanishad (as translated in Alistair Shearer's book *The Upanishads*): "Pürüsha (the Creator) spoke, saying, "I am," and thus I'ness was born. And even now, when a person is asked "Who is it?" he replies first, 'It is I,' then adds his name. But then Pürüsha became frightened, as even now we become frightened when alone. He thought to himself: "Since there is nothing but myself, what is there to be frightened of?" Thereupon his fears dissolved, as he realized they were groundless. For verily, fear is born of duality."

The Garden of Eden

Genesis 2-8 states: "Now the Lord God had planted a garden in the east, in Eden; and there he put the man he had formed." Verse 2-10 describes the location of Eden in more detail: "A river watering the garden flowed from Eden; from there it was separated into four headwaters. The name of the first is the Pishon; it winds through the entire land of Havilah, where there is gold. The name of the second river is the Gihon; it winds through the entire land of Cush. The name of the third river is the Tigris; it runs along the east side of Asshur. And the fourth river is the Euphrates. The Lord God took the man and put him in the Garden of Eden to work it and take care of it."

The Learning Channel presented a very well researched program in 2003 by David Rohl, who had spent quite some time investigating the actual location of Eden, and Rohl was interviewed on the Learning Channel's web site. He was asked about evidence regarding the Garden of Eden's physical location being narrowed down to the region of Tabriz in Iran. Rohl said: "The arguments for placing the traditional site of the original Garden of Eden in the region of Tabriz are, in a sense, interrelated and follow a logical path of deduction — each clue coming from the previous one. However, the starting point for the investigation has to be the four rivers of Eden (mentioned in the second chapter of Genesis), which had their sources in Eden. Two of these rivers —the Perath (Euphrates) and Hiddekel (Tigris) have always been known. They have their headwaters (Hebrew roshim) in the mountains of eastern Turkey around Lake Van. The trick was to identify the other two rivers — the Gihon and Pishon. We have now been able to show that they are the Gaihun-Aras and Kezel-Uizhun, both flowing into the Caspian Sea. They have their headwaters around Lake Urmia.

So Eden was situated in the region where the sources of these four rivers are still located today — in other words in the mountains of Ararat (Assyrian Urartu) around the two great salt lakes of Van and Urmia. The next step was to look for the Garden of Eden in the eastern part of Eden, where Genesis 2:8 tells us it was located. There is only one large valley due east of Lake Urmia, hemmed in on three sides by snowcapped mountains — and that is the Adji Chay Valley, at the heart of which stands the ancient city of Tabriz.

Rohl also stated that Reginald Walker was the first to recognize western Iran as the area in which the author of the book of Genesis set the Eden legend. Walker is said to have been a scholar who specialized in linguistics — in particular, toponyms (the names of places and their etymologies). He was the one who made the link between the biblical River Gihon and the River Aras when he found out that the Arabic geographers, following the post-Islamic invasion of Persia, knew this river as the Gaihun. Walker then went on to equate the Pishon with the Uizhun by replacing the ancient Iranian "U" with a Semitic "P" (such a phonetic change is attested in the region) to give us an original biblical Pizhun or Pishun.

However, though the Genesis myth used a real geographical location for Eden, it is still myth. Genesis 3-24 states: "After he drove the man out, he placed on the east side of the Garden of Eden cherubim and a flaming sword flashing back and forth to guard the way to the tree of life." There is no part of that land that is now uninhabitable because of either a gate or cherubim, so it is clear that the entire story of Eden was a myth. It was a beautiful myth, however, likely created at the time of the Babylonian exile of the Jews. The real connotation of the Genesis myth is to visualize a pure land, free of evil, a land of innocence, and beauty. The geographical coordinates were used to give some kind of credibility to the myth. The two cherubim represent the duality of our egotistical nature, which prevents us from seeing the pure land. There are many myths which use real geographical locations. For instance, the myth of the Hindu god Rāma uses the city of Ayōdhya in India as the site of Lord Rāma's capital city. Ayōdhya is now the center of a major Hindu-Muslim conflict. Apparently there was a Rāma temple which is now the site of a mosque, built at the time of Mughal (Mogul) King Babur, by destroying the existing temple and building a mosque over it. Hindus want the temple back, but the Indian Supreme Court has put a stay on any changes. It seems to me that since it has been a mosque for hundreds of years, the current owners have full authority over the property. In any case, aside from the mosque/temple, there is no evidence whatsoever in Ayōdhya of the remnants of a great palace in the city.

Mankind's 'Punishment.'

God creates the tree of knowledge, and declares to Adam and Eve that its fruit is forbidden. Eve is enticed by the serpent to eat the fruit, and she does. In punishment, God declares to eve: "I will greatly increase your pains in childbearing; with pain you will give birth to children. Your desire will be for your husband, and he will rule over you."

One wonders how a loving God could create such temptation and then, just because Eve yields to the temptation, mete out such severe punishment for all of womankind, for all of eternity. There is a much more subtle interpretation. It appears to me that the story was carefully crafted to show the result of disobedience to God. A way of looking at this story is that suffering is part of human life, and that it is only humans who "know" suffering. It does not seem to me that animals go through pregnancy in fear of the pain of labor, but humans do, with knowledge, memory and perception. Suffering is multiplied by memory of the past and anticipation of the future. The "punishment" for knowledge, or the consequence, really, is awareness of suffering. I believe that this is the sensible way to look at the story, and not to think that God is so cruel as to inflict torment on people for eternity. It was brilliant on the part of the storyteller, however, to have come up with such a concept of suffering caused by disobedience to God.

The Bible states that man was made in the image of God. Trying to relate this to the fact that the Bible also states that God fashioned man out of dust and then breathed life into him, it is very difficult to try and fit the two ideas together. Therefore, the idea that God made man in his image has been interpreted in a variety of ways. In the tradition of ancient India, God transformed himself into all of creation by primordial sacrifice. The word sacrifice has various connotations for people, but the Vedic view is not just simply an offering, but transformation. It is supreme self-sacrifice. The Creator did not simply just sit back and create things, he offered himself up in sacrifice, and the result of the sacrifice was the manifestation of all of creation as we know it. Indeed, the practice of burnt offerings, as performed in ancient Judaism and Hinduism, is a practice of "reversing" this primordial sacrifice: to transform what is precious to us, through the medium of fire, back to the higher state that is with God and is God. When we talk, therefore, of God making man in his own image, indeed, it is not just man, but all of creation that is made in God's image.

I see "God's image," simply put, to equate to the quaint phrase "chip off the old block." The maker of Steinway pianos, in its brochure on its smaller pianos, states that the manufacturer simply makes less of it, but does not put any the less into it. That is the company's way of saying that whether large or small, each piano made by the company has the same quality, the same characteristics! I see the same principle apply to the nature of each of us. Whether large or small, the visible Universe is composed of nothing but pieces of that infinite being. Indeed, there is not a second that the living influence of the Creator is not present in each one of us to sustain us in life. We may vainly go around saying that we are this or that, or that we do this or that, but we are oblivious to the fact that our very core, our very essence, our very life itself, is nothing but a living fragment of the Supreme creator. It is only through great contemplation and meditation that this conclusion comes to us. Otherwise, all we see is an infinite number of things and creatures, with no common connection between them all. We see diversity where there really ought to be unity. The Tao Te Ching said it so wonderfully that from the One came the ten thousand things. However, the most incredible fact, according to the Üpanishads, which are part of the Hindu Vĕdas, is that having so created all of what is seen and indeed unseen, the Creator remains full and complete in integrity and wholeness, in everything as well as transcending everything. Creation is then part of a greater fullness and completeness, with no separation from the Creator.

I therefore see the teaching of the Bible that man was made in God's image, to be a statement made by a prophet with a deep understanding of the nature of God and man. However, it is a statement, like those of mystics in general, that means much more than it seems. The more literal and mundane interpretation, would be to think of a giant anthropomorphic being "up there somewhere" who creates man, using a miniature version of His giant anthropomorphic form, then pulls out a rib and creates woman. This is a quaint tale, but like much of the chapter of Genesis, it must not be taken literally. There is so much more satisfactory an understanding to be obtained if one looks a little deeper. There are scholars who believe that Eve being created out of a rib taken from Adam is a mistranslation, the correct translation being that Eve was created out of one *side* of Adam. The writers of the Bible therefore taught the idea that primordial man was androgynous, and Eve, the female, was separated from the male. This is represented in Hinduism by God being represented as the androgynous *Ardhanarishvara*, or half-male and half-female. In biological terms, the process is the same as one cell dividing into two by breaking off one side of itself, following which the two halves become two whole cells.

Noah and the Flood

The Bible story of Noah and the flood is a most fascinating one. The Bible has us believe that God created the flood to destroy all of creation, particularly humanity, because "God saw that the wickedness of man was great in the earth, and that every imagination of the thoughts of his heart was only evil continually." To accept that God actually did so, is to entirely miss the point of the Bible.

William Ryan and Walter Pitman, in their book *Noah's Flood: The new scientific discoveries about the event that changed history* and in a related TV program on Noah's flood, have presented a very dramatic and revealing account of research into the flood. They have shown quite conclusively, based upon their own, as well as that the research of others that the flood occurred in the Black Sea. Prior to 5500 BCE, the time of the flood, this body of water was a fresh water lake, the surface of which was around 400 feet below the current level. With the end of the ice age and the melting of large glaciers, the water in the Mediterranean Sea rose sufficiently to burst through the Bosporus, which in those days was a natural dam rather than being the channel it is now. This huge torrent, which they describe as exceeding two hundred times the flow over the Niagara Falls, covered miles and miles of the land around the Black Sea, destroying the civilizations that had developed in the area. This flooding occurred in just a few days, with the water occupying as much as a mile of land in just a day.

This was an awesome, horrendous flood, probably one of the greatest of catastrophes that human beings have ever encountered. It is likely that many people managed to escape with their lives, with perhaps a minimum of belongings. There is evidence of a very significant migration out of the Black Sea area into areas mostly to the South such as Mesopotamia, but with some to the North as well. Mounds from old settlements reveal layers of settlement with evidence of a new culture, that date back to soon after the flood. It appears likely that the tales of the flood originated from these settlers, and made their way to so many civilizations over the years.

The Epic of Gilgamesh was first discovered in the Library of Ashurbanipal, a 7th century BCE Babylonian King. It is likely, however, that the Epic was based upon Sumerian legends that dated back much before that. In this legend, the heroic King Gilgamesh, in his quest for immortality, speaks to a sage called Utnapishtim. The sage came to know of the God Enlil's intent to destroy the world. In those days the world teemed with people who were noisy and they made such a clamor that the gods could no longer sleep. The god Enlil heard the clamor and he said to the other gods that they needed to exterminate mankind. So the gods agreed to exterminate mankind. Utnapishtim therefore, under the guidance of the Goddess Ea, built a vessel, square in shape, one hundred and twenty cubits (length from elbow to fingertip) in length per side, consisting of seven levels, to hold the seed of all creatures.

After the furious winds and floods that effectively destroyed all of mankind except for the chosen few, the gods were much dismayed. Then Ea opened her mouth and spoke to warrior Enlil, (translated by N.K.Sandars) "Wisest of gods, hero Enlil, how could you so senselessly bring down the flood?"

"Lay upon the sinner his sin,
Lay upon the transgressor his transgression,
Punish him a little when he breaks loose,
Do not drive him too hard or he perishes.
Would that a lion had ravaged mankind
Rather than the flood,
Would that a wolf had ravaged mankind
Rather than the flood,
Would that famine had wasted the world
Rather than the flood,
Would that pestilence had wasted mankind
Rather than the flood."

In the biblical legend of Noah, however, God expresses no real regret, but makes his assurance not to create a flood ever again by displaying a rainbow. In the Epic of Gilgamesh, the goddess flings her necklace into the sky, turning them into stars to promise that never again would a flood destroy mankind.

The Epic of Gilgamesh, likely of Sumerian origin, probably preceded the Biblical account by more than two thousand years. Noah's Ark was three hundred cubits long and fifty cubits wide, but Utnapishtim's was one hundred cubits square. In the Bible, once the floodwaters subside, Noah sends a raven, and then a dove, the latter three times. In Gilgamesh's Epic, the Sage sends a dove, then a swallow, and then a raven. The general similarities between the two legends are much more than coincidental; the Biblical account was adapted from the Gilgamesh legend.

It is clear that the flooding of the Black Sea was probably one of the greatest natural catastrophes that affected the Old World over the past several thousand years. To the people of those days, it may indeed have seemed to be a disaster sent upon mankind by wrathful beings of the heavens. To a polytheistic culture, it was the wrath of the gods that caused it, and to the monotheistic Hebrews, it was God's expression of disgust for humanity that led to the flood from which only Noah, his relatives, and the contents of the Ark were saved. I see the flood and its aftermath as a grand setting for storytellers to preach about the anger of God against the errant ways of mankind, and need for humankind to mend its ways. It is a natural human tendency to try and "wipe the slate clean" and start anew; this was projected on to God as having done the same thing.

While I quite enjoy the story of Noah and his Ark, we should understand the significance of the myth. God, of supreme wisdom and understanding, could not possibly manifest behavior human enough, to have anger enough, to destroy all of his own precious creation simply because his creatures were no longer pure by his standards. If anyone believes that God really did so, it is their privilege, but in so doing they would have completely missed the point of the writers of the Bible: their fear and awe of God was expressed in this tale of Noah. To take the tale to heart is to appreciate, and empathize with, that fear and awe. To truly believe that God actually caused the flood to drown all of creation is not only to miss the point, but also to try and make something credible out of what is not.

My wife and I stayed at home when a furious hurricane swept into our town. The ocean waters rose eleven feet above the normal level and surrounded our house. It was frightening to be there, with winds of over one hundred miles per hour, and waist-deep water all around the house. The situation not only caused a great sense of fear, but a tremendous feeling of awe towards the raw power of nature. It induced a feeling of great humility and our powerlessness in the face of the power of nature. It is no wonder that in many cultures, the power of nature is personified in the Goddess, represented sometimes as a fierce, bloodthirsty female. It is my feeling that the flood epics, whether from the Bible or elsewhere, must be taken as a great lesson in humility that we must take when considering the awesome power of God as revealed through nature. The destructive force of nature is something that can never be explained. There is no "Godly intent" in this destruction; besides, such forces were present long before humanity populated the entire earth. When a tidal wave engulfs a town, we must realize that the town just happens to be in the way. When a prophet states in a holy book that such events are an expression of the "wrath of God," he has simply bowed his head in undisputed surrender to the awesome power of the force of nature, which in turn derives from the power of God.

The Hebrew Patriarchs

The patriarch of the Jewish people, also of Christians and Muslims, was Abraham; Avraham to Hebrews, and Ibrahim to Muslims. The essential syllable in this name is "brahm." There is great similarity between this word and "Brahman," the Hindu concept of the supreme formless being that is the ultimate reality. The root of "Brahman" is "brh," or that from which all grows. There is also a god called Brahma, different from the Supreme Brahman. And in the Semitic tradition, it was Abraham, from whom the great monotheistic traditions of the ancient Middle Eastern world arose and grew. Abraham is the Patriarch, the very first of those chosen by God. At first he was just Abram, but afterwards he became Abraham. His wife was a Pagan Sarai to begin with, and as Acharya S points out, the name's root is similar to that of the Goddess Sarasvati, Brahma's spouse, and she becomes a biblical Sarah. In Sanskrit, Aham (pronounced ahum) means I or Me. God often refers to himself as Aham in Sanskrit. Brahm-Aham, I am Brahma the God. I wonder: could it not be that Abram becomes Abraham, Abram-Aham, once he became inspired by God? Of course, Hebrew does not use the Sanskrit word 'Aham;' however, the myth of Abraham and Sarah might have had a Hindu/Pagan origin.

Acharya S. speaks of Abraham and Sarah in her book, *The Christ Conspiracy*: "Although Abraham is held up as the patriarch of the Hebrews and Arabs, the original Abraham and Sarah were the same as the Indian God Brahma and his spouse the goddess Sarasvathi, the "Queen of Heaven," and the story of Abraham's migration is reflective of a Brahmanical tribe leaving India at the end of the age of Taurus. This identification of Abraham and Sarah as Indian gods did not escape the notice of the Jesuit missionaries in India; indeed, it was they who first pointed it out. (Godfrey Higgins in his book *Anacalypsis*)

Concerning the patriarch and his wife, Barbara Walker states in her book *The Woman's Encyclopedia of Myths and Secrets*: "This name meaning Father Brahm" seems to have been a Semitic version of India's patriarchal god Brahma; he was also the Islamic Abrama, founder of Mecca. But Islamic legends say Abraham was a late intruder into the shrine of the Ka'bah. He bought it from the priestesses of its original Goddess. Sarah, "the Queen," was one of the Goddess' titles, which became a name of Abraham's biblical wife. In the tale of Isaac's near-killing, Abraham assumed the role of sacrificial priest in the druidic style, to wash Jehovah's sacred trees with the blood of the son: an ancient custom, of which the sacrifice of Jesus was only a late variant."

Acharya S continues: "Abraham also seems to have been related to the Persian evil God Ahriman, whose name was originally Abriman. Furthermore, Graham states, "The Babylonians also had their Abraham, only they spelt it Abarama. He was a farmer and mythological contemporary with Abraham….Regarding details of the Abramic story, Barbara Walker says: "The biblical mother-shrine Mamre at Hebron included a sacred oak in a female-symbolic grove. Old Testament scribes pretended it was the home of Abraham, although even in the fourth century A.D. it was still a Pagan site, dedicated to the worship of idols." Furthermore, Abram's "Ur of the Chaldees" apparently does not originally refer to the Ur in Mesopotamia and to the Middle Eastern Chaldean culture, but to an earlier rendition in India, where Higgins, for one, found the proto-Hebraic Chaldee language. Regarding Sarah, Walker relates that the "original name of Israel meant 'the tribe of Sarah.' Her name was formerly Sara'i, the Queen, a name of the Great Goddess in Nabataean inscription. Priests changed her name to Sarah in the sixth century BCE. These stories serve not as chronicles of individuals but of gods and tribes such that, as Walker further relates, "Sarah was the maternal goddess of the 'Abraham' tribe that formed an alliance with Egypt in the 3rd Millenium BC. Hence the story of Abraham and Sarah in Egypt."

Acharya S. writes in another chapter: "Another inhabitant of the crossroads of Sumeria was purported to be the biblical "patriarch" Abraham, whose story in fact reflects the merger of the Aryan/Egyptian cultures. As demonstrated, the Abraham myth is paralleled in India, such that the "Ur of the Chaldees" apparently represents not the Sumerian city but an "Ur of the Culdees" in India, and the story of Abraham's migration to Harran reflects the movement of an Aryan Brahmanical tribe into the Levant. The Abraham myth evidently represents the fanatic patriarchal followers of Brahma leaving India during a war over gender brought about by the change of the equinoctial ages, i.e., that from Taurus to Aries. This Brahmanic tribe ostensibly migrated from the Indian region of Oudh (Judea), possibly from the village of Mathura, westward through Persia, ending up in Goshen, "the house of the sun," i.e., Heliopolis in Egypt, where it established a place named Maturea/Mathura. As the tribe migrated from India, it named various landmarks wherever it settled by the same or similar name as those of its homeland. The Abramites of Brahmans later moved back into Canaan from Egypt to create their own nation, dividing the land and extant peoples into the 12 zodiacal sections under "Jacob," or Seth the Supplanter, and his "sons," who were in reality tribal gods. Among numerous etymological examples to support this migration theory, many of which have already been provided, Higgins points out that Hebrews are called Yehudi, and that the Sanskrit word 'Yuddha' means warrior, which the Yehudi certainly professed to be in their sacred texts. In addition, the father of Krishna was Yadu/Yuda/Yudi, or Judi, and the word 'Shaitan'-'adversary,' whence comes 'Satan'- is the same in Hebrew and Sanskrit. Higgins further states that the cradle of Buddhist and Jainist faith was in the Indian town of Jessalmer, evidently the same as Jerusalem, which, as we have seen, is also found in Egypt. The connection continues, as Higgins finds the Syro-Hebrew-Christian savior god/apostle Tammuz/Thomas not only in India but also in Egypt: "Tamus was the name of the chief Egyptian deity: the same as Thamus of Syria." It is likely that migrations between Africa/Egypt and India been occurring many thousands of years ago and that these cultures shared a common root."

Was Abraham really a historical figure? In their book *The Bible Unearthed* by Israel Finkelstein and Neil Asher Silberman, Israeli Archeologists, is a section titled "The failed search for the historical Abraham." They write that Kings 6:1 indicates that the Exodus occurred 480 years before the construction of the Temple. And that the Israelites were enslaved for 430 years in Egypt according to Exodus 12:40. They made further calculations and arrived at a date of around 2100 BCE as the time Abraham left for Canaan. They write: "Of course, there were some clear problems with accepting this dating for precise historical reconstruction, not the least of which were the extraordinarily long life spans of Abraham, Isaac, and Jacob, which all far exceeded a hundred years. In addition, the later genealogies that traced Jacob's descendants were confusing, if not plain contradictory. Moses and Aaron, for example, were identified as fourth-generation descendants of Jacob's son Levi, while Joshua, a contemporary of Moses and Aaron, was declared to be a twelfth generation descendant of Joseph, another of Jacob's sons. This was hardly a minor discrepancy."

They quote the American scholar William F. Albright as initially believing that the age of the patriarchs was accurate. However, Albright's theory proved to be unfruitful: "He and his colleagues thus began to search for evidence for the presence of pastoral groups of Mesopotamian origin roaming throughout Canaan around 2000 BCE. Yet the search for the historical patriarchs was ultimately unsuccessful, since none of the periods around the biblical suggested date provided a completely compatible background to the biblical stories. The assumed westward migration of groups from Mesopotamia toward Canaan-the so-called Amorite migration, in which Albright placed the arrival of Abraham and his family-was later shown to be illusory. Archeology completely disproved the contention that a sudden, massive population movement had taken place at that time."

The myth of the patriarch Abraham, however, is not simply just a story; it is the allegorical myth of a great covenant, or agreement, between God and a people who identified themselves with a certain way of thinking, attitude and way of life. The authors conclude their chapter with wonderful insight: "The great genius of the seventh century creators of this national epic was the way in which they wove the earlier stories together without stripping them of their humanity or individual distinctiveness. Abraham, Isaac, and Jacob remain at the same time vivid spiritual portraits and the metaphorical ancestors of the people of Israel. And the twelve sons of Jacob were brought into the tradition as junior members of more complete genealogy. In the artistry of the biblical narrative, the children of Abraham, Isaac, and Jacob were indeed made into a single family. It was the power of legend that united them—in a manner far more powerful and timeless than the fleeting adventures of a few historical individuals herding sheep in the highlands of Canaan could ever have done."

The essential point, as the authors have beautifully put it, is that they were "metaphorical ancestors." The God-chosen lineage was Abraham-Isaac-Jacob, the flagships of the fleet. A Hindu equivalent would be Manu, the primordial Man, the lawgiver and his descendants. No amount of research proving that Abraham was not a historical person but a mythical ancestor of the Jews will ever take away from the inspiration that Jews have upon reading of the exploits of the patriarchs.

The important message of the Abraham myth is, I believe, hidden in the directive that God apparently gave to Abraham in Genesis 12: "I will make you into a great nation and I will bless you. I will make your name great and you will be a blessing. I will bless those who bless you and will curse those who curse you. All people on earth will be blessed through you." This statement was accompanied by the directive to leave his country, people, and the shelter of his father, to a land that God was to show him. I believe there is a message of great implication in these words. To attain knowledge of God, we have to abandon everything we ever knew or know, and go on into unknown territory deep within our minds, with only *one and only* compass, guide and mentor: God. All greatness can and will come once we set sail with God as our wind and guide. From the one who understood this, others were to learn also, and over the years, entire nations were to learn this secret and were to be so blessed. The curse on those who cursed Abraham simply means that such people would remain in ignorance and never achieve that inner knowledge of God that only surrender to God would provide. This was the mystical teaching for the Jews created by their forebears. The same teaching was adopted by Christians and Muslims in later years. There was something unique and deeply inspiring about the Abraham story, and Abraham is, not surprisingly, adopted as the patriarch of all these people of the three great faiths.

The Exodus

According to the Hebrew Bible, the Hebrews had moved to Egypt and flourished, but later were enslaved by a Pharaoh. Moses, their beloved prophet, rescued them from bondage. In the biblical story, God sends, through Moses, ten different catastrophes on Egypt. After the tenth, where every first born male Egyptian dies, the Pharaoh releases the Hebrews. They reach the Red Sea, (thought by scholars to have been the 'sea of reeds" rather than the Red Sea, and God parts the waters of the sea for them to cross. Meanwhile, the Pharaoh sends his chariots after the Hebrews, and as they roll into the path created in the middle of the sea, the sea closes in on them and drowns them. The Hebrews then wander in the desert for forty years, fed by manna from heaven, and arrive at Canaan. Under the leadership of Joshua, they attack Canaan, whose walls magically fall to the trumpet blasts of Joshua's men. Thus it was that Canaan became Israel.

Interesting legend, but did all of this really happen? Israel Finkelstein and Neil Asher Silberman, in their book *The Bible Unearthed*, show that there is no archeological evidence for the Exodus, the wandering in the desert, and the invasion of Canaan. "The saga of Israel's exodus from Egypt is neither historical truth nor literary fiction. It is a powerful expression of memory and hope born in a world in the midst of change. The confrontation between Moses and Pharaoh mirrored the momentous confrontation between the young King Josiah and the newly crowned pharaoh Necho. To pin this biblical image down to a single date is to betray the story's deepest meaning. Passover proves to be not a single event but a continuing experience of national resistance against the powers that be." The Exodus myth was an allegorical myth meant to have a unifying influence on the Jews, to give them a common identity and "history." Finkelstein and Silberman show that the Israelites were native Canaanites who later formed a unified group with a common philosophy and religion.

Many scholars, even Jewish clerics, have been coming to the conclusion that the Moses story is a mythical one. Teresa Watanabe, Religion Writer for the LA Times, wrote an excellent review of the subject in the April 13th, 2001 issue of the paper. She reported that many Rabbis, such as Rabbi David Wolpe of the Sinai Temple in Westwood, CA, have started teaching their congregants to re-consider the history of Israel as written in the Bible. She quotes authors as questioning the prevailing theory that Israel came to be as written in the Bible; rather that it emerged peacefully out of Canaan--modern-day Lebanon, southern Syria, Jordan and the West Bank of Israel. Under this theory, the Canaanites who took on a new identity as Israelites were perhaps joined or led by a small group of Semites from Egypt--explaining a possible source of the Exodus story. As they expanded their settlement, they may have begun to clash with neighbors, perhaps providing elements of reasons for the conflicts recorded in Joshua and Judges.

She quotes William Dever, a professor of Near Eastern archeology and anthropology at the University of Arizona as saying that scholars have known this for a long time. Dever has said that Egypt's voluminous ancient records contained not one mention of Israelites in the country, although one 1210 BC inscription did mention them in Canaan, and that virtually no scholar accepts the biblical figure of 600,000 men fleeing Egypt, which would have meant that including women and children there would have been a few million people,. The ancient desert at the time could not support so many nomads, scholars say, and the powerful Egyptian state kept tight security over the area, guarded by fortresses.

Also, in 1999, she reports, Israeli archeologist Ze'ev Herzog of Tel Aviv University set off a furor in Israel by writing in a popular magazine that stories of the patriarchs were myths and that neither the Exodus nor Joshua's conquests ever occurred. Herzog, Finkelstein and others have of course had to deal with fierce criticism and protest; it is a very touchy subject. The world is determined to construe myth as history, and will only consider "evidence" that even remotely suggests that these beloved myths are true, and completely ignore evidence which reveals the opposite.

The Mysterious Moses

Moses (Moshe) is piously believed to be the God-empowered man who rescues the nation of Israel from slavery. However, it can be easily discovered that the entire story was a Hebrew myth. Acharya S., in her book *The Christ Conspiracy*, states: "The legend of Moses, rather than being that of a historical Hebrew lawgiver, is found from the Mediterranean to India, with the character having different names and races depending on the locale: "Manu" is the Indian legislator. "Nemo the lawgiver," who brought down the tablets from the Mountain of God, hails from Babylon. "Mises" is found in Syria, where he was pulled out of a basket floating in a river. Mises also had tablets of stone upon which laws were written, and a rod with which he did miracles, including parting waters and leading his army across the sea. In addition, "Manes the lawgiver" took the stage in Egypt, and "Minos" was the Cretan reformer." She quotes Louis Jacolliot as tracing the original Moses to the Indian Manu: "This name of Manu, or Manes…is not a substantive, applying to an individual man; its Sanskrit significance is *the man, par excellence,* the legislator. It is a title aspired to by all the leaders of men in antiquity." She continues: "Like Moses, the Indian God Krishna was placed by his mother in a reed boat and set adrift in a river to be discovered by another woman. The Akkadian Sargon also was placed in a reed basket and set adrift to save his life. In fact, "The name Moses is Egyptian and comes from *mo,* the Egyptian word for water, and *uses,* meaning saved from water, in this case, primordial. Thus, the title Moses could be applied to any of these various heroes saved from the water.

These references show clearly that Moshe was a mythical figure idolized by the nation of Israel to be their rescuer, their leader. Moshe was, and always will be, a source of inspiration and strength. The fact that he was not historical does not take away from this inspiration, because he embodied all that was ideal for the Hebrew nation. With him Hebrew monotheism was reborn, re-established. There were no tablets of stone in reality; rather, they were the ideas, the commandments, of the Hebrew scribes "written in stone." As discussed elsewhere, the "Ten Commandments" were chosen as the guiding principles of a newly formed nation. And ironically, as mentioned above, the directive "Thou shalt not kill" apparently had no real meaning in practice, because the

Hebrew God constantly commanded his people to kill people who were of other faiths. However, such a commandment, as has been discussed elsewhere in the book, was entirely myth.

Kashmir—A (Jewish) Paradise?

Holger Kersten, in his book *Jesus lived in India*, reveals what he feels is fascinating evidence of the intimate link of the Hebrew people to Kashmir in India. In the Old Testament, Deuteronomy Chapter 34, it is written: "Then Moses climbed Mount Nebo from the plains of Moab to the top of Pisgah, across from Jericho. There the Lord showed him the whole land…this is the land I promised on oath to Abraham, Isaac and Jacob when I said I will give it to your descendants. I have let you see it with your eyes, but you will not cross over into it. And Moses the servant of the Lord, died there in Moab. He buried him in Moab, in the valley opposite Beth Peor, but to this day no one knows where his grave is."

Kersten states that he has found these sites mentioned in Deuteronomy in Kashmir, India. In the book *Jesus Lived in India* he writes: "Beth-peor later became called Behat-poor and now Bandipur. Mount Pisgah and Mount Nebo are adjacent to the plains of Mowu, or Moab. 12 Kilometers from Bandipur (Beth-peor) is the village of Aham-Sharif, and from there, one has to walk to reach the little village of Buth at the foot of Mount Nebo. Above the village is a garden like area, with a stone column about a meter high, which is said to be the tombstone of Moses. Apparently the gravesite has been reverently tended to for over 2700 years. There are also sites named Muqam-I-Musa, 'the place of Moses.' In a town called Bijbihara, south of Srinagar, a place on the riverbank is still referred to as 'Moses' bath-place, where there is a magic stone called KaKa-Bal or Sang-I-Musa, or 'Stone of Moses.'" Eventually, he states, the ten lost tribes of Israel settled in Kashmir and its surrounding areas.

However, as discussed above, Acharya S. and others have shown that Moses was a mythical figure, not really based on a historical one. If indeed there was a significant Jewish presence in Kashmir, it is not at all surprising that the name of Moses was given to geographical sites. The name Moses has remained as the embodiment of a supreme human being in the Jewish heritage. The name is also revered in Islam, which could explain the prevalence of objects or sites bearing the name of Moses.

Enter Jesus

The focal point of Christianity, however, is Jesus the Christ (the anointed.) Jesus, the Chosen of the chosen. For believers, he is love and light incarnate, yet so misunderstood and misrepresented. He is the one figure who has dominated the history of the western world, indeed a large part of humanity: nearly two billion people at this time, or one-third of humanity.

Scholars now seem to have a variety of views about Jesus. Hershel Shanks, in *The Mystery and Meaning of the Dead Sea Scrolls*, writes: "Armed with refined methods of literary criticism and the insights of archaeology, anthropology, and sociology, as well as new texts (especially the Dead Sea Scrolls), scholars are publishing numerous lives of Jesus that often differ markedly from one another: Jesus is seen as a Jewish revolutionary, a political agitator, a follower of the Cynic philosophy, a magician, an apocalyptic prophet, a popular sage, a holy man or charismatic, a Galilean rabbi, a wily politician, even a trance-inducing psychotherapist, and, of course, a messiah. No consensus has emerged."

Christians accept the gospels, including the four canonical gospels, the epistles of Paul and the Acts of the Apostles, as revelation directly handed down by God, as though dictated by God and written down by scribes. They seldom explore the actual history of the formation of the Church and the countless different "gospels" that circulated around the world in the first two centuries of our era. And seldom do they think of the amount of editing of the "God-given gospels" that was carried out until the authorities were satisfied that they were suitable to be placed as the Canon: a process that took nearly four hundred years if not more.

Who started Christianity—and why?

In this book, I have at times referred to Jesus as though he was a historical person, as it is simpler to do so. After all, when quoting from the Hindu scripture called the Bhagavad-Gita or 'Song of the Lord,' it is easier to simply say "Krishna said" though it is very likely that the entire book was spiritual fiction: a sage called Vyäsa wrote it with a play-like theme of Lord Krishna as the teacher and Arjuna the warrior as student. For a devout Hindu, it is not necessary to prove or disprove the historical significance of Krishna; what is important is the message. It is a divine message, composed by someone very inspired.

The New Testament, however, is a collection of several books. Getting a "canon" together was truly a formidable task. It is something that took a few hundred years to achieve. Scholars have shown that in the first couple of hundred years of our era, there were numerous "gospels" in circulation, and finally the Church had most of them burned as heresy, to allow only the ones we know at this time.

If Jesus is a fictional figure, then what is his exact nature? In their remarkable book *The Jesus Mysteries,* Freke and Gandy write: "The more we studied the various versions of the myth of Osiris/Dionysus, the more it became obvious that the story of Jesus had all the characteristics of this perennial tale. Even by event, we found we were able to construct Jesus' supposed biography from mythic motifs previously relating to Osiris/Dionysus:

Osiris-Dionysus is God made flesh, the savior and Son of God.
His father is God and his mother is a mortal virgin.
He is born in a cave or humble cowshed on Dec. 25th before 3 shepherds.
He offers his followers a chance to be born again through baptism.
He miraculously turns water into wine at a wedding.
He rides triumphantly into town on a donkey while people wave palm leaves to honor him.
He dies at Easter-time as a sacrifice for the sins of the world.
After his death he descends into the Earth, and then on the third day he rises from the dead and ascends to heaven in glory.
His followers await his return as the judge during the Last Days.
His death and resurrection are celebrated by a ritual meal of bread and wine, which symbolize his body and blood."

The above characteristics of the gods Osiris of Egypt and Dionysius of Greece appear to rule out the idea that Christianity is unique; rather, it is based not on a historical 'savior,' but on Pagan motifs well known in those days. The work of several authors has shown that what is now considered to be Christianity was the work, among others, of Greek-speaking Jews of Alexandria, called Therapeutae, who were profoundly influenced by Pagan thinking and understanding. Freke and Gandy in their book *Jesus Mysteries* go into the extensive history of the Jews in Alexandria, and the blending of Jewish and Hellenistic culture. They believe that the Therapeutae of Alexandria were what they called proto-Christians. Alexandria was the center of Pagan mysticism in late antiquity, had the largest Jewish population outside Judea, and was the home of the greatest masters of the Christian gnosis during the first few centuries CE. They believe that Alexandria was the most obvious place for the Jesus Mysteries to have been created.

The story of Jesus is based upon earlier myths of dying-resurrecting god-men including Osiris of Egypt and Dionysus of Greece. The Greeks could not simply adopt the myth of Osiris, so they adapted the story of Osiris to a minor deity called Dionysus. Freke and Gandy write: "In this way, the Greeks were introduced to the Egyptian Mysteries in a form that seemed indigenous to themselves." However, the Alexandrian Jews, adopting earlier myths, could not use any "gods" as they only had one, Jehovah. Freke and Gandy state: "The Jews had dispensed with all gods and goddesses, and worshiped only their one God, Jehovah. But while Jehovah could be equated with Plato's Supreme Oneness, he did not have a mythological biography like the Pagan gods, which could be adapted to become the Osiris-Dionysus myth. Unlike other cultures the Jews had no minor deities, so there was only one Jewish mythological figure who could possibly be transformed into Osiris-Dionysus: the Messiah....The construction of the Jesus story suggests that the creators of the Jewish Mysteries took the only option available to them and synthesized the dying and resurrecting godman of the Mysteries with the Jewish Messiah. The gospels clearly state that Jesus is the Messiah. He is said to have been born in Bethlehem from the line of David--just as the Messiah must be. He is called the Messiah by Peter. He is even named Joshua (Jesus in Greek), which was the expected name of the Messiah. Yet Jesus the Messiah is actually only a thin veil concealing the quite different figure of Jesus the dying and resurrecting godman."

For traditional Jews the Messiah, who was expected to come with victory over their enemies, it was entirely unacceptable that he would die by crucifixion, or die in any manner at all. In Judaism the Messiah was not thought of as someone who would save them by his own sacrificial death, which is a phenomenon unique to Pagan dying-resurrecting gods. Therefore, Jesus is not meant to represent the Jewish messiah but the godman of the Mysteries who represents victory over the limitations of the body.

Barbara Watterson, a European Egyptologist, writes in her book *Gods of Ancient Egypt:* "Osiris is probably the best known of all Egyptian gods. His appeal lay in the belief that he had lived on earth as a man who brought nothing but good to mankind but who was betrayed and murdered. His resurrection and the hope of eternal life that he held out to everyone further enhanced his popularity, which was unrivalled until Roman times when the popularity of his wife, Isis, gained ground. Only the advent of Jesus Christ, who brought the same message to mankind, eclipsed the fame of this the most sympathetic of all the deities in the Egyptian pantheon."

The "mysteries" are not mere myths. They are stories with a message, usually taught in secret societies involved in mysticism. Hans Kung writes in his book *Christianity and the World Religions*: "One thing, at least, is clear: 'Mysticism,' in the original *literal sense,* comes from the Greek *myein*, to close (the mouth). The "mysteries" are, therefore, secrets, secret teachings, secret cults, which one does not speak about in the presence of the uninitiated. One closes one's mouth in order to seek salvation within oneself. And silence is recommended to those who wish to draw near to the mystery. Renunciation of the world, turning inward, immediate union with the Absolute-these have long been viewed as the characteristics of mysticism." For the mystics who created the Jesus myth, Jesus was the Messiah because he transcended death. His victory was not a military one over the enemies of the Jews, but the greatest victory of all; victory of life over death. For the members of the Jesus cult, he was the symbol of the quest for immortality, the greatest quest in life.

The Gnostic Gospels

If we were to carefully study the history of the Gnostic gospels discovered a few decades ago, we would realize that during the first two to three hundred years of this era the Middle East was in great turmoil. There were hundreds of various sects of Christians, each claiming to have the "true" teachings of Jesus. It has been found that the Dead Sea Scrolls had literature somewhat similar to Gnostic work. The earliest Christian literature is Gnostic, and the "historical" information was patched in later, creating "literalist Christianity." Of all Gnostic work, the best known is the gospel of Thomas. Indeed, the authors of the Jesus Seminar have made it the fifth gospel. The gospel consists of paragraphs called Logia, meaning thought or teaching, which start with the words

"Jesus said." A lot of what is written in that gospel does correspond to what is written in the gospels of the New Testament. Tradition has it that Thomas was close enough to Jesus to be called his twin. This gospel (translated by Bentley Layton in his book *The Gnostic Scriptures*) starts with: "These are the obscure sayings that the living Jesus uttered and which didymus (twin) Jude Thomas wrote down. And he (Jesus) said, "Whoever finds the meaning of these sayings will not taste death."

Freke and Gandy write in *The Jesus Mysteries* that the Gnostics were the great intellectuals of early Christianity. Valentinus, for example, was a highly educated Alexandrian philosopher and poet, elected Bishop of Egypt. He was an influential figure in early Christianity, and the church leader Irenaeus apparently deplored the fact that many Christians, including some leaders, had sought initiation from him. They point out that other leaders of literalist Christianity such as Tertullian admired Valentinus, and that St. Jerome admired the Gnostic Marcion as a sage.

It may well be that it was the Gnostics who first created the gospel story in a very simple form, with the theme of the "anointed one" who dies to his earthly nature and "resurrects" into a higher spiritual state. Perhaps elements of a quasi-historical story came bit by bit, embellished by those who got to know the story. Literalist Christianity was born when a group of people or a church insisted that the story was absolutely historical, and it turns out that the Roman Emperors backed the literalist church, the Roman Catholic Church. The Gnostics were likely dismayed at their mystery religion being converted into a quasi-historical drama, and conflict developed. Eventually, the literalist Church had to eradicate the Gnostics and all traces of the Gnostic origins of Christianity.

From Gnosticism to Literalist Christianity

The creators of the story of the New Testament had to create a historical background for the story of Jesus to make the entire story seemingly credible. Paul's writings, among the earliest of Christian writing, make no mention whatsoever of the historical Jesus, because such a historical setting had not yet been created. Freke and Gandy state: "Yet Jesus could not be said to have existed in the distant past like the Pagan Mystery godman, because such a Messiah could not bring political salvation to his people now. He would have to be portrayed as coming in the recent past, as this alone would make him relevant." They continue: "The Jewish godman was given the name Joshua/Jesus after the Exodus Joshua ben

Nun, whose name means "Jesus son of the fish." This is perfect for a savior figure designed for the new astrological Age of Pisces, symbolized by the fish. The time chosen for Jesus' "birth" links him to an important astrological conjunction in 7 BCE, which ushered in the new age of Pisces. This stellar conjunction also becomes the star that prefigures the birth of the godman in Pagan myth. Thus Jesus symbolically becomes the new savior for a New Age."

Other considerations also came into play. Freke and Gandy write: "According to Mathew, Jesus is born in the reign of Herod, who tries to have him killed as a baby to prevent him becoming king of the Jews. Herod, who died in 4 BCE, was a puppet of the Romans and completely loathed by the Jews. Bringing the infant Jesus into immediate conflict with the hated king already fits Jesus into the mode of the "just man unjustly accused" and portrays him as the Messiah come to defend the Jews." They then show how Luke makes a similar point, yet uses a different date, the time of the census of 6 CE. "By then the Romans had finally annexed Judea and the census was to enable them to directly tax the Jews. Judea no longer even had its own puppet administration, but was now ruled by a Roman governor. This led to desperate hopes that the Messiah would arise to protect his people and by placing Jesus' birth at this time, Luke implies that this hope has been fulfilled." Pontius Pilate was also a historical person who was hated by the Jews, and had even defiled the temple at Jerusalem.

Regarding the historical context of the death of Jesus at the direction of Pontius Pilate, Freke and Gandy write: "According to Josephus and Philo, Pilate was particularly detested by the Jews. He had violated Jewish religious taboos many times, including being the first Roman to defile the Jerusalem temple. Pilate therefore had to be the executive who finally directs the proceedings against Jesus. However, choosing Pilate as the character who was seemingly in charge of the proceedings caused serious historical problems of documentation, as apart from the gospels there are no Roman records of his actions.

Focusing in on Jesus: Prayer or Meditation?

One of the important points of this chapter is that we don't need a historically verifiable Jesus in order to meditate on God using his name. The name Jesus has become established as a spiritually viable word that denotes God; as established as any "God" known to man. Justin

O'Brien, in his book *A Meeting of Mystic Paths--Christianity and Yoga* writes that a prayer practice, which is a meditative prayer, was described in the Russian version of the Philokalia, a compendium of teachings and diaries from the Desert Fathers, the Greek Fathers, and theologians of Byzantine spirituality, from St. Anthony in the third century up to modern times. "The method, known as The Jesus prayer, consists of the simple, invariable formula: "Lord Jesus Christ, Son of God, have mercy upon me" repeated again and again. The inspiration for the formula is grounded in the Bible and the meditations of the Greek fathers. In 1351 an Orthodox Council officially approved the doctrinal justification for the prayer. This ecclesiastical achievement was largely due to the defending efforts of a fourteenth-century monk, Gregory Palamas of Athos, who later died as the Archbishop of Thessalonica in 1359." O'Brien states that the purpose of the Jesus prayer is not merely ritualistic or devotional, but a primary means for growth in self-knowledge. He states: "In the Jesus prayer an interior transformation is also sought that leads to what the Greek Fathers called *theosis,* or the spiritualization of the personality. Hesychasm, a spiritual tradition that dates back to the third century, uses the Jesus formula as one of its forms of inner prayer. The Hesychast monks (Hesychast means "the tranquil one") were especially noted for using this meditation as the chief means for their spiritual development. They combined prayer and meditation with breathing techniques as instructed by the monk Nicephorus the Solitary: "You know, brother, how we breathe: we breathe the air in and out. On this is based the life of the body and on this depends its warmth. So sitting down in your cell, collect your mind, lead it into the path of the breath along which the air enters in, constrain it to enter the heart together with the inhaled air, and keep it there. Keep it there, but do not leave it silent and idle; instead, give it the following prayer: "Lord Jesus Christ, Son of God, have mercy upon me." Let this be its constant occupation, never to be abandoned. These are the words of this blessed Father, uttered for the purpose of teaching the mind, under the influence of this natural method, to abandon its usual circling, captivity and dissipation and to return the attention to itself, and through such attention to reunite with itself, and in this way to become one with prayer and, together with prayer, to descend into the heart and to remain there forever."

Manuel Dunn Mascetti, author of the excellent book *Christian Mysticism* writes: "The deep mystical experience of these men and women in the desert, which became the kernel of orthodox mysticism, is one that speaks powerfully to the modern world: hesychasm. This is the quiet prayer in which one recites the name of Jesus in faith and love. The word itself comes from *hesychia*, literally meaning 'quiet.' Hesychasm is a method that induces an altered state of consciousness similar to that produced by the recitation of mantras in Buddhism or Hinduism, in which the mind is stilled and the whole energy of body, mind and spirit is focused toward deepening the intimacy with God." The author explains further: "The prayer of the heart, as hesychia came to be called, is a meditation in five parts:

--Entering a state of quiet without reading, thinking, reasoning, or imagining.
--Repeating the Jesus prayer with faith and love and absolute concentration
--Regulating the breathing so it becomes rhythmical and at the same time fixing one's gaze on the heart, the stomach, or the navel, allowing the mind to sink back into the heart--aligning mental, spiritual and physical energies into the contemplation of Oneness
--Feeling inner warmth arising that may develop into the sensation that a fire is burning inside the heart
--Attaining deification, or theosis, the state of God-within, through absolute contemplation. The goal of *hesychia* is to unite one's heart with the heart of God, so that the quality of God-consciousness begins to arise in the individual who is practicing this meditation."

Mascetti also writes: "The contemporary Greek mystic and psychologist Hierotheos Vlachos summarizes the teachings of the Church Fathers in this respect: Saint Gregory the Theologian regarded hesychasm as essential for attaining communion with God. "It is necessary to be still in order to have clear converse with God and gradually bring the mind back from its wanderings." With stillness a man purifies his sense and his heart. So he knows God, and this knowledge of God is his salvation."

Mascetti then concludes: "Hesychasm flourished, and continues to flourish, in the desert monasteries and at the holy mountain in northern Greece, where monks from many parts of the world spend a life or prayer and fasting."

The Sufis use the method of meditation on the heart, but of course, do not use the Jesus prayer described above. Pathanjali, an Indian Sage who lived in the second century BCE, who wrote the famous Yoga Sutras, stated that meditation on the heart is an effective way of attaining spirituality. Therefore, aside from the use of the phrase "Jesus Christ, Son of God," the spiritual traditions of various religions are very similar. Indeed, I see the very word "Jesus," derived from the Greek *Iesous*, to very simply be a word connoting the embodiment of God's energy in the form of "the anointed one," which in a way is a mystical concept. Even without referring to an historical person, it has spiritual significance. The Gnostic sages who founded Christianity certainly had such a meaning in mind when they began the use of the word.

The Jesus prayer is an excellent example of combining prayer and meditation. *The statement is a prayer, and repetition is a meditation technique* described in the Indian tradition as Mantra Yoga, or the practice of repetition of a Mantra or sacred word/phrase. Such Mantras are best taught by a teacher who guides the student in its use. The word *Jesu* can be effectively used as a Mantra. If divided into two syllables, 'Yay' and 'Soo,' with the first used on the in-breath and the second in the out-breath, this word is a very effective, powerful, easy-to-use Mantra. The key is to progressively relax with every breath and every syllable, until there is nothing but the breath and the mantra. Visualizations of figures, such as a cross, could be used as well, but I believe that just the word is sufficient to induce concentration and a meditative state. Jesu simply means Jesus, and meditation on the word is very Christian a practice. Despite it being a simple word, it has the ability to awaken latent spiritual states. I have used an 'angelic Christ figure on a Cross' as a mental concentration object, and found that when that concentration deepens into meditation, there is just the object, a vast space around me, and myself. This reveals a kind of trinity that could be interpreted as the Father (shining Christ figure), Son (myself) and the Holy Spirit (vast space). This however does not exactly correspond to the usual Christian trinity, where the Christian practitioner himself is not part of the trinity; he is outside, prayerfully hoping that he will be accepted by the trinity some day. The actual practice of meditation will remove any doubts as to whether this technique works for the reader. Christian mystics have consistently relayed the message that merging with the Christ is not only possible, it is desirable, and something that ought to be achieved. Sadly, however, most churches have forbidden meditative practices and have taught their congregants that meditation is not for them. One lady told me firmly that demons occupy the blank mind that meditation induces. My response to that is that if people have faith in demons, then surely they will occupy their minds.

The use of mystery myths by initiates in the Jesus Mysteries, or those of Osiris/Dionysus was an entirely different practice, and required a teacher to guide carefully chosen initiates into the inner mystery. The physical death of Jesus symbolizes the dropping away of the physical realm and limitations of the initiate, and the resurrection symbolizes the entry into the higher realms of the Spirit. Not much is known of the secretive practices involved in the inner mysteries. Whether the inner mysteries involved using Mantras is not well known. The latter develops a state of concentration which then deepens into a state of higher realization; a mystery myth likely involves visualizing the deity as a being of light, and then merging with that light. Or it might even have been something that is deeply contemplated upon just as in a Zen koan, thereby developing higher states of awareness.

Transcending Biblical Boundaries

As I see it, it is perfectly possible to love and revere the Bible and yet not have any need to insist that it reveals the only absolute truth about humanity, creation, and all related subjects. In many cultures, ancient legends about creation are loved and still taught to wide eyed children, who grow up to cherish them, yet enjoy the learning of scientific exposition and understanding. Aside from fundamentalists, the rest of the world is happily able to reconcile the two. For instance, if man was created from a clot, as the Qur'an states, one wonders how or why God created blood before creating man. Or if we accept the idea that man was created from semen, we must just reverently accept that semen was created out of water and earth, and man (woman as well) was fashioned out of semen. The Brihadäranyaka Üpanishad (translated by Alistair Shearer) explores this: "A tree when felled sprouts again from the root. But from what root is man reborn when he is cut down by death? Do not say semen, for that comes from the living-as trees spring up from seeds of trees that have not died." The Üpanishad goes on to answer that the Supreme Brahman, or infinite God, is the root of man's existence. Therefore the "creation of man from semen" is just a metaphor; it refers to the creation of man from "the essence of man."

Jean-Jacques Rousseau, in his book *The Creed of a Priest of Savoy* stated what he felt to be undesirable doctrine: "If, then, it taught us only absurd and reasonless things, if it inspired in us only feelings of aversion for our fellows and fear for ourselves, if it painted for us only a God wrathful, jealous, vengeful, partial, and hating man; a God of war and combats, always ready to destroy and strike down, always talking of torments and penalties, and boasting of punishing even the innocent, my heart would not be drawn toward that terrible God.." By "it" he was referring to the Bible. I see the Bible as inspired writing by Jewish writers who were so repulsed by what they felt was unacceptable social behavior, that they were inspired to project their feelings to a personal God who projected their desire for social order. The God of the Bible is formless, can never be represented by anything but his Holy Name, and has numerous edicts, requirements and laws. Indeed, this God, whose name YHVH, consisting of the four letters, the tetragrammaton, is a name that must not be pronounced. Though referred to as Yahweh, and incorrectly as Jehovah, the Hebrew God is referred to in conversation as Hashem, or the Name; in liturgy as Adonai or Elohim. This mythical God seemingly takes away land from whoever was not of the "chosen," and helps his followers destroy their enemies. One might wonder how the One and only God of the entire Universe would help sustain one race of man by destroying others. The answer, as I have often said, is that such a myth was created to give direction to the Jewish people. God does not take from some people and give to others. The word "chosen," as discussed above, however, must correctly be interpreted to mean that Jewish visionaries chose a certain way of life and law, and having implemented it, became those who have chosen what they feel to be the biblical way to God.

Christians and the Jews

To me it is extreme irony that the Bible, being composed of Jewish ideas, Jewish inspiration, Jewish legend, and the essence of Jewish culture, has been "adopted" by Christians who subsequently have shown nothing but disdain for the Jewish people. It is not just irony, it is extreme sadness, and injustice as well. The "Father," prayed to by Christians, is none other than the Lord God of the Jews. The "Father" that Jesus spoke of is a loving father, and while it is true that the God as described in many sections of the Old Testament is a fierce, vengeful, jealous God, there are numerous sections of the Old Testament where God is depicted as a merciful, loving God. Freke and Gandy point out in their book *The Jesus Mysteries* that literalist Christians did want to keep the Old Testament: they regarded it as relating a divine history, thereby substantiating the claim that the New Testament was equally valid. They write: "Keeping the Old Testament also meant they could claim, as Tertullian does, that Christianity "rests on the very ancient books of the Jews" and that these are far older than any book, city, cult, or race of the Pagan world. As literalist Christianity became more and more Romanized, the blame for the death of Jesus was shifted from the Roman governor Pilate to the Jewish nation as a whole. In the gospel of Mathew, the Jewish crowd, which demands that Jesus be put to death, is made to chant: "His blood be on us and on our children." They quote a scholar's words: "The legacy of these words has been terrible. They have been cited to justify centuries of Christian persecution of the Jews. It is significant that only at the recent Vatican council has a formal declaration been made exonerating subsequent generations of Jews from responsibility for the murder of Christ." It is such irony because for Gnostics, the death of a god-man is an important event which precedes his resurrection. Therefore, it is important that we not dwell on who was responsible for the "death" of Jesus. The overcoming of death is the great message of hope for humanity. The gospels, likely created by Jewish mystics, were meant to teach a vital message that orthodoxy was to be shunned, while acquiring a spiritual understanding through the mystery of the resurrection.

The "Lost" years of Jesus

One of most intriguing aspects of the Jesus story was that of his "lost years," from the age of twelve to the age of around thirty when he started his mission in Palestine. Jesus' disappearance from the scene at age twelve and his reappearance at age thirty, is considered by many authors to confirm the fact that he was a mythical character, and not historically real. However, other authors seem to have their own interesting theories, which are worthwhile exploring just out of interest. There are very many "Jesus was here" stories in the world, and the stories of "Jesus in India" are certainly fascinating. It is not at all surprising that variants of the Jesus story are to be found in India, as there always has been much interchange between the people of the Middle East and India.

I have quoted the ancient Hebrew connection to India as described by Holger Kersten in his book *Jesus lived in India*. Kersten reveals an intimate link between Northern India, particularly Kashmir, and the Jewish people. He feels that that Jesus was a historical figure, known and fondly remembered and referred to as the Prophet Issa, as Yuz Asaf in Persia, and so on. Kersten feels that Jesus traveled in India during his "lost years." Elizabeth Clare Prophet, in her book *The Lost Years of Jesus* describes Jesus traveling as far south in India as to what is called Orissa today. Apparently, he was welcomed by the priestly caste until he started arguing that the Vĕda, the Hindu sacred scripture, ought to have been taught to everybody, including the lowest caste. And indeed, he is said to have actually done so, thereby inciting hatred from the upper caste people who conspired to have him assassinated; it has been part of Hindu custom that the teaching of the Vĕda be limited to the "twice born" only. The lowest caste were not entitled to be taught the Vĕda, as they were not "twice born."

Prophet states that two Russians, Nicholas Notovich, and years later, Nicholas Roerich, found an ancient, 1500-year-old document which Notovich called *Life of Saint Issa*. The document called starts with the story of Moses and the Pharoah, and continues with various narratives about the Israelites. It then speaks of the birth of Issa as an incarnation of God. Issa grows up, and at the age of fourteen, arrives in India, then called Sind. Issa learns much from the Indian priests, but later on, becomes teacher to them instead.

An extract of the text reads: "Issa bade them (the lower two castes) "Worship not idols. Do not consider yourself first. Do not humiliate your neighbor. Help the poor. Sustain the feeble. Do evil to no one. Do not covet that which you do not possess but which is possessed by others...not only shall you not perform human offerings, but also you must not slaughter animals, because all is given for the use of man. Do not steal the goods of others, because that would be usurpation from your near one. Do not cheat, that you may in turn not be wronged. Do not worship the sun-it is but a part of the universe. As long as the nations were without priests, they were ruled by the natural laws and preserved the purity of their soul."

Apparently Issa (Jesus) incurred the wrath of the priests who conspired to assassinate him, so he traveled back to Israel, spending time in Persia and having the same problems again. The original of this document, if there ever really was one, is apparently no longer available. It is a fascinating story, but obviously created as a myth, because it would have been impossible for a biographer to have traveled with Jesus across India and the Middle East to document all these happenings. There are very many "Jesus was here" legends worldwide, some as far north as Scotland. It is not surprising, as the character of Jesus is central to one of the most powerful religions in the world, and also a character accepted by Islam as a great prophet. The story *Life of Saint Issa*, if indeed there was such a document, was likely yet another apocryphal text, but centered on Jesus in India.

I see the creators of the Jesus myth as characterizing him to be a "guru in spirit," a mystical character who taught the importance of love, compassion, proper behavior, and complete devotion to God. There is no question whatsoever that Jesus was one of the most fascinating of mythical, mystical characters. He was a held by the Gnostics to be the very body of compassion and light.

Merging with the Christ

Ramakrishna was one of the greatest of Indian mystics and spiritual leaders of the nineteenth century. He would spend stretches of time deeply immersed in practicing various religions. Here is an excerpt from the book *Ramakrishna and his disciples* by Christopher Isherwood, revealing a brief period when Ramakrishna was completely immersed into being a Christian:

"At length, on the evening of the third day (of immersion into Christian practice), while he was walking in the forest hermitage, he saw a tall, stately man with a fair complexion coming towards him, regarding him steadfastly as he did so. Ramakrishna knew him at once to be a foreigner. He had large eyes of uncommon brilliance and his face was beautiful, despite the fact that his nose was slightly flattened at the tip. At first, Ramakrishna wondered who this stranger could be. Then a voice from within told him, 'This is Jesus the Christ, the great yogi, the loving Son of God and one with his Father, who shed his heart's blood and suffered tortures for the salvation of mankind! Jesus then embraced Ramakrishna and passed into his body. Ramakrishna remained convinced, from that day onward, that Jesus was truly a divine incarnation." The phenomenon of merging with a deity is referred to in Hinduism as merging with the "Ishta Dĕvata," the practitioner's "preferred form of God." Ramakrishna taught us that there are numerous paths to the Divine, and if practiced whole-heartedly, they all lead us to what is really our common destination. There are many stories of devotees of various gods such as Krishna, who have visions of such gods and merge with them. Ramakrishna was able to visualize not only Jesus, and blend into him in just three days, but other "God-forms" as well. This appears to me to be the essence of Gnostic Christianity, but is anathema to literalist Christianity. We need to remember that Ramakrishna was not an ordinary human being. He was referred to as Paramahamsa, or 'Great Swan." A swan is a symbol of a very accomplished being who has achieved a near-divine state. Interestingly, in the Indian way of thought, Jesus is a Paramahamsa, a supreme guru.

This incident helps us realize, or understand, the nature of Jesus and similar "gods." They are not in some far away heaven looking down upon us. They are accumulations of spiritual energy that we generate, and are with us and around us at all times. The word Christ, derived from the Greek word Christos, refers to a spiritual concentration of energy that Gnostic initiates focused on to achieve oneness with God. The Buddhist tradition calls them "bodhisattvas." Such beings do not necessarily have to have been historical figures, only metaphysical. It would be more appropriate to think of them as similar to the energy of radio or light waves. We are surrounded by radio waves and cosmic rays and other manifestations of energy every second, but do not know it; not unless we "tune in," to radio for instance. Prayer and meditation is the way to tune in to the energy of these beings. Prayer tunes in, and meditation allows us to be inspired and taught by the higher being. The inner mind, or consciousness, is the communication link. After all, we can not see God or hear God, not with our normal hearing. From the inner mind comes to us all the revelation and inspiration that we need, indeed desperately need! Prayer to the spirit of Jesus, in my view, can be very fruitful and fulfilling, despite Jesus never having been a historical figure. Christians have historically found great solace in prayer to the spirit of Jesus. This must not be discouraged or disparaged as misguided, because the spiritual support that is so derived is real. A person's personal deity is that person's source of solace, comfort and strength. It is a very personal practice, and no one has the right to question someone else's practice.

The Essence of Christianity

The essence of Christianity is to have Jesus the Christ in our hearts. The end result of the process is that we radiate the power of Christ towards those around us. The day we start radiating the power is the day we stop being Bible-thumping fanatics, considering ourselves superior to those who are 'non-Christian' and stop claiming that we are saved and others are not. This latter process is that of judging, something those who have Christ on the mind, but not yet in the heart, are highly prone to do. Jesus did teach us to take the log out of our eye before trying to take the splinter out of our brother's eye, but few people realize that judging someone not to be 'Christian' is to do just that. There is an enormous difference between having Christ on the mind and Christ in the heart.

81

The end result of having Christ in the heart is no different from being enlightened in the Buddhist tradition, or a state of Samadhi in the Hindu tradition. Once in that state, not a word need be said: our very appearance and manner speak for themselves.

This process of judging is extremely common among fundamentalist Christians. It is impossible to discuss anything with such people. They never see the state of spiritual achievement as being possible for followers of other religions. If one does not state in the exact words: "I have accepted Jesus Christ as my savior" then one is not "saved." The very burden that such people take trying to save others is usually their own undoing, causing them needless anxiety and needless distress to others. For goodness' sake, God the creator is surely going to find a way to allow for each and every one of us to eventually be redeemed. It is *His* burden, not ours. Devout Christians usually cling to the words of Jesus (John, 14:6) "I am the way and the truth and the life. No one comes to the Father except through me." While Christians are convinced that Jesus claimed that he was the way to God, they are not aware of the fact that the founder of virtually every religion spoke very similar words. One way of looking at this situation is this: God, the supreme power governing the universe, has radiated His power through countless enlightened human beings. When such beings say, "I am the Way," it is that power speaking, not the limited human form through which it speaks. The truth is that each one of us is capable of radiating God's power and light, and I believe that this was the essential message of Jesus as taught by the creators of the Jesus Myth, yet that essential message has been taken literally by millions of Christians ever since.

Ernest Holmes, who lived 1887-1960, of whom Norman Vincent Peale said: "I believe God was in this man, Ernest Holmes," wrote in his book *Science of Mind:* "Jesus answered, 'I am the way the truth and the life.' Again he is referring to the individual "I" the son of the eternal "I am." This Son is the way to the Father. We approach reality through our own natures and through no other source. "No man cometh unto the Father but by me." God is within and it is here that we meet Him. The inward gaze alone can reveal the Father."

Holmes continues in another section: "When Jesus said, 'No man cometh unto the Father but by me,' of course, he meant the 'I am'. This 'I am', then, means the inner Reality of every man's nature, and when we stop to figure it out, how can we come unto God, the Living Spirit, except through the avenues of our own consciousness, which is the only approach to God we could possibly have? It is another way of saying that the only way we shall ever approach reality is by uncovering the Divinity already latent within our own consciousness, in our own soul, in the center of our own being. Every man is divine and the Christ way is the way of the unfolding of his Divinity through his humanity; the uncovering of his spiritual individuality and the use that his personal man, or his personality, makes of it. Meditation is for the purpose of consciously recognizing man's divinity and uncovering it."

Therefore, it was the 'I am', God the Father, within Jesus speaking as the son, who is God's fragment embedded, incarnated. The Son is the way to the Father. Each one of us is equally endowed with the Son, and this is the most essential message of Jesus. Our inner/greater consciousness is the way to the Divine. It IS the divine. It must be recognized, realized, and then we will realize that it is the way, the truth, and the life.

Most Christians quote the Bible as justification for the truth that Jesus is the only son of the Supreme Lord. This is somewhat circular logic, however, to state that Jesus is Lord, the proof being that he said so, in books written by unknown authors. Even if there really lived a Jesus, the gospels were written so long after Jesus, and it is not possible to know the exact words that Jesus used. His words would have been in Aramaic, then translated into Greek, and then again into Latin. In any case, much of what is written in the New Testament is considered by various authors to be atypical of what would have been the "real message" of Jesus. Separating the wheat from the chaff proves very difficult. Thomas Jefferson, the third President of the United States, expressed his great concern in a letter to John Adams, the second President, dated January 24th, 1814: "The whole history of these books (the gospels) is so defective and doubtful that it seems vain to attempt minute enquiry into it: and such tricks have been played with their text, and with the texts of other books relating to them, that we have a right, from that cause, to entertain much doubt what parts of them are genuine. In the New Testament there is internal evidence that parts of it have proceeded from an extraordinary man; and that other parts are of the fabric of very inferior minds. It is as easy to separate those parts, as to pick out diamonds from dunghills." As President Jefferson said, it is relatively easy to identify with the universal spirituality of many of the teachings in the Bible; I see such words as diamonds, those spoken by a true guru, one who has discovered God's presence within him. A supreme teacher

83

has the light of God within him or her, and is able to teach the truth to others in order that they may discover the same light within themselves. The writer of the gospel of Thomas has Jesus saying that unless we discover ourselves, we are in poverty, and we are the poverty. It is very easy for followers to create an icon or idol out of such a teacher instead, and this has happened very many times in the history of humanity.

Christianity and the Indian Tradition

It is now important to proceed to the similarity of the teachings of Jesus with the teachings of ancient India. The intimate link between India and the rest of the ancient world is often forgotten. There is no mention of India in the Bible, as there was no such name during those days. Elaine Pagels, in her superb book *The Gnostic Gospels*, states that many scholars have wondered about the high likelihood of there being Buddhist and Hindu influences on the philosophy of the Gnostics. Sanskrit, Greek, and Latin are considered sister languages, and indeed there are those who feel that Sanskrit was the most ancient of the three languages. Take for instance the word trini, which is the Sanskrit word that means three. Add the letters ty and you get trinity. Purohit is Sanskrit for Priest, and Kshetra is Sanskrit for theater, or stage (on which the Play of Life occurs). Deva is a word for God, and note how its root is used in the word devotion or divine. However, it is now well known that the Bible consists of gospels chosen by the Church to be the essential canon, (the word kanoon in India refers to law, derived from Arabic and Urdu, a Persian-derived language) and most other gospels were either hidden or destroyed. Aside from being mentioned as one of the twelve apostles, Thomas is hardly mentioned. Yet the gospel of St. Thomas, retrieved from the Nag Hammadi Library, consists entirely of Logia, or the words of Jesus. The Sanskrit word Dve means two, and Didymos is Greek for twin. Thomas has been referred to as the "twin of Jesus."

The story of St. Thomas coming to India is very ancient, but quite shrouded in mystery. No historians have ever been able to accurately date Thomas' arrival in India. Acharya S. maintains that Thomas Christianity was a product of Indians of the Malabar Coast who had already adopted the Tammuz religion of Egypt. In the Indian Christian tradition, St. Thomas is said to have arrived in India with the gospel long before it arrived in Europe. He arrived at the West Coast, now called Kerala, on a slave ship. He established churches, traveled across the country, and finally arrived at Madras on the East Coast. It was there that he was subject to martyrdom. His legacy remains, however, with the San Thome Cathedral in Mylapore dedicated to him, and a monument on a hill called St. Thomas Mount, next to the airport. If Jesus was a mythical figure, with no real "apostles," who was Thomas? Perhaps he was a teacher of the Jesus mysteries; stories of god-men who died and were resurrected to life were by no means alien to Indians, who likely accepted the mystery myth wholeheartedly and perpetuated its practice. More research and attempts to document the actual year in which 'Thomas' arrived in India would be invaluable. The *Acts of Thomas,* an apocryphal text, says that Thomas got chosen by lot to go to India. Thomas was said to be the twin of the Lord in the gospel, which as I see it has a hidden meaning: The Lord breaks a part of himself away to accomplish something in a far-away land. At that time, according to the gospel, an Indian King Gundaphoros decided to bring a carpenter from abroad. Jesus happened to meet the emissary sent by the King, and sold his twin Thomas to serve the King, who ordered Thomas to build a palace and gave him money for the work. Instead of building the palace, Thomas gave the money to the poor and spent his time preaching. Gundaphoros had Thomas imprisoned, but Thomas revealed the palace he had built for him in heaven, after which he released Thomas. The apostle then traveled across India until the time he was martyred. According to the gospel, his body was moved to the west. This story obviously conflicts with the one that has Thomas arriving at the Malabar Coast but not as a slave, and eventually being martyred at Madras on the east coast where a shrine is said to mark the place where he was buried. Since it is a fact that Thomas Christianity is a very ancient religion in South India, it is more than likely that Thomas was one of the teachers of the Jesus mysteries who chose to travel to India to teach. After all, there is an established community of Jews in that part of India; it is perfectly plausible that a Jewish mystic came to India with a mystery myth. People are enthralled by myth, and the Jesus myth is most certainly a captivating one.

All Christian prayers end with the word Amen. The ancient Sanskrit word 'Aum,' (often shortened to Om) bears very close resemblance to the words Amen, Amin, or Oommen. Aum is considered to be the word that represents the Infinite, the Creator. St. John starts his gospel with "In the beginning was the Word, and the Word was with God, and the word was God." In Christian thought, this "Word" was said to be Jesus. But it can easily be said that the Word, translated from the Greek 'Logos,' simply just represents an idea, or thought, of the Supreme. Many scholars and mystics have stated that Aum is "The Word."

A deep understanding of Yoga and Buddhism makes it easy to understand the teachings of the Gnostics who created the myth of Jesus. Both the parables and other teachings then become clear. The gospel of St. Luke, 11:34-36, states: "The light of the body is the eye: therefore when your eye is single, your whole body also is full of light; but when your eye is evil, your body also is full of darkness. Make sure, therefore, that the light which is in you is not darkness. If your whole body therefore becomes full of light, having no part dark, the whole shall be full of light, as when the bright shining of a candle gives you light." In mystic meaning, the reference to "thine eye be single" clearly refers to the third, all seeing eye that is referred to in Hinduism. God, for those who worship Him as Shiva, is the one with the all-seeing third eye. Verse 36 means that when we become enlightened with the power of understanding, then we are bright enough to shed light on to, and for, those around us who have not understood. Stephanie Noble, in her wonderful book *Tapping the Wisdom within,* tells us that to her, the phrase 'enlighten me' means 'In Light, in me.'

Or the saying "lest ye be born again of water and Spirit:" Dvija is the ancient Sanskrit word for "twice born." To undergo purification, a ceremony including being baptized with water and recitation of the Scriptures is an important part of Hindu custom. After this ceremony, one becomes Dvija, or twice born. Baptism is a custom that is far older than Christianity, and was practiced by the Essenes. And the word Issa, the word that referred to Jesus, Iesous in Greek, quite likely is a different spelling or pronunciation for the word Isha, short for Ishwara, a word that means 'the expressed, or manifest, power of God, or simply, God for short. "Born of water and Spirit" could also simply mean to elevate ourselves to a higher ethereal, spiritual, stratum, represented by water and spirit. The Tao Te Ching, the magnificent old Chinese wisdom book, gives to water the supreme quality of being completely yielding, yet being extremely powerful.

The mystics who created the myth of Jesus saw the kingdom of God with the mystic vision of the Seers of the East. God's presence is here and now, and energizes every molecule of matter on earth, on water, and in air. In the gospel of St. Luke, it is said: "Once, having been asked by the Pharisees when the kingdom of God would come, Jesus replied, "The kingdom of God does not come with your careful observation, nor will people say, 'Here it is,' or 'there it is,' because the kingdom of God is within you." A variation on that statement is to be found in the gospel of Thomas, Logion 113: "They are not going to say, 'here it is,' or 'there it is.' Rather, the kingdom of the Father is spread out over the earth, and people do not see it."

In the gospel of Thomas, Logion 3, (as translated by Bentley Layton) he teaches this much more dramatically. Jesus said, "If those who lead you say to you, 'See, the kingdom is in heaven,' then the birds of heaven will precede you. If they say to you, 'It is in the sea,' then the fish will precede you. But the kingdom is inside of you. And it is outside of you. When you become acquainted with yourselves, then you will be recognized. And you will understand that it is you who are children of the living father. But if you do not become acquainted with yourselves, then you are in poverty, and it is you who are the poverty."

Profound words, indeed! This is the essential teaching of the Hindu Ūpanishads. The universe, as taught by the Ūpanishads, consists of one primordial force, which permeates all that is both seen an unseen. This force also transforms itself to all that is seen, both living and inert matter. This force is referred to as Brahman, vaguely reminiscent of the concept of Yahweh, "I am that I am." In the Chandōgya Ūpanishad, Svĕtakĕtu asked of his teacher: "Please, Sir, tell me more of this teaching." The teacher asked him to take some salt, put it in a container of water, and return to him the next day. The teacher asked him to show him the salt, which of course the pupil could not; it had all dissolved and was not visible. The teacher asked the pupil to taste the water to confirm that the salt had dissolved, which he did. Yet the salt was not visible. "Similarly," said the teacher, "We do not perceive pure being permeating everything, but in truth it is there. That being, the subtlest essence of everything, the supreme reality, the source of all that is manifest, that is our essence, and thou art that, Svĕtakĕtu!"

Jesus also used the parable of the mustard seed to describe the kingdom of God, and this parable is remarkably similar to the teaching of the banyan seed in the Chandōgya Ūpanishad, dating to a thousand years earlier. In Mathew 13-31, Jesus says: "The kingdom of heaven is like a mustard seed, which a man took and planted in his field. Though it is the smallest of all your seeds, yet when it grows, it is the largest of garden plants and becomes a tree, so that the birds of the air come and perch in its branches." In the parallel teaching in the Ūpanishad, dating to eight hundred or more years BCE, Svetaketu questions his father about the supreme God Brahman, and the teacher, his father Uddälaka Aruna, tells his son to pick a fig from a banyan tree. "Split it open and tell me what you see inside." "Many tiny seeds, Sir." "Take one of them and split it open and tell me what you see inside." "Nothing at all, Sir," replies Svetaketu. Then the father said, "The subtlest essence of the fig which to you as nothing, my son, is the very nothing from which this mighty banyan tree has arisen. That being which is the subtlest essence of everything, the supreme reality, the Atman (Self) of all that exists, is also the essence of your being; and thou are That, Svĕtakĕtu!"

For St. Paul, however, the "kingdom," is a future happening: "For the Lord himself will come down from heaven, with a loud command, with the voice of the archangel and with the trumpet call of God, and the dead in Christ will rise first. After that, we who are still alive and are left will be caught up together with them in the clouds to meet the Lord in the air. And so we will be with the Lord forever." (Thessalonians I) However, many of Paul's epistles are now known to be forgeries, and this paragraph may possibly be a forgery, or it could have Gnostic implications, because those "dead in Christ" may refer to those who attained Gnostic Knowledge before they died.

It is so much easier to truly understand Jesus or Christianity when one takes India and its ancient religions into consideration. There is an amazing similarity between the teachings of the Buddha who lived around 560 BCE, and those of Jesus. The Buddha taught love and compassion, and elimination of anger and hate, to be the way to eternal joy. Both these divine teachers emphasized that a change in our attitude and behavior is the key step toward leading a blessed life. Kersten and Grubar, in their superb book *The Original Jesus-The Buddhist sources of Christianity*, emphasize the point, the incredible similarity between the teachings of the two teachers. The most crucial teaching of the mystics who created the character of Jesus, in my view, is to achieve a total transformation of our selves. It is not just possible; it is an absolute requirement, that such a transformation take place. We will be the darkness if we do not.

The Beatitudes

One of the most important teachings of Jesus consists of the Beatitudes, also called the Sermon on the Mount. In the gospel of St. Luke, however, the sermon does not happen on a mountain. Scholars have shown that the Beatitudes are based on existing thought, including ideas from the Old Testament. Some authors are not convinced that all the nine (eight, if verse 11 is considered separate from verse 10) beatitudes were actually spoken by Jesus, perhaps only four, but in any case, put together, they constitute quite a formidable teaching. *The Sermon on the Mount according to Vĕdanta* by Swami Prabhavananda is a book devoted to comparing the beatitudes to the philosophy of the Hindu tradition. Justin O'Brien, author of the book *A Meeting of Mystic paths, Christianity and Yoga* also evaluates the beatitudes with a comparative viewpoint. Let us consider each of the beatitudes (Mathew 5:3):

Blessed are the poor in spirit, for theirs is the kingdom of heaven.

The essence of this teaching is also the paramount Buddhist teaching of non-attachment, as well as an important teaching in the Hindu Bhagavad-Gita; it is considered to be crucial to achieving a state of spirituality. Our lives often revolve around material possessions. The idea is not to abandon all we have and live in a forest, but to transcend any attachment to our possessions. A Buddhist scholar once said that when he sees a beautiful crystal vase, he immediately imagines it to be lying shattered in a hundred pieces, after which he no longer finds himself attached to it.

Blessed are those who mourn, for they will be comforted.

There does not appear to be any hidden meaning in this statement, except that for those of faith, comfort is always at hand. It offers solace for someone in distress, someone grieving, and someone who has lost hope. It gives *reason* for faith.

Blessed are the meek, for they will inherit the earth.

The gospel writer likely took this from psalm 37:11. One of the important teachings of the Tao Te Ching, is that the hallmark of a sage is his or her humility. "Pride comes before a fall," as the old proverb says; pride is one of the "seven deadly sins." One cannot help but remember that wonderful poem of Percy Shelley, "Ozymandias," in which just the legs of a statue of a king, long dead, stand in the desert with the rest of the body missing. "My name is Ozymandias, King of Kings," says the inscription on the pedestal, "Look on my Works, ye Mighty, and despair!" The poet goes on to describe the great irony: "Nothing beside remains. Round the decay of that colossal wreck, boundless and bare, the lone and level sands stretch far away." It was Gandhi who said that tyrants never succeed in the end. Like Ozymandias, they pass away too.

Blessed are those who hunger and thirst for righteousness, for they will be filled.

In the Buddhist tradition, it is taught as "Samma Sankalpa," or right resolve or determination. We must make a determined quest for what is right, and in the Hindu tradition, it is of supreme importance to seek knowledge of the Dharma, or the laws of what is right and wrong, and try to follow them. J. Krishnamurti, one of the greatest of modern philosophers, always felt that there must be a passion to our quest for spiritual understanding. He once said: "You know, passion is necessary to understand truth—I am using the word passion in its full significance—because to feel strongly, to feel deeply, with all your being, is essential; otherwise that strange thing called reality will never come to you."

Blessed are the merciful, for they will be shown mercy.

One of the most important characteristics of God, Allah, as described by Mohammed, is that He is always merciful. A related word is compassion, an important word in Buddhist thought. The greatest of Kings were always ones who were considered to be not only just, but merciful as well. One of the meanings of the word mercy as written in Merriam-Webster's dictionary is "a blessing that is an act of divine favor or compassion." This beatitude should be interpreted in reverse order, to say: God is merciful to you, therefore be merciful to others. It is the end-result of forgiveness.

Blessed are the pure in heart, for they will see God.

In the Yoga tradition, it is taught that "Saucha, or purity, is part of five pre-requisites for attaining spirituality, called the Niyamas, or Observances: the others being Santosha (deep contentment), Tapas (austerity), Svädhyäya (study of scriptures), and Ishwara-Pränidhänäni, (surrender of ourselves to God). In the Buddhist tradition, a mind which is free from the extremes of attachment and aversion becomes pure, and such a mind is capable of achieving enlightenment.

Blessed are the peacemakers, for they will be called sons of God.

War is the end result of greed and hate; in contrast, peace is the end product of love, compassion, understanding, and elimination of clinging to borders, boundaries, religious and racial differences. Islamic terrorists, or any terrorists for that matter, in their quest for 'holy' war, will never understand the crucial importance of this beatitude. Desiring only the promised paradise in heaven, they leave behind the chaos of a hell on earth with their nefarious deeds, and in the end they will defeat their own purpose. Terrorists cannot ever destroy a nation.

Blessed are those who are persecuted because of righteousness, for theirs is the kingdom of heaven. Blessed are you when people insult you, persecute you and falsely say all kinds of evil against you because of me.

This beatitude is considered typical of the teachings of Jesus, as the mystics who created the Jesus myth were iconoclastic, and rejected rigid rules. The Buddha and his followers were often the targets of ridicule and persecution, because he challenged the authority of those in power. The prophet Muhammad was persecuted also. However, sadly, the followers of Jesus and Muhammad have been the culprits responsible for the persecution and death of millions of people across the world. And in countries like Sri Lanka and Burma, Buddhists have tragically been guilty of the persecution of the minority Tamils.

Jesus and Children

Jesus gave great emphasis to the purity and innocence of children. The Tao Te Ching, dating to five hundred years before, also gave such emphasis. John C.H. Wu translates verse 55:

"One who is steeped in virtue is akin to a new-born babe.
Wasps and poisonous serpents do not sting it,
Nor fierce beasts seize it,
Nor birds of prey maul it.
Its bones are tender, its sinews soft,
But its grip is firm.
It has not known the union of the male and the female,

Growing in its wholeness, and keeping its vitality in its
Perfect integrity.
It howls and screams all day long without getting hoarse,
Because it embodies perfect harmony."

In Luke 18:18, there is a charming episode: "People were also bringing
babies to Jesus to have him touch them. When the disciples saw this,
they rebuked them. But Jesus called the children to him and said, "Let
the little children come to me, and do not hinder them, for the kingdom
of God belongs to such as these. I tell you the truth; anyone who will not
receive the kingdom of God like a little child will never enter it."

The essence of the teachings of these sages, (both likely mythical) Lao-
Tzu and Jesus, is that as we grow up we lose our purity and innocence,
and build upon it layers and layers of misunderstanding. Children are
entirely full of trust and love, and have wide-open minds, absorb what
is taught. But we adults have pre-conceived notions, and have learned
to dislike and to judge. Innocence, to me, is to dwell in the Tao, to dwell
in the Kingdom, which is a realm of purity in which we are capable of
dwelling, here and now. It is within us, not elsewhere. It is pure Mind. It
is what the Buddhists call Buddha-nature. Children manifest this purity
and joy; they manifest pure love, which is why it is so easy to love them.
Meditative practice helps us become aware of this deepest core of purity
that is an integral part of our nature, something that we forget as we grow
up. Knowledge that is imparted by books, teachers, and others, is relative
knowledge. Knowledge that transcends, in contrast, is something that
we must return to, and become like children again. A state of being in
which to live is to be at play, called "leela" in the Hindu tradition. All of
life itself is nothing but God's play. Understanding it is not possible. It is
only possible to delight in the play itself.

Jesus as the embodiment of love

The essence of the teaching of the writers of the various gospels is,
simply, *love.* Love for all other human beings, i.e. our neighbors.
Bruce Bawer, in his book *Stealing Jesus-How Fundamentalism betrays
Christianity* writes: "An exhaustive study entitled *The faith of the early
Fathers*, which enjoys the official approval of the Roman Catholic
Church, identifies no fewer than 1046 distinct doctrines that were
propounded by one or more of the early church fathers. These doctrines
concern such matters as the authority of scripture, tradition, and the

church, the nature of God and Jesus, the soul, faith, hope, sin, grace, justification, the sacraments, worship, death, judgment, and heaven. Of these 1046 doctrines, only nine concern love. Love figures far less frequently in the works of most of the church fathers, in fact, than almost every other subject treated by them." It is possible, therefore, to absorb the most essential teachings of the Gnostic Sages who created the character of Jesus, and rule out all the other "creations" or doctrines of the literalist church. Love for all is Christianity of the heart, and all other doctrines are Christianity of the head.

Conclusion

To summarize, the mystical teachings of the Jewish sages speaking through the character of Jesus are no different from the mystical teachings of the various great teachers and sages the world has known. It took a few hundred years for various authorities to come to an agreement on the canon of the Bible. Scholars feel that the mystical myth was taught first, very similar to the mystery myths of the Pagan gods Osiris and Dionysus. The historical aspects of the story were patched in later, although with numerous errors in accuracy. These errors, however, need not take away from the gospels' ability to help us attain a state of purity, contentment, understanding, and love. They teach us to look within ourselves, to attain a state of spirituality that is our birthright. In his wonderful book *You Are the Light: Rediscovering the Eastern Jesus,* John Martin Sahäjänanda, a Camaldolese monk living in South India, reminds us that Jesus clearly said that *we* are the light of the world, not just Jesus. It is time that we learned that while we can allow these spirit guides to help us attain that state, the state to be achieved is uniform to all of us. It is a state of being. This state transcends religions. There is room in this state for the teachings of all the sages who have ever lived. There is room in this state for the Tao, the Dhammapada, the Bible, the Vĕdas, the Qur'an, and an infinite number of scriptures yet to be found or written. The Bible is truly as vast as an ocean. It is possible to go 'verse-berry-picking' and find phrases, paragraphs or parables that suit just about anything one wants to say. But in the end, all we would do is wind up throwing these verse-berries at each other in anger, and the verse-berries then turn into something much harder and crueler, such as arrows, bullets and bombs. Such weapons originate from the misguided habit of picking bits and pieces of wisdom and promoting them as the infinite truth. The truth is one, and let us all see that as the goal. Scripture points to the goal; let us not worship the scripture instead. Brother John Martin

Sahäjänanda looks at the biblical statement in the Gospel of Mathew 4: 17 "The Kingdom of God is at hand, repent" in a very different way, one reminiscent of the Gnostic viewpoint. For him, the Kingdom is the ocean of God that we are already immersed in; "at hand," or "near," as the NIV version translates it, is a misleading concept. The kingdom is right here, right now, there is no future coming to wait for. For him, to "repent" is to attain a state of metanoia, the Greek word from which "repent" is derived. To attain metanoia is to be enlightened, to attain Gnosis, Jnana, and personally sense, feel, and resonate with God within and around us.

CHAPTER FOUR:
ISLAM, THE JEWELED SWORD

He is All. He is Love.
He is All-Love. He is Al-lah.

Take the words "I love" and repeat them over and over. See how close to the word "Allah" it gets. Allah is a very ancient word for God. It is a *Pagan* name. Caesar E. Farah in "Islam" writes: "Allah, the paramount deity of Pagan Arabia, was the target of worship in varying degrees of intensity from the southernmost tip of Arabia to the Mediterranean." It is interesting to note that to speak the syllable "llah," you must press the tongue on the front of the hard palate. This tongue position is an important part of some Taoist meditative techniques. I doubt, therefore, that it was mere coincidence that the word Allah came to represent God. Farah continues: There were hundreds of such deities in Pagan Arabia; the Ka'bah alone at one time housed three hundred and sixty seven of them. Of all those mentioned in the Qur'an, four appeared to be the most popularly revered on the eve of Islam: al-'Uzzah (Power), al-Lat (the Goddess), and Manah (Fate); all three female deities, popularly worshipped by the tribes of the Hijaz, were regarded as the daughters of Allah (the God) who headed the Arabian pantheon when Muhammad began to preach." "To the Babylonians he was "Il," to the Canaanites and later the Israelites he was "El;" the South Arabians worshipped him as "Ilah," and the Bedouins as "Al-Illah" (the deity). With Muhammad, he becomes Allah, God of the worlds, of all believers, the one and only who admits of no associates or consorts in the worship of Him."

The above, however, reveals the relative superficiality of "monotheism," because you start with several Pagan gods, get rid of all of them (particularly the daughters of Allah) except one, and there you have "monotheism." There does not appear to be anything superior in such a practice as compared to the seemingly inferior understanding of polytheism. I call it 'monotheistic polytheism.' And indeed, later on in Islam, the practice of praying to various saints takes the place of "lesser gods," so the practice of polytheism continues in a different form. It also reveals the fact that the ideas of Islam are a continuum, an evolution of thought. A fundamentalist Muslim may think that the entire world was ignorant of the true nature of God until He revealed His true nature and word through Muhammad in the Qur'an. Even Muhammad, however,

95

never did claim that God revealed a fresh new message, just whatever He had tried to reveal through various prophets: that there is only one power in the Universe.

In his book *The Son of Man,* Andrew Harvey quotes a verse from the Bible, one the beatitudes, in 'Peshitta,' an ancient Aramaic dialect, that uses a very similar word for God: "Tubwayhun layleyn dadkeyn b'lebhon d'hinnon nehzun Alaha," translated in the King James Version as 'Blessed are the pure in heart for they shall see God.'

Allah was later given many respectful names. Other religions also have names for the one supreme power, such as YHVH in the Judaic tradition and BRHMN, (pronounced Brhmŭn) in the Hindu tradition. As did the Hindu sages of old, Muhammad saw beyond the many and saw the One: which is why he consistently praised Jewish prophets who had sensed that truth. Hindu sages thousands of years earlier, who had also seen into the truth of the one reality, said in the Rig Vĕda: "Truth is one, sages call Him by different names."

Inner and Outer Islam

I have tried various ways in which to comprehend Islam, to try and find a pattern that fits, a picture that describes it in full, and I found it an elusive goal, until I thought of this: Islam is like a glass globe. The globe itself is outer Islam, and the vast emptiness in the middle is inner Islam. On the globe is etched and painted the numerous Surahs (verses) of the Qur'an, and the various Hadiths, or traditions, of Islam. The etchings and paintings, like representations of nature, reveal both beauty and ugliness. There is gentleness, and there is brutality. They form a tightly woven masterpiece, the representation of which cannot be moved or rearranged, or the glass will break. Outer Islam is as rigid, and yet as delicate, as the glass of this globe. It cannot be probed, or challenged in any way. To break it is to hurt the sensibility of Muslims who revere and admire this globe. It is easy to break, as the pictures and etchings are complete and tightly knit on its surface. There can be no erasing, modifying, or changing what is on it; it must be accepted as it is. You could be critical of it, but like any great painting, if you make even the slightest modification, you have ruined it forever. It must not be touched. This Hadith is part of outer Islam:

"Abu Hurairah, May Allah be pleased with him, reported:
The Messenger of Allah (may peace be upon him) said: I have been
commanded to fight against people until they testify that there is no
god but Allah, and he who professes it is guaranteed the protection of
his property and life on my behalf except for a right warrant, and his
affairs rest with Allah."

The theme of outer Islam appears to be: "I am the one great God Allah.
Believe and submit to me, and believe in the Day of Judgment, and you
will be granted paradise in the after-life. If not, I will cast you into the
burning fires of hell forever." I personally reject the concept of a Day of
Judgment, and I certainly do not believe in eternal hellfire. I therefore
reject the core theme of what appears to be "outer" Islam. Outer Islam is
the part of Islam where a limited deity who calls himself Allah dictates
all kinds of things into a book called the Qur'an, including brutal and
barbaric commandments such as the cutting off of the fingertips of
unbelievers.

However, the concept of surrender to God, if considered to be the core
theme of "inner" Islam, is most acceptable. Not a surrender to a sky-
god deity called Allah "up there" somewhere, but to the supreme one
energy/power pervading the entire universe, call it Allah or what you
will. Inner Islam is like the profound emptiness within the globe. It is
a void that defies content. It can neither be challenged, nor needs to
be. It is a yielding emptiness that yet contains all the fullness within.
It offers the great truth of containing whatever is poured into it; it
is all encompassing. Its profound and yet simple truth of letting go,
surrendering to the Supreme, is identical to Hindu Bhakti, Japanese
Zen, Chinese Tao, and Tibetan Mahamudra. It is the path of surrender.
Its process is as simple as an ice cube melting in water. You are the ice
cube and Allah the water. There is naught to do but melt. That is the only
truth of inner Islam. It is a complete letting-go, accompanied by deep
relaxation. Accomplished masters of Tai Chi, Chi Kung Yoga and similar
arts have understood the meaning of this concept. Without surrender
one cannot succeed in such arts. Once understood, the glass globe that
surrounds this vast full emptiness is also understood and accepted: the
greatest value of a vessel is not its shape or form, nor is what is engraved
on it, but the space that it offers to hold within it whatever is given to it.

The eternal truth of inner Islam is the same as what has been taught for
millennia in the Hindu Üpanishads, that there is nothing but one eternal

Reality, Truth and Power. The Kĕna Üpanishad states: "That which cannot be conceived by the mind, but by which, they say, the mind is conceived—know That alone as Brahman, and *not that which people here worship*." Muhammad had the same quarrel with the people at the Ka'bah: he felt that people were not worshiping what he felt was the 'true God.' But regretfully, Muhammad did not have the wisdom to teach the difference and let people gradually mature spiritually; his actions were to simply destroy practices that did not conform to his understanding. Deity worship is as old as humanity, and it will always be practiced. Islam practices the worship of holy relics of saints, which take the place of deities represented by images.

Inner Islam yields; outer Islam forces the yielding. Inner Islam is vast; outer Islam is extremely limited. Inner Islam asks for surrender to God; outer Islam demands surrender to Islam. Therefore, it is crucial that the world, particularly the Islamic world, starts thinking of the vast difference between the two. It is time we realized that in one form or another, all religions practice surrender to God. The Bhagavad-Gîta, one of Hinduism's most beloved scriptures, says (Chapter VII:20): "Those whose wisdom has been stolen by this or that desire, go to other gods, following this or that rite, led by their own nature." Yet, God is said to have said in understanding in the following verses: "Whatsoever form any devotee desires to worship with faith—that faith of his, I will make firm and resolute. Endued with that faith, he engages in the worship of that dĕva (a deity, or god-form) and from it he obtains fulfillments of his desire; all this is what I have ordained. Verily the fruit that accrues to those men of little intelligence is finite. The worshipers of the devas go to the devas, but My devotees come to Me." The "Me" refers to the cosmic One Supreme. I see no difference between the essence of Islam and this profound teaching expounded in the Gîta. Therefore, there need not be, there must *not* be, any more reason for Islam to subdue other religions in order to project the true nature of worship of God. Verse 2:256 of the Qur'an says that there must not be any compulsion in religion, and has been quoted countless times by apologists; however, such people seem to conveniently forget the words that follow in the same verse: "The right direction is henceforth distinct from error. And he who rejects false deities and believes in Allah has grasped a firm handhold which will never break." A mystical interpretation of this verse is that from within us, is the best guidance of all; however, a literal interpretation is that only the deity Allah, with the words in the Qur'an, can be relied upon to provide the right guidance.

Much of the Qur'an is written in allegory, and with contemplation the meaning of some of those Surahs can be discerned. It is said that there may be as many as seventy-seven layers of understanding which could be obtained from the verses of the Qur'an. Indeed verse 3:7 of the Qur'an states that some of its Surahs are direct, clear, basic, and self evident, while also stating that some parts of the Qur'an are allegorical truths. It sternly warns people to avoid searching for meanings that they do not comprehend, and therefore cause confusion. "No one knows the hidden meanings except God," the Surah states, but then admits that "none will grasp the message except men of understanding." It is my understanding that the Surahs that have blunt, fiery messages of warning are for people of simple belief and faith; other verses with allegorical teachings are also to be found in the Qur'an that in keeping with the mystical truth that God pervades all, and we need to let go to God in surrender. The Persian/Urdu word for God is Huda, and the Sanskrit word for heart/soul is Hrudaya. The similarity of the two words is no coincidence. God is in our hearts. Ancient cultures enjoyed the commonality of the language of the heart; we now seem to revel in the differences of the languages of our heads.

The Path of Surrender

The word Islam means to surrender to God. Salat, or Namaaz, is the term that refers to prayer in Islam. There is a prescribed manner of performing Namaaz consisting of a sequence of postures accompanied by prescribed prayers. One of the postures involved in the performance of Namaaz is for the person to be sitting on the legs in a kneeling position, palms up, with elbows halfway bent, in a gesture of submission. This posture is appealing in its very nature: it is neither begging, nor withdrawing; it is halfway in between, in a neutral state of supreme submission yet with dignity and composure. Yet another pose is to go down on hands and knees in prostration, part of the sequence of Namaaz. This is the same as that of a yoga posture called the child's pose or prayer pose. The position is highly valuable in inducing a great state of relaxation and devotion. I see a profound sense of humility and prayerfulness being developed by the practice of Namaaz. The Namaaz posture is not unique to Islam, however; for the followers of Hinduism and Buddhism are very familiar with the posture. The Sanskrit word "Prapatthi" means surrender or submission, expressed in virtually the same posture. Tibetan Buddhists perform thousands of prostrations over a period of time as part of a yoga intensive. Performing a series of prostrations steadies the mind, induces a state of humility, and a state of surrender to a greater Being.

The concept of surrender to God as being the theme, the crux, the most vital aspect of Islam, cannot be overemphasized. Donald Altman writes in his book *Art of the Inner Meal:* "Surrender also has a lot to do with the essence of the word Islam, whose roots of Silm and Saläm not only mean 'peace,' but convey the idea of surrender as well. This surrender is the giving up of oneself to live in peace-with God, with the community, and with oneself." He continues: "Muslims also pray several times a day-and many of their prayers, even many daily actions, start with the words that mean "In the name of God, who is most gracious and most merciful." In the larger sense, this allows them to begin almost any action 'in the name of God' or with God in mind. This powerful intention is recited often-whether one is boiling a pot of tea, preparing a meal, driving to the market, or getting ready to do almost anything. Consider this for a moment: Isn't this really a gentle, peaceful way of surrendering the outcome of our actions to God? Here is a way of letting go of our need for worldly control. After all, surrender to God is the cornerstone of faith."

Altman then goes on to differentiate between surrender and submission. There is a subtle difference between the two concepts, and Altman clarifies: "To submit to anything, is to allow yourself to be subjected to the authority of another without your permission, control, will, or judgment. Surrender, on the other hand, can be experienced as a process of faith, and in this sense is actually a choice. By choosing to surrender we may actually be gaining-not losing-greater freedom, control, and access to deeper parts of ourselves."

Outer Islam wants you to submit to that religion, but inner Islam wants you to surrender to God.

Spiritually, the concept of surrender to God is of the utmost importance. Sadly, in history, Muslims have demanded submission from others to their religion Islam, sword in hand. Surrender to God comes from deep within, and should never be forced. Forced submission to Islam is a crime against humanity and an abomination, in contrast to the act of spontaneous surrender to God, which is the most beautiful act that a human being could perform.

The word Islam, as I interpret it, simply means "surrender to God that derives inner and outer peace." Outer Islam involves surrender to the will of God as spoken through the Qur'an. A generally held belief would be that Islam consists of surrendering to God the Islamic way, in the acceptance of every word of the Qur'an as the final word of God and in the upholding of the five pillars of Islam. Inner Islam, which is truly the Islam to be practiced, consists of surrender to God from within, and has little or nothing to do with the Qur'an or religious Islamic practice. It is open to all, indeed desirable by all. The actual practice of "surrender to the will of God" would seemingly be open to interpretation. How do we know God's will? To the question of if it is from the words of the Qur'an or the Hadith, the answer is an emphatic 'no.' God's will can be known every moment, by each one of us, if we only develop the art. We could practice any of various mystic paths that have been taught over the years. Taoist flow, Buddhist mindfulness, Hindu renunciation, Christian Gnosis, all of these paths have tried to teach us, and help us attain knowledge of the will of God. God is within us and around us at every moment. We have the inner guidance of God available at all times, yet we go around oblivious to it. If we relax the mind, and develop the practice of mindfulness, we are then subject to guidance from a greater mind/wisdom from within. This constitutes true surrender to the will of God. This is true Islam.

The Qur'an

The Qur'an is stated in the Islamic tradition to be the "word of God" divinely revealed to Muhammad through the angel Gabriel. It is said that Muhammad was in a cave when the angel Gabriel spoke to him and asked him to "recite." It is also said that Muhammad was illiterate, and yet started reciting after the angel, and thus the Qur'an was revealed. Such is the nature of myth. Myth also has it that the same angel appeared hundreds of years earlier to Mary and stated in the gospel of Luke 1: 30-35 that she will become pregnant, and had to call the child Jesus. The angel said that Jesus would be great and called the Son of God. Yet the angel Gabriel is said to have dictated the Qur'an, which most emphatically states that Jesus was not the Son of God. This great contradiction indicates that myth changes with time and with culture and with the persons who are inspired to create it. All the great scriptures of the world were revealed to mystics, and myth was "revelation" appropriate to the times, and blended in with existing thought. Muslims, however, accept that the Qur'an is the direct unaltered word of God.

Even to think that an element of myth could be involved would be blasphemy. Poetry, in contrast, was considered to be the work of *Jinn,* or spirits. Caesar Farah writes: "Rhetorical oratory and poetry constituted for the Bedouin a dearly cherished source of aesthetic pleasure. He was easily swayed by the power of speech and rhythm and aroused beyond compare by the eloquence of his tongue. Hence poetry and oratory provided the best incitement to valorous deeds on the battlefield. The Qur'an preserves the rhetorical wealth of the Arab's pre-Islamic heritage; indeed, rhetorical oratory proved itself a strong energizing force in times of war. He who commanded the right world at a crucial moment could bring victory to his tribe. Poetry served as a weapon of "psychological warfare" aimed at demoralizing the enemy through derision. But such powers of eloquence were not for all to share and employ; they were gifts of the spirits (jinn)." Farah adds a footnote: "Muhammad had a strong antipathy for poets, whom he accused of being inspired by the Jinn; the Arabic term for poet, "sha'ir," stands for "he who senses" by extrasensory means." Surah 36 of the Qur'an states: "We have taught Muhammad no poetry, nor does it become him to be a poet. This is but a warning: an eloquent Qur'an to admonish the living and to pass judgment on the unbelievers." In the Indian Islamic tradition, inspired by Sufis, Shairi, or poetry, is greatly appreciated and enjoyed; it could be romantic or religious, but just the beauty of rhyme, mostly in Urdu, a blend of Farsi (Persian) and Hindi, induces a state of rapture. I submit that poetry is divinely inspired.

There is no doubt whatsoever that the Qur'an itself served as a "weapon of psychological warfare." Its recitation in Arabic is said to have mystical power over anyone who listens to it enchanted. But one man's poetry is another's dull prose. The Qur'an is said to be God's word while all poetry just the work of inferior spirits, to be derided. I submit that the Qur'an is no superior, and indeed not inferior, to the divinely inspired poems of countless inspired poets such as Rabindranath Tagore. Whether we speak of the Qur'an, or any poems whatsoever that have captured the hearts and minds of people for thousands of years, it is all the work of humans who were/are truly inspired. One great example of divinely inspired poetry is the Vĕda, the Holy Scripture of the Hindus. They are said to be "Shruti," or "that which is heard." This is in contrast to "Smrithi," or "that which was composed." The Vĕdas are not considered to be the creation of man, but what sages heard directly from God. However, this is a pious belief; it appears to me that neither the Vĕdas nor the Qur'an are the "direct word of God." They are all inspired poetry

102

and prose. Interestingly, in the world of Islam, particularly among the Iranian people, poets such as Hafez and Rumi and poetry in general are still highly regarded, despite fundamentalist Islamic rule.

Leon Uris, in his remarkable book *The Haj,* gives an extremely comprehensive list of items covered in the Qur'an: "The Koran has many other things besides punishments and rewards. It gives us instructions about fornication, adultery, disobedient peoples, alms, murder, corruption, insults, debtors, the pit, divorce, blame casting, dowries, persecution, fasting, the Day of the Burning, fighting, backsliding, backbiting, covetousness, gambling, infanticide, burying infants, heathenism, inheritance laws, how to sleep, menstruation, parental duties, wet-nursing, marital intercourse, oaths, dissension, orphans, eating in others' houses, prayer times and requirements, the evil eye, ownership of horses, suckling, the scene of the judgment, prohibition of wine and alcohol, renegades, retaliations, Satan, repentance, slanderers, treatment of slaves, widows' wills, thievery, suspicion, usury, cunning, transgression, omens, diets and food laws, prayers of the evil, sexual abstinence, unscrupulous business practices, vanity, raising the dead, sexual dishonor, eunuchs, motherhood, regulations for keeping concubines, blood clots, enemies, evil spirits, why Muhammad must be believed, vanquishing the Greeks, veiling the woman's face, cattle, fraud, niggardliness, idolatry, Allah's powers of imposing death, hypocrites, breaking bonds with kin, temptation, avarice, ritual washing, head shaving and other rules for pilgrims, fate of sinners, those who disbelieve, conspiracy, treatment of enemies and women refugees, lewdness, pregnant camels, slinkers, rain, perversity, plots and counterplots, world unity, and mercy."

Perhaps the verse that best summarizes the message of the Qur'an resides in the Surah Al-Furqan 25:62: "The true servants of the Merciful are those who walk humbly on the earth and say: 'Peace!' to the ignorant whom they meet; who pass the night standing and on their knees in adoration of their lord; who say: Lord, ward off from us the punishment of hell, for its punishment is everlasting: an evil dwelling and resting-place; who are neither extravagant nor miserly but keep an even stature; who invoke no other god besides Allah and do not kill except for a just cause (manslaughter is forbidden by Allah); who do not commit adultery (those who do will be subject to double punishment on the Day of Judgment, unless they repent); who do not bear false witness and do not lose their dignity when listening to insulting abuse; who do not turn

103

a blind eye and a deaf ear to the revelations of their Lord when they are reminded of them; who say: "Lord, give us joy in our wives and children and make us examples to others. Such people shall be rewarded with paradise for their strength of mind. In paradise they shall find a welcome and a greeting, and there they shall abide for ever: a blessed dwelling and a blessed resting-place."

However, the message of the Qur'an can also very easily be construed as a threat to humanity: a threat of death or maiming in this life, and eternal hell-fire in the next life, for those who do not submit to the God Allah or accept the Qur'an as His word. Verse 5:33 states: "Those that make war against Allah and His apostle and cause disturbance in the land shall be put to death or crucified or have their hands and feet cut off on alternate sides, or be banished from the country. They shall be held to shame in this world and sternly punished in the next; except those that repent before you overcome them. For you must know that Allah is forgiving and merciful." The sheer brutality of these words rules out, as far as I am concerned, that these are God's words. If they are, I have no use for such a God; and in any case, if one and several verses in the Qur'an are not really God's word, the entire book is to be rejected as God's word. To even suggest cutting off someone's right hand and left foot, is the ultimate in cruelty; from what demonic source, I wonder, does such cruelty come? Ironically, this verse comes right after verse 5:32 that teaches the gravity of murder: "We taught the Israelites that whoever kills a human being, except as a punishment for murder or other wicked crimes, should be looked upon as though he had killed all mankind; and that whoever saved a human life should be regarded as though he had saved all mankind." Of course, apologists would immediately remind us of the "except those that repent before you overcome them" clause, but during a battle, losers don't usually submit to the winners unless the battle is done. And it appears that once the non-believers are overcome in battle, then no mercy will be shown, and the inhuman punishments recommended above will be meted out. Historically, Islamic armies have not shown much mercy. The Qur'an is a most frustrating book to fathom. While parts of it reveal pure and simple spirituality, much of it is steeped in primitive dogma that chokes all freedom and joy out of human existence.

What do we expect from a prophet?

Islam has been called the "Straight path," which if referring to the most essential aspect of the religion, is an accurate description; sadly, however, it is much more a path that is as curved as the scimitars that were used to enforce it. It is a path strewn with countless bodies of massacred non-Muslims *and Muslims,* and countless amputated hands and feet, done at the "direction of God."

Ibn Warraq, in his book *Why I am not a Muslim* writes: "Muir's *Life of Mahomet* appeared between 1856-61, in four volumes, based on the original Muslim sources, the very sources whose reliability was questioned in the last chapter, but which Muir accepted as worthy of attention. Muir was to pass a judgment on Muhammad's character that was to be repeated over and over again by subsequent scholars. The scholar divided Muhammad's life into two periods, the Meccan period and the Medinan period; during the first period, in Mecca, Muhammad was a religiously motivated, sincere seeker after truth; but in the second period, Muhammad the man shows his feet of clay, and is corrupted by power and worldly ambitions. Muir went on to say that so long as the Koran remained the standard of belief, certain evils would continue to flow: "Polygamy, divorce, and slavery strike at the root of public morals, poison domestic life, and disorganize society; while the veil removes the female sex from its just position and influence in the world…freedom of thought and private judgment are crushed and annihilated. Toleration is unknown, and the possibility of free and liberal institutions foreclosed… ." Muir's final judgment is "The sword of Mahomet and the Coran (Koran) are the most stubborn enemies of civilization, liberty, and truth, which the world has yet known."

It is well known that Muhammad resorted to enormous violence in order to establish his message. Ibn Warraq writes of Muhammad's battles in his book *Why I Am Not A Muslim.* He states that Muslims attacked at Nakhla during the sacred month, when bloodshed was normally forbidden. A Meccan was killed, two were taken prisoner, and much booty was carried back to Medina. However, Muhammad apparently did receive a part of the spoils and a ransom of forty ounces of silver for each prisoner. He also "received" a revelation from God justifying the action: "They will ask you concerning the sacred months, whether they may war therein. Say: Warring therein is grievous; but to obstruct the way of God and to deny Him, to hinder men from the holy temple, and to expel His people from there, that is more grievous than slaughter."

Ibn Warraq then describes that in 627 the Meccans and their allies began their attack on Medina. It was a siege that lasted two weeks, and the Jewish tribe of Medina, the Banu Qurayza, surrendered. Muhammad ordered them to be killed. Warraq quotes Muir: "During the night, trenches sufficient to contain the dead bodies of the men, were dug across the market place of the city. In the morning, Mahomet himself a spectator of the tragedy, commanded the male captives to be brought forth in companies of five or six at a time. Each company as it came up was made to sit down in a row on the brink of the trench destined for its grave, there beheaded, and the bodies cast therein...The butchery begun in the morning, lasted all day, and continued by torchlight till the evening. The booty was divided, slave girls given as presents, women sold, and property auctioned. And yes, a revelation came down from heaven justifying the stern punishment meted out to the Jews (Surah 33.25): "And He has caused those Jews that assisted them to descend from their strongholds. And he struck terror into their hearts. Some you slaughtered and some you took prisoner.""

It seems entirely unacceptable that a prophet should slaughter men in such a brutal manner, and then come up with a "revelation" that it was divinely ordained. It is equally unacceptable that such "revelations" were indeed the word of God. The Meccan passages of the Qur'an reveal tolerance; the Medinan passages recommend killing, decapitating, and maiming. For ever verse or two that teaches tolerance and patience, the Qur'an has a verse that teaches violence against the non-believers. God never orders the slaying of people. In the chapter on Christianity I discussed at length the mythical nature of God's directives against the enemies of the Israelites, and indeed against Israelites who did not follow his commandments. World myth is indeed full of directives against the "enemies" of the deity in that myth.

Muhammad took on many more wives than was allowed his followers. In verse 33:50, at which time he had nine wives as well as many slave girls, he came up with a "revelation" which authorized this: "Prophet, We have made lawful to you the wives to whom you have granted dowries and the slave-girls whom Allah has given you as booty; the daughters of your paternal and maternal uncles and of your paternal maternal aunts who fled with you; and the other women who gave themselves to you and whom you wished to take in marriage. This privilege is yours alone, being granted to no other believer."

Muhammad therefore allowed himself several wives, eleven in all, and stated that he had divine authority to do so. Many people have a problem with this, but I personally do not. After all, many men with mystic powers also have a strong attraction towards women. Besides, after he married his first wife, he remained monogamous until her death; he married many of his subsequent wives who became widows when his colleagues were killed in battle, or married women who were offered as wives as part of treaties. On occasion, tradition has it, he got into some difficulty. On one occasion, it is said, Muhammad became involved with one his concubines, Maria the Coptic maid. He was supposed to have been with Hafsa, one of his wives, who was apparently away but came back unexpectedly. She was furious, it is said, and told this to Aisha, and threatened to expose the event to everyone in the household. A 'revelation' promptly came, stating that what he had done was proper. Surah 66:1 states: "Prophet, why do you prohibit that which Allah has made lawful to you, in seeking to please your wives? Allah is forgiving and merciful." The revelation (Surah 66:4-5) chastised Hafsa and Aisha: "If you two turn to Allah in repentance you shall be pardoned; but if you conspire against him, know that Allah is the protector of the prophet, and of Gabriel, and of the righteous among the faithful. The angels too are his helpers. If the prophet divorces you, his Lord will give him in your place better wives than yourselves, submissive to Allah and full of faith, devout, obedient, and given to fasting; both widows and virgins." Unbelievably, Muslims have faithfully accepted this verse as the word of God. I cannot but help consider it to be a bit of verse contrived by Muhammad to get himself out of a jam with his wives; some of what is written in the Qur'an does not exactly seem to be 'divinely directed.' However, it is known that he took extremely good care of his wives, and treated them with great respect and affection; he would always rise when one of them entered the room. Countless men in power have preferred to have multiple wives, including kings of the Hebrew Bible. Several modern gurus have gotten into deep trouble getting involved with several women while advising their followers to follow rules of either celibacy or strict chastity. Muhammad lived the way he wanted to, with nothing to hide.

Muhammad surely could be said to be one of the most remarkable persons in history. It is extremely likely that he had great charisma and was able to inspire countless followers both into spirituality as well as into battle. He has brought to humanity a message that has become accepted as the word of God by more than a billion people. While charismatic, he still lived a frugal life. He surely was a mystic, as the verses of the Qur'an as chanted in Arabic are said to have a mesmerizing effect on those who listen to them. And he is one of countless spiritual leaders who had a fondness for women; while those in a monogamous world got into great trouble because of it, he did not because of being in a polygamous world. Despite the brutality mentioned above, he certainly was a very brave warrior and a very effective military leader. Uniting the warring tribes of Arabia under the one banner of Islam was an achievement that perhaps no one else could have done.

The Five Pillars of Islam

This section reviews the Five Pillars, or tenets, of Islam, we must try and see whether there are any of the tenets that ought to be universal for all people, and discuss how they could be viewed from a world viewpoint.

1. Shahada, or the profession of faith: *There is no God but Allah, and Muhammad is his prophet.*

In Arabic, the Shahada recites *La Ilaha Illa'llah:* which for me translates to 'there is no other than the One who is without another.' I see the teaching of Islam to actually be very simple: abandon any ideas of God derived from any prior human source whatsoever, and to let go and surrender to the formless infinite that surrounds us and pervades us all the time. This approach appears to be virtually identical to the teachings of the Üpanishads of India except for the fact that the word Brahman (That from which everything grows) is used instead of the word Allah. Sadly, except perhaps for the understanding of Sufi mystics who realize this, a fundamentalist approach to Islam would preclude any such equivalent. The word would have to be Allah. Therein would end any dialogue or consideration of identical teachings that arose elsewhere. It is time, therefore, for non-Muslims, particularly Hindus, to become comfortable with, and accepting of, the word Allah as an equivalent word that describes this wonderful invisible presence that is all around us, and is the core of our being. And equally so, it is time for Muslims to accept that there are religions such as Hinduism that have exact equivalents for the description of Allah, particularly Hindu words such as Brahman, Bhagavän, or Îshvara.

Islam's severe intolerance of what the Qur'an refers to as unbelievers, and idolatry, is well known. Any religion that involved the use of icons, images or idols had to be destroyed. No doubt the intention was to eliminate what Muhammad thought to be ignorant worship of idols, which the Qur'an refers to as unthinking objects not capable of accepting devotion. India, therefore, has been the biggest target of attack for Muslim warriors ever since. This is a supreme tragedy, because Hindus believe in God being formless and infinite, but invoked by prayer into an icon or image simply for the purpose of prayer. There are many Hindu rituals that involve immersion of such forms in rivers afterwards, in the humble gesture of accepting that the Infinite cannot be limited to man-made forms. There may never be reconciliation between the two religions, but one can only hope and pray that the followers of each will try and understand the beliefs of the others. I personally find that the sentiment "there is no God but God" to be valid, and full of veneration and respect. Whether it is Christians who call Jesus the son of God, something that Muhammad rejected vehemently, or Hindus who invoke God's energy into images that they worship, all must realize that truly, all of it is but varied manifestation of God. Anything else is just a contrivance, a way of thinking or believing, something that is of value in their practice. Whatever the practice, we must remember that there is but one truth, one changeless entity that is in, and that is, the universe, and that is God. This is the teaching of inner Islam that outer Islam has covered with severely harsh and repressive teachings aimed at destroying those who practice a Pagan or Hindu way of worship.

The Hindu religion is considered by many to be epitome of idolatry. However, it is not too well known that in the ancient days of Vedic Hinduism, idolatry was seldom practiced. The major mode of worship was through sacrifices, not unlike that practiced in Semitic religions such as Judaism. A verse in the seventh chapter of the Rig Věda, one of Hinduism's most precious texts, asks Lord Indra, then Chief among the gods, to destroy idolaters: "Slay, Indra, the male demon! Slay the witch who joyously triumphs in her magic. Let the idolaters fall with broken necks. May they not see any more the rising of the sun." However, Hinduism is a collection of various practices, and has changed over the millennia. Image worship, discussed in detail in the chapter on Hinduism, is an established practice in Hinduism and not to be considered an ignorant form of worship. Besides, image worship, part of devotional religion or Bhakthi Yoga, is only a small aspect of the Hindu life, which involves a variety of practices such as doing good work as Karma Yoga, contemplating the true nature of God in the practice of Jnäna Yoga, and most importantly, training our minds in the meditative art of Raja Yoga, at which time God's power and energy are personally experienced by the practitioner.

The Qur'an, overall, is extremely intolerant. Verse 3:85 categorically states: "It is not acceptable for a man to choose a religion other than Islam; in the world to come he will be one of the lost." Verse 2:256 appears to be more tolerant, saying "There shall be no compulsion in religion." However, as mentioned above, on reading further, we realize that the sentence likely addresses Muslims to keep their resolve against Pagan pressure, to fight Pagans and other non-Muslims trying to dissuade Muslims from their path: "True guidance is now distinct from error. He that renounces idol-worship and puts his faith in Allah shall grasp a firm handle that will never break. Allah hears all and knows all."

As to Christianity, the core belief of that religion was unacceptable to the Qur'an. Verse 4:171: "O People of the Book! Commit no excesses in your religion, nor say of God aught but the truth. Christ Jesus the son of Mary was only a messenger of God, and His word, which He bestowed on Mary, and a spirit proceeding from Him: so believe in God and His messengers. Say not "trinity": desist. It will be better for you, for God is one God: glory be to Him, above having a son." Verses 19:88-92 are more emphatic: "They say: 'God most gracious has begotten a son.' Indeed this is a most monstrous thing you have said! Upon mentioning that God has begotten a Son the skies are ready to burst, and the earth ready to split asunder and the mountains to fall down in utter ruin; for it is not in keeping with the majesty of God most gracious that He should beget a son." However, miraculously, *while a baby in the cradle,* Jesus apparently said: (Verses 19:30-31) "I am indeed a servant of God, who gave me revelation and made me a prophet; and He has made me blessed wherever I am, and has provided for me prayer and charity as long as I live." Finally, verse 4:157 completely contradicts what the New Testament states: "They said in boast, 'We killed Christ Jesus the son of Mary, the apostle of God'--but they really did not kill him, did not crucify him; it was made to appear so to them. And those who disagree about this may be full of doubt, with no certain knowledge, and have only conjecture, but surely, they did not kill him. No, God raised him up unto himself; and God is exalted in power and is wise." Scholars seem unclear as to whether the Qur'an says God created an illusion of a crucifixion and physically raised Jesus to Himself, or merely exalted his status to that of a true prophet.

To accept Muhammad as the messenger is to accept that Muhammad is a unique being who brings this teaching to us. The word messenger, or rasul, is very much a Semitic word. However, it would be quite unacceptable to non-Muslims to accept that Muhammad is God's only prophet, or the "Seal of the prophets." Hinduism teaches that each of us has the potential to radiate God's wisdom and love, and to become a "Guru." The word rishi, or sage, a word of Sanskrit origin, may possibly have a similar origin as the word rasul. In any case, as in Islam, which accepts Abraham, Moses and Jesus to be rasul, there were at least seven rishis in Hindu legend. Indeed the Qur'an accepts that God has sent apostles to every nation. Would a new secular Islam for the next millennium allow that there were prophets among people who were not 'of the book,' and that there are as many potential sources of Godly wisdom as there are humans on earth? Not likely, but it must be hoped that followers of Islam will realize that they cannot make others submit to the idea that Muhammad is the only prophet. But equally so, it must be that non-Muslims gracefully accept the fact that Muhammad did have remarkable inspiration, enough to record a most remarkable collection of literature.

One way of looking at the concept of "Muhammad is His prophet" is to realize that the ancients reciting original poetry or scripture would often include their name in the poem to reveal authorship. We could look at the statement as "There is no God but God, and remember that Muhammad is the one you have heard this message from"

The Bible, long before Muhammad, had very clear directives about submission to God. Job 22:21 states: "Submit to God and be at peace with him; in this way prosperity will come to you. Accept instruction from his mouth and lay up his words in your heart. If you return to the Almighty, you will be restored." Psalm 82 complains: "But My people would not listen to Me; Israel would not submit to Me. So I gave them over to their stubborn hearts to follow their own devices."

2: Salät, or prayer, five times a day:
The most valuable teaching of Islam is absolute and total elimination of our ego, in order to allow our entire being to be guided by God. Legend has it that Allah demanded that we pray fifty times a day and that Moses

negotiated this down to five times to make it practical for people to follow. It would seem to be most desirable, however, to go through every moment of life in a state of prayerfulness. The practice of mindfulness, as taught by the Buddha, tries to achieve this state.

Islamic practice hinges on the proper practice of Salät five times a day as the proper practice. The Qur'an states: (11:114) "Recite your prayers morning and evening, and at night also." (Qur'an 17:78) Recite your prayers at sunset, at nightfall, and at dawn; the dawn prayer has its witnesses. Pray during the night as well, an additional duty for the fulfillment of which your Lord may exalt you to an honorable station." Noontime prayer has mention in the Qur'an, (verse 30:18): "Therefore give glory to Allah morning and evening, Praise be to Him in the heavens and the earth, at twilight and at noon."

Prayer five times a day is difficult to institute as a universal practice, as it is often impractical to interrupt work to spread out a prayer mat and go through the ritual of prayer. Can a Muslim settle for prayer just morning and night, as stated in verse 11:114, or is it more appropriate to insist on all the prayer times as collected from various other verses? Hadith, or tradition, insists on the accepted five times. It appears to me that one would not be wrong following verse 11:114 and perform prayer morning and night, and at night when there is more time. Twilight is a superb time for prayer.

3: Zakäh, or Charity:
A tax of two and one-half percent was fixed as the tax to help the poor and needy. There was quite some resistance in the early days of Islam to this tax, but once the religion was firmly established, the tax became an established part of life. In a way, it could be stated that Muhammad instituted the first welfare state of the Arabian area. However, this was by no means unique in world history, as countless kings have tried to institute laws that allowed for the care of the poor and needy.

Recipients were those in immediate need, slaves trying to buy their freedom, debtors finding it very difficult to meet their obligations, strangers and wayfarers and those who collect and distribute these donations. Most nations these days do try and incorporate caring for the poor and needy within their social structure. In the secular United States, for instance, a variable amount of collected taxes goes towards the welfare and health care of the elderly, disabled, and the poor. It would no longer be practical to fix an amount of 2.5% toward this end, *but we can safely assume that for all practical purposes, the directive of the prophet is being met in this regard.*

4: Sawm, or fasting, during the holy month of Ramadan:
The holy month of Ramadan, the month that the Qur'an was revealed, is to be observed by all Muslims. From dawn to dusk during the holy month, a Muslim is to fast, avoiding food and drink, and is to avoid sexual intercourse. Overeating at night negates the great value of the fast, and sadly enough, too many people do just that. Fasting has been the practice of various religions, and truly not exclusive to Islam alone. It would be worthwhile for non-Muslims to try and observe the daytime fast for at least one day during the month of Ramadan not only as a token of respect for Muslims, but to experience the practice first-hand. A similar yet effective practice is to wait, after any meal, until we are hungry before eating again. A stomach full of food causes lethargy and torpor, while hunger invokes an alert state of mind. Avoidance of overeating is equally important; indeed I doubt the value of any religious or spiritual practice done within an hour after a meal!

5: Hajj, or pilgrimage, to Mecca:
In Islam, Mecca is the most holy of places, and the Ka'bah, (kaba simply means cube, the shrine being a cube-shaped structure) the holiest of holy shrines. It is located within the Grand mosque of Mecca. Legend has it that the Ka'bah was built by Adam, rebuilt by Abraham as the holy place of God, and was restored back to its holiness by Muhammad. Adam and Abraham are likely to have been mythical characters, and the Ka'bah was an important center of Pagan worship from time immemorial. Visitors to the Ka'bah wear two pieces of seamless white cloth, many have their head shaved, and perform a circum-ambulation of the shrine, and express adoration to a black stone, very much like Hindus have always done in their temples. While we must respect the Muslims' sentiment toward Mecca, Muslims must be willing to accept that those practicing other religions find other places to be equally holy. For instance, Jerusalem is holy for Jews and Christians; Varanasi is holy for Hindus, and so on. Muslims in the past have committed destruction of the holy places and shrines of others, but in all fairness, Crusaders and others have destroyed Islamic holy shrines as well. This must end for all time. It is known that Muhammad initially accepted Jerusalem as the most Holy place, but after his conflicts with the Jews of Medina, he changed the most Holy place of Islam to Mecca. Qiblah is a term used by Muslims to denote the direction

in which they face when praying. The change in Qiblah was explained in the Qur'an, Surah 2:142: "Foolish people will say: 'What has turned them from the Qiblah to which they were used?' Say: To God belongs both east and west; He guides whom He will to a way that is straight."

In other words, there is no particular direction that is any more sacred than the other. I see the ground under my feet as the holiest place in the world, which means that any place that I am, or will be in, is holy. Just look at the magnificence of the skies at dawn, with all shades of crimson, red and orange, and the awe that it inspires, inspires us to pray just looking at the splendor. We pray to the one God *with* the dawn, though in those days our "idolatrous" ancestors attributed this majesty to a goddess of the dawn. For goodness' sake, what difference does it make? Our ancestors obviously were more subject to venerate these wondrous beauties of nature, and their direction of worship simply depended on wherever God's awesome power was displayed, such as volcanoes, rivers, oceans, forests, mountains, and so on. Who could not be moved by the Psalm's writer who wrote in Psalm 37:6: "He will make your righteousness shine like the dawn, the justice of your cause like the noonday sun." And in Psalm 121-1 we read: "I will lift up my eyes unto the hills, from which comes my help." But the true Qiblah is *inwards*.

The Qur'an does order the destruction of the shrines of idolaters, but so does the Old Testament in the Bible order the execution of those who pray to the sun or moon or stars. These are all scriptures dating back a very long time, and it is time to set aside some of the directives in them. Their purpose then must have been entirely different from the state of the world now. It is possible that Muhammad was dealing with unscrupulous "priests" extorting money from gullible people claiming to be able to communicate to various "deities," which likely occurred in many primitive religions. The essence of Hinduism is that while during Pooja the energy of God is invoked into images, after the ceremony, God is thanked, and released from the image. The latter may even be immersed into a river, or destroyed. Such a practice, rather than being "ignorant idolatry," is the result of very profound thinking and planning for people to find a way to relate to the infinite formless Divine. Islam is said to be the "straight Path" requiring no mediator, but Hinduism is fully aware of this approach as well, implementing this in various practices of Yoga that do not require the use of priests or images or temples. Indeed, for that matter, the best "straight Path," in my view, is Zen.

The Qur'an: Inspired or Revealed?

Every syllable written in the Qur'an is said to be the actual word of Allah, the one Supreme God of the Universe. The Hindus believe the same of the Vĕdas, and the Jews the Torah. The message in these various scriptures is so varied in content. How is one to interpret all of this? Who are we to believe? To me there appears to be a vast difference between the terms divinely revealed and divinely inspired. Seeing enormous difference between the various "revealed" scriptures of the various religions, it seems clear to me that all these are divinely inspired scripture, rather than being of two kinds, revealed and inspired. Even the poetry of Nobel Prize winning poet Rabindranath Tagore appears to be divinely inspired. Inspired work such as the Qur'an appears to have content very unique to the people and culture of the times. The God as described in it is all-powerful and all encompassing, frightfully infuriated by what is described as idolatry and dedication to "false" Gods, somewhat similar to the jealous zealous God of the Old Testament. The message of the Qur'an is that there is no God but God, and Muhammad has brought forth this particular scripture never before revealed to the people around him, and a revelation to be carried forth for eternity. Complete submission to this God is demanded, or on judgment day all non-believers are to be punished in hell-fire. In contrast, Hinduism has, for millennia, offered a much more graceful revelation of monotheism:

This excerpt from the Rig Vĕda, a Hindu scripture dating back to around 5000 BCE, reveals the depth of understanding of God even in those days:

"What God shall we adore with our offering?
He who gives vital energy (präna) and manly vigor, whose commands
even gods obey, whose shade is life eternal, he who is the Lord of death.
What God shall we adore with our offering?
He who by His grandeur has emerged the sovereign of every living thing
that breathes and sleeps; He who is Lord of two-footed man and four-
footed creatures.
What God shall we worship with our offering?
By right the snow-capped mountains, the rivers and the sea belong to
him; they are his possession. The four directions and these heavenly
regions are his extended arms.
What God shall we adore with our offering?"

The phrase "whose commands even gods obey" is a clear statement that God is one, and "gods" are simply angelic beings that exist only in the light of the one Supreme.

The Hindu Üpanishads, appended to the Vĕdas, dating to 800 BCE or earlier, at least 1300 years before Muhammad, reveal in most majestic poetry and prose that there is but one uniform force pervading the entire universe. Any "gods" that people have worshipped, often represented in images, are but just focuses of energy, limited manifestations of this one cosmic energy called Brahman. This force pervades all that is living or non-living, moving or stationary. We humans are nothing but a flowering of that energy. Ignorance leads us to think and behave as individuals, while ultimate knowledge makes us realize the unity. Deep understanding leads us to submission, to allow the greater force to pervade. Submission is the essence of the expression of this true knowledge. Submission is Islam. There was, therefore, very clear revelation, or "inspired understanding," in Hinduism that still endures today after almost three thousand years.

The Vĕdas, however, do not teach of either eternal hell for non-believers or eternal paradise for "believers." Ignorance leads to rebirth in the earthly or other realms, and absolute knowledge leads to the mind, and therefore the individual, being eternally freed from being reborn into any realm whatsoever.

During the early Vedic times, quite likely prior to the first millennium BCE, the Aryans worshipped several gods, simply as aspects of the supreme One. The Üpanishads, which were appended to the Vĕdas, then appeared, which further confirmed the supreme wisdom of there being only one absolute force in the universe. By the end of the first millennium CE in India, this had given way to the "path of devotion," very much involving the invoking of supernatural energy into images which were then allowed to give "darshan," or blessing energy, into devotees. Such worship is the equivalent of focusing the sun's rays using a convex lens, and far from "ignorant idolatry." This time period unfortunately also coincided with the aggressive spread of Islam by its followers, who massacred the "idolaters" including Buddhists who venerated or even worshiped images of the Buddha. Countless temples housing enshrined images were destroyed. Such destruction continues today. The book *Lajja:Shame* by Dr. Taslima Nasrin describes the destruction of countless Hindu shrines in Bangla Desh. The irony is that there are many verses in the Qur'an encouraging followers to be tolerant of the "ignorant practices." Allah is merciful and compassionate; He has to be; the "ignorant" are His creation, are they not? How could He order their destruction? It is my fervent hope and prayer that the world will resist fanatics who only read the sections of the Qur'an ordering destruction of "unbelievers," and ignoring equally valid words of tolerance, compassion and mercy. The words 'I love' and 'Allah' are too similar to be just coincidence.

Cruel Punishments in Islam

The Qur'an prescribes very primitive and cruel punishment not just for criminals, but for those who do not accept Islam as the true religion. In Surah 8:12, we read: "Allah revealed His will to the angels, saying: "I shall be with you. Give courage to the believers. I shall cast terror into the hearts of infidels. Strike off their heads, and cut off their fingertips!" The latter act is one of downright barbaric brutality, as fingertips are extremely sensitive, and cutting them off is an act that would cause unbelievable pain. Having sutured many finger wounds in emergency departments, I know how sensitive the fingers are. It is truly a tragedy that such a verse is to be found in the Qur'an, giving inspiration and support to terrorists and fundamentalists to cause such horrific torture on non-Muslims. An even greater tragedy is to accept that God said these words. Indeed the previous verse Surah 8:11, strengthens the resolve for a Muslim: "Remember He induced a trance-like state on you, to give you a calm directly from Himself, and he caused rain to descend on you to cleanse you and remove the stains of Satan, to strengthen your resolve and make firm your stance." Cutting off of fingertips is not something done on the battlefield; it is an act that can only be done on someone bound and tied, and therefore an act of mutilation done to a prisoner, essentially so he would never wield a sword again. After Khomeini came to power in Iran, his men committed an assortment of acts of torture on those who were formerly in power. They used every form of torture described in the Qur'an as promised to unbelievers in hell.

Even theft calls for extremely brutal punishment. Verse 3:38 states: "As for the man or woman who is guilty of theft, cut off their hands to punish them for their crimes. That is the punishment enjoined by Allah. He is mighty and wise. But whoever repents and mends his ways after committing evil shall be pardoned by Allah. Allah is forgiving and merciful." But being pardoned by Allah does not save the most unfortunate person's hands, apparently. I find it entirely unacceptable that such brutality can be brought forth in a 'holy book.' However, the Old Testament of the Bible also condones brutal punishment, and it is known that Muhammad obtained quite some inspiration from the Bible. Stoning to death, for instance, is a Biblical punishment prescribed for adultery and other offenses. In the known history of the Jews, however, such punishment is rare; in the known history of Islam, on the contrary, it is well known.

Punishment does not end in life, either, for the person who refuses to submit to Islam. Verse 44:46 onward states: "The fruit of the Zaqqum-tree shall be the sinner's food. Like dregs of oil, like scalding water, it shall simmer in his belly. A voice will cry: 'seize him and drag him into the depths of hell. Then pour boiling water over his head, saying; "Taste this, illustrious and honorable man! This is the punishment you doubted."" And 40:72: "Those who have denied the scriptures and the message which We have sent with Our apostles shall know the truth hereafter: when with chains and shackles around their necks they shall be dragged through boiling water and burnt in the fire of Hell."

Another threat in verses 78:21-25 is quite sickening as well: "Truly, hell is a place of ambush, a dwelling place for the transgressors, where they will abide for ages. They shall taste nothing cool, nor any drink, except for boiling water and icy cold cloudy fluid (variously translated as slop, dirty wound discharges, and such by various translators)."

The Qur'an, therefore, is replete with verses scattered across it, promising all kinds of fiendish punishments in life and in the life after, for those refusing to adopt Islam as their religion. These verses have been the inspiration for so much cruelty inflicted on innocent people of other religions. "God's" promises of the tortures of hell must be rejected as traditional understanding and belief of people of those times, and not taken literally. Besides, even other religions speak of the tortures of hell. In Hinduism, a period in hell is for those who are cruel or evil, and cause pain, suffering or death to others; even for those, it is not an eternal punishment, but of a duration in proportion to the extent of their evil. God is gracious, merciful. He sees people adoring Him in their own way in their own religion. Therefore it is my prayer that Muslims will realize that no human being can ever judge as to who deserves hell, and an even greater prayer that they will certainly stop causing hell on earth to those of other religions whom they wrongly consider to be "unbelievers."

Islam and Christianity

Islam has its own version of what Christianity really ought to be all about, and its own stories about Jesus. The Qur'an states in a most determined manner that Jesus was not a Son of God, only an apostle. Verse 4:171 states: "O People of the Book! Commit no excesses in your religion, and do not say anything about God but the truth. Jesus the son of Mary was only an Apostle of God and his Word, which He bestowed on Mary, and a Spirit proceeding from Him. So believe in God and his apostles. God is but one God, not three. Glory be to Him, who is exalted above having a son." Therefore Islam has been at odds with Christianity ever since.

There are some stories concerning Jesus that are not to be found in the Bible. For instance, the Qur'an states in verse 19:30 that Jesus spoke from his cradle: "I am indeed a servant of God, who hath given me revelation and made me a prophet." The Qur'an is very firm that Jesus was not a Son of God, only a prophet. Interestingly, this episode concerning Jesus is simply a modification of a fable regarding Jesus from the apocryphal First Gospel of the Infancy of Jesus Christ. According to that Gospel, Jesus spoke from his cradle, stating that he was Jesus, the Son of God. It appears that the Qur'an takes that fable and modifies it to make Jesus state that he was a prophet rather than the Son of God. Verse 3:51 has Jesus exclaim "It is God who is my Lord, and yours; Worship Him, for this is a Way that is straight." Verses 3:48-49 state that God would teach Jesus the Book and Wisdom, the Law and the Gospel, make a clay bird, breathe into it and make it come alive, and perform miracles under God's direction.

It appears that the source for the Qur'an story of Jesus bringing a clay bird alive is the Thomas gospel of the Infancy of Jesus Christ, an apocryphal text. In that, Jesus takes some soft clay from the bank of a stream, and created twelve sparrows. He then clapped his hands, directing the sparrows to fly away, and they did. Therefore it appears that the Qur'an is doing no more than repeating an ancient fable.

Christians generally cannot tolerate the Islamic belief that Jesus was no more than yet another prophet, for to them Jesus is the Son of God who is the redeemer. There appears to be no reconciliation between the two viewpoints. Or is there? The Gnostics created the mythical character of Jesus to teach love, compassion and forgiveness, much as the Jews created myths of various prophets to teach aspects of Jewish wisdom. Perhaps we could take it that the Qur'an admonishes people to accept and learn the message, and not worship the prophet. The Qur'an seemingly speaks of Jesus as a genuine figure of history, a prophet who did live on earth and do miraculous things. On the other hand, the Qur'an equates Jesus with all the other prophets before him. The prophets were mythical; perhaps the Qur'an lets our level of understanding interpret as to whether we accept the prophets as historical or simply just learn their teachings. There is no historical basis for Jesus, as is discussed in the chapter on Christianity. Therefore I feel that the Qur'an's 'revelation' about Jesus was simply a modification of earlier Christian myth, with newer 'Islamic myth.' The Qur'an's version of the Jesus story is neither Gnostic in understanding, nor is it based on historical truth. The creators of the Jesus myth did not create a prophet; they created a deity, an embodiment of God who speaks what they thought was divine truth. The Qur'an of course would forbid any such practice, and would rather we simply just listen to what it considers to be God's message brought time and time again through various prophets.

An Unjust War

While it is well known that Muhammad the prophet and his followers resorted to the sword to quite an extent, we must remember that they, the early Muslims, were severely persecuted and oppressed. Perhaps Muhammad, in his fervor of having discovered what he felt in his heart was the proper path, was forced to resort to violence to resist violent persecution, and become a warrior. Jihad is to fight oppression and the freedom to be in peace and to worship in the manner that feels right and proper. Krishna, in the Hindu Bhagavad-Gita, says to Arjuna: (verses 2: 31-34) "Further, looking at your own duty you ought not to waver, for there is nothing higher for a warrior than a righteous war. Happy indeed are the warriors who are called to fight in such a battle, which comes of itself as an gateway to heaven. But, if you will not fight this righteous war, you will have abandoned your own duty and fame, and you shall incur sin. People too, will remember your everlasting dishonor; and to one who has been honored, dishonor is worse than death." The Qur'an also emphasizes at times that aggression is only to be undertaken in defense, as Surah 2:190 states: "Fight for the sake of Allah those that fight against you, but do not attack them first. Allah does not love the aggressors." However, the words that follow give Muslims free reign to destroy non-Muslims: "Fight against them until idolatry is no more and Allah's religion reigns supreme. But if they mend their ways, fight none except the evil-doers." This verse eliminates any possibility of reconciliation between Muslims and others: Allah's religion has to be forcefully instituted wherever possible. It is my prayer that such verses will be disregarded.

What is great irony is that Muslims have lost sight of that original clamor for liberty to practice their faith without oppression, and now oppress those who do not believe in the Qur'an or in Islam. It will have to be up to those of us who have courage, to maintain dialogue with the Muslim world, to truly see the light as revealed by the prophet, that God is one, God is all, God is everything, all we need to do is to let go our egos in deep submission, and that is all. God is love and mercy and compassion, and our behavior must be in keeping with that ideal. No matter what some parts of the Qur'an state about killing enemies and idolaters and "unbelievers," the essence of Islam is deep humility and an even deeper letting go, submission, to the greater power that surrounds us every second of our lives. The brutal killing of innocents being carried out by Islamic terrorists can only stop if the Muslim world speaks out boldly that there is no heaven for the killers of the innocent. The Qur'an also has powerful statement against corruption which unfortunately is quite prevalent even in Islamic nations today, as in verse 2:189: "Do not usurp one another's property by unjust means, not bribe with it the judges in order that you may knowingly and wrongfully deprive others of their possession." It appears that Islamic Kashmiri terrorists, who have driven hundreds of thousands of Hindus from their homes or killed them, have no use for such words of wisdom.

Islam as a religion is a very powerful force in the world today, and will likely continue to be so for many generations to come. People brought up in the fundamentalist part of that tradition will never see things in any light but that of the Islamic viewpoint. Their women will always be subordinated, hidden behind veils, and will never be an active part of public life. Such a pity that women must be hidden away to help men avoid temptation. It appears to me that such men ought to wear blindfolds instead! Even our ancestors of tens of thousands of years ago had women actively participate in hunting their prey as well as giving birth and nurturing the young. Women in virtually all other cultures take a major role in both family and social life. The female is actually the crowning glory of all creation, it is she who is the part of life that generates fresh new life and helps perpetuate the human race. This is why the energy of the cosmos is worshipped as female in many cultures. For them, the energy of life is female; it is the Goddess. Not for the Taliban of Afghanistan, however. They continue to intimidate, rape, and kill the women of Afghanistan. Afghan women have got together to create a Women's Bill of Rights, demanding that Afghan women be treated as humans, and not sold into marital slavery or traded as compensation for crimes by families. The brutalization of women in Afghanistan is publicized in the West, but it is not likely that newspapers in Islamic countries discuss their plight. To further add to Afghan women's problems, the Afghan government is in the process of courting the Taliban to join in the reconstruction of Afghanistan. This means that the women of Afghanistan will always be treated as second class citizens—or worse.

Women's rights in the Islamic world are sure to be promoted by the 2003 Nobel Peace prize being awarded to an Iranian woman and judge, Shirin Ebadi, the first Muslim woman to be awarded the prize. Ebadi had spent decades promoting the rights of women and children in Iran. She pressed for justice in the case of Arian Golshani, a nine year old girl abused and killed by three family members, including her father and a stepbrother. Arian was just 8 years old, and weighed 35 pounds when she was tortured to death by her father. She had been beaten in the head and face, burned by cigarettes, and had knife wounds over her entire body. She also suffered bone fractures over the years that never healed properly, because she had never received medical attention. Iranian law prevents a father from being convicted for killing his own child, and despite Ebadi's work, the law has not been changed. Arian's father was given a two year sentence for causing injury, but not for killing her. There still is much to be done in Islamic countries like Iran and Pakistan, where women are denied justice. The Iranian Parliament has passed a law giving custody of children with unfit parents to relatives or orphanages, but apparently Ebadi is trying to get a law passed that allows the mother custody when the father is considered unfit. Pakistani women who are raped have virtually no recourse in courts of law, because according to the law in that country, four male witnesses are required to substantiate their claim. No rapist is going to ever assemble four male witnesses when he commits the crime; such a law goes against all good sense, and is an outrage against humanity.

Islamic leaders often incite Muslims into hatred and intolerance of non-Muslims. At the tenth session of the Islamic Summit conference held on October 16, 2003, Dr. Mahathir bin Mohamad, Prime Minister of Malaysia, gave a speech that was applauded by attending members with a standing ovation. The entire speech dripped with paranoia against what Mahathir felt was a worldwide conspiracy against Muslims and Islam. He seemed to think that Muslims worldwide are oppressed and exploited by "them," which often appeared to mean Jews, and parts of his speech pointedly mentioned Jews as the enemy of Muslims. The theme of his talk was "We are all Muslims. We are all oppressed. We are all being humiliated."

Mahathir seemed to be worried sick that Jews are going to destroy the Muslim world. He said: "We are actually very strong. 1.3 billion people cannot be simply wiped out. The Europeans killed 6 million Jews out of 12 million. But today the Jews rule this world by proxy. They get others to fight and die for them....we may not be able to do that." The implication seemed to be that non-Jews were fighting on behalf of the Jews, but Muslims would have to fight for themselves. Mahathir hoped that at least a third of the Islamic world would unite in its fight against the Jews. In any case, the world is most certainly not intent on "wiping out" Muslims, and Mahathir's statements surely promote unwarranted fear and paranoia among Muslims.

Mahathir then came up with his own version of history: "We are up against a people who think. They survived 2000 years of pogroms not by hitting back, but by thinking. They invented and successfully promoted socialism, communism, human rights and democracy so that persecuting them would appear to be wrong, so they may enjoy equal rights with others. With these they have now gained control of the most powerful countries and they, this tiny community, have become a world power. We cannot fight them through brawn alone. We must use our brains also." It is difficult to comprehend that the prime minister of a country could make such an asinine statement that Jews invented democracy in order to protect themselves. On the other hand, perhaps we should not be surprised. Muslim paranoia appears to be reaching towards new heights. Why would the prime minister of Malaysia want to fight Jews, anyhow? Even if he sympathized with the Palestinian Arab cause, the statements that he made were purely incendiary and anti-Semitic, and served no good as far as achieving a peaceful end to the Palestinian conflict. Until the Muslim world stops applauding such rants, rather than raving about them, there surely will be no end to the conflict between the Islamic world and the rest of humanity.

123

In the same way that Europeans, weary of the severely oppressive way of the Church, moved to the Americas, it can only be hoped that a newer, more secular Islam will develop over the years to come. An Islam that builds on the simple and beautiful concepts taught in some of the verses of the Qur'an, while eliminating the hate and intolerance that has been characteristic of Islam in the past. The definition of "unbelievers" must evolve. The Qur'an, verse 43:89, states: "The Apostle says: 'Lord, these men are unbelievers.'" To which God replies "Bear with them and wish them peace. They shall before long know their error." The biggest problem is: who is to judge as to who is in error?

The true essence of Islam is that of accepting that the one God that pervades the universe is most compassionate and merciful. The use of the sword and the gun has no element of compassion or mercy. I can see no paradise for those who cause so much pain and suffering, particularly in the name of God.

On the other hand, there have been countless wonderful Islamic mystics who have delighted us with sublime poetry. This poem by Rumi is a superb example:

"I tried to find Him on the Christian cross, but He was not there;
I went to the temple of the Hindus and to the old pagodas,
But I could not find a trace of Him anywhere.
I searched on the mountains and in the valleys,
But neither in the heights nor in the depths
Was I able to find Him.
I went to the Ka'bah in Mecca, but He was not there either.
I questioned the scholars and philosophers,
But He was beyond their understanding.
I then looked into my heart, it was there where
He dwelled that I saw Him;
He was nowhere else to be found."

What profound words! In them is the essence of mysticism, different from the traditional teachings of any particular religion including Islam. There are many books written about the Sufi mystics within Islam. I would think that the Sufis could be considered similar to Yoga practitioners within Hinduism. They are different, and sometimes bordering on being heretic, yet somehow acceptable because they are entirely and totally devoted to Allah. The teachings of the Sufi masters, and many sections of the Qur'an, contain gems that we could pick up and utilize in developing an understanding of a way of being that is the subject of this book. A way that any one of us can joyfully follow.

CHAPTER FIVE:
A THOUSAND RELIGIONS IN ONE:
HINDUISM

In the fall of 1999, the Southern Baptist Convention created a brochure entitled "Diväli, Festival of Light". Here is an excerpt:

"More than 900 million people are lost in the hopeless darkness of Hinduism, worshiping 330 million gods and goddesses created by the imagination of men and women searching for a source of truth and strength....Hindus believe that all people are trapped in a vicious circle of birth, death and reincarnation, and that the only hope of escape is by achieving unity with the gods. They seek power and blessing through worship of gods and goddesses and the demonic powers that lay behind them....

....Hindus find it difficult to come to Christ. Most cannot believe because they have not heard the truth of the gospel. Also, most Hindus do not have a concept of sin or of personal responsibility, nor do they have a concept of a creator God. Yet, when the gospel is clearly presented in a culturally relevant way, many do respond to Jesus.

We invite you to join us in praying specifically for several unreached Hindu people groups as they celebrate Diväli, the Festival of Lights. May the light of Jesus Christ break in upon the darkness that entraps these who worship gods, which are not God.

This introduction was followed by what they called *Intentional Prayer:*

1. Pray that Hindus who celebrate the festival of lights would become aware of the darkness in their hearts that no lamp can dispel.
2. Ask God to show Hindus that their worship of and prayers to the gods ultimately are futile.
3. Pray that Christians will have opportunity to explain why they do not participate in Diväli and to give bold testimony about Jesus, the Light."

Needless to say, there was a storm of protest by Hindus, and the White House under President Clinton accused the Southern Baptist Convention of perpetuating religious hatred through its evangelism efforts. SBC

President Paige Patterson had the audacity to respond: "Apparently, because the President has very few convictions, he harbors deep resentment against those who do. I would say that the president or his press secretary or both have once again demonstrated that the one thing for which they have no regard is truth." The entire fiasco demonstrated that not only did the SBC show blatant disregard for any kind of sensitivity toward Hindus, but also that they showed disrespect toward the President of the United States. President Clinton did, and does, have a deep conviction: that of respect for all people and their freedom to follow the fundamental constitutional guidance of the United States in practicing their own religion free from oppression. Such a conviction is infinitely superior to the "conviction" of the Southern Baptists, which is a parochial, limited and narrow one. And the truth, which they accused the President of not having any regard for, is that the SBC does nothing but incite hatred from people of other religions whom they treat with such derision.

The SBC did, however, submit an apology later. Its web site states: "The IMB (International Mission Board) has since issued a statement expressing regret about the reaction, while explaining its intent. The language in the prayer guide was chosen to communicate to Southern Baptists, not Hindus" the statement said, "and the truths in it, as we understand them, are rooted in the Bible, the book we believe to be God's revealed Word. It is distressing to us that elements of the guide may have offended our Hindu neighbors and for that we are profoundly sorry. We understand that the good news of God's saving love in Jesus, the Savior, may be offensive to some but never was it our intent to express that love in an offensive way."

The statement "Hindus believe that all people are trapped in a vicious circle of birth, death and reincarnation, and that the only hope of escape is by achieving unity with the gods." is a gross misunderstanding. Hindus believe that humans get into a cycle of rebirth because of their desires and the evil karma of their past lives. However, they believe that Moksha, or attaining blissful unity with God, (the "gods", or "devas" are considered to be heavenly beings that help direct the way to the Supreme, and are not ends in themselves), leading to a cessation of the cycle of rebirth, is the ultimate goal of life. To the statement "They seek power and blessing through worship of gods and goddesses and the demonic powers that lay behind them", the response is that Hindus clearly differentiate between divine powers and demonic ones. The gods are called dĕvas, and demons are called räkshasas. The statement "most Hindus do not have a concept of sin or of personal responsibility, nor do they have a concept of a creator God" is a gross insult. Hindus are extremely conscious of sinful acts, consider them to be terribly bad karma, and avoid them in the practice of ahimsa, or non-violence. They have a deeply religiously inspired motivation in the avoidance of violence and killing. As to a creator God, Hindus very much believe that the universe originated from one supreme God.

However, Hindus need to pay attention to such serious criticism. And it is not just Baptists who level criticism against Hinduism; it sometimes comes from within. A letter by a Dr. Viswanath P. Kurup published in the July-Aug-Sept 2002 issue of *Hinduism Today* magazine ought to alert us to the plight of Hindu temples. The doctor and a Swami Pranavananda of Vivekananda Kutir, Rameswaram, were on a tour of temples. He reported pleasant experiences at Kathmandu, and at Belur Math, home of the Ramakrishna Mission, and at the nearby Dakshinĕswar temple. However, moving south, his experiences at the Lingaräj and Jagannäth temples in Bhuvanêswar and Püri caused great upset. They had to deal with a great deal of abuse from the Pandas, hereditary priests, and Püjaris who perform the ceremonies. They wrote: "Here these Pandas and Püjaris control everything in and around the temples and cause serious harm to the devotees congregating at the temples. They ruthlessly pressure and abuse visitors for the sake of filling their purses. Although we were ready to pay anything they asked for, still our plight was not different. In front of every temple deity they demanded huge amounts of money for services we did not want to perform for one reason or other, and, on failing to meet their demands, we were subjected to abusive and profane insults. We could not visualize how such acts of terror could happen in a place of holiness and worship. In these temples we never got any peace of mind, nor could we worship the God with humility. They also used obnoxious language toward Swami Pranavananda and threatened him for aiding us out of their trap. We left both temples with tears in our eyes. What a paradox. Expecting to worship in peace at the abode of the presiding almighty, what we gained instead was eroding of our faith, nervousness and frustration. The same treatment was repeated when we visited a few of the major temples in Tamil Nädu."

When I was a teenager, I decided to visit a temple in Mangalore, India. The priest insisted that I go first to the temple tank to wash my feet. However, the tank was overgrown with slimy moss, so I slid right into the tank. Coming out furious, I decided that I had had enough. I did not visit a temple again for several years. I felt that God's energy could never be resident in such places, so I did not visit temples for several years. Hindu temple priests are often arrogant, and their temples are, in many cases, places of greed and ungodliness. Until Hindus boycott temples where priests practice such abuse, there will never be any change or improvement in their behavior. And until all people including "untouchables" are admitted freely and treated with respect, Hindu temples can never be considered to be 'places of God.' It is well known that money can buy special worship ceremonies at temples at which time the priests are very attentive, but since the vast majority of temple-goers are poor and leave very little in contributions, priests tend to treat the public at large with disdain, saving special attention for the people who substantially support the institution. A Western church-type congregational approach will not work in India, because such an institution demands a middle class that can contribute a certain percentage of its income. In India the wealthy support the temples, and the vast majority doesn't contribute enough to support the temple at all; they simply cannot afford to, explaining the brusque treatment by the priests. In the Christian tradition, a congregation, or a group of people, bring in a pastor or priest who is paid an adequate salary, and he or she serves that community, spending time with all the congregants. Hindu priests operate differently. They perform services at the temple which is open to anyone (except for untouchables, as mentioned above) and indeed some temples have huge crowds going into them. Since there is no set fee to just go through, the priests have to arrange darshan (a view of the deity) for all those people, most of whom cannot afford to pay.

Fortunately, visiting temples is only a small part of Hindu life, and not the guiding spirit of the religion. There are numerous smaller temples where the priests know the devotees, and treat them with kindness. Even if the priests seem authoritative, people seem to tolerate such behavior, as their faith in the deity of the temple is so great that it does not discourage them. Also, most Hindus are part of communities that have their own guru, and they establish affiliation with the temples associated with such gurus. But all said and done, priestly behavior does not seem to dissuade people from going to temples: their faith and devotion overlooks all obstacles. Therefore it is likely that things are not going to change very soon.

In any case, judging Hinduism by the behavior of priests would be similar to denouncing Catholicism because of acts of abuse committed by some priests. Hindu religious practice largely consists of personal devotional practice at home called "Pooja." Hindu philosophy, mythology, and proper moral behavior taught from childhood, all play an important part of Hindu life. Hinduism is truly a vast religion, with an enormous collection of religious practices, and Hindus go about their devotion to God including visiting temples, oblivious to the behavior of some priests.

Variety in Hindu Practice

People often think they have understood Hinduism, but need to realize that they likely have not really understood it. It is like trying to say that in a play, any one of the scenes or characters constitutes the entire play. We cannot possibly take several thousands of years of religious and mystical practice and the results thereof, written or orally transmitted, and blend them all into one uniform practice. Scholars have called it a "way of life," others have called it the 'Sanāthana Dharma' (which means the Eternal Truth) but call it what you may, the essential nature of Hinduism is difficult to comprehend.

One of the most striking things about Hinduism is its seeming contradictions. At times it is in a state of joyful uncertainty, and at other times it can be obsessively dogmatic. But respect for varied opinions has always been a hallmark of Hinduism. For example, the following seemingly contradictory ideas may be expressed by Hindus:

God is one. God is many. God is one and many. God is immanent. God is transcendent. God is both immanent and transcendent. God must be worshipped in form. God need not be worshipped in form. God must be worshipped both in form and without form. Man has a soul. Man's soul is a part of God. Man's soul is apart from God. Devotion is the way to God. Knowledge is the way to God. Meditation is the way to God. Physical force is the way to God. Breath is the way to God. Celibacy is essential. Celibacy hinders the Way. Action is the Way. Renunciation is the Way. Renunciation in Action is the Way.

All of these ideas have been argued back and forth for a few thousand years now. If you look very carefully at the paradox in each of the two or three sentences, you will suddenly smile and realize that we are battling each other's ideas, and then you realize that one is right, and the other is right, they are both right! And that is when you become a guru!! A true guru would never insist that s/he has all the answers; you would be lovingly told that you would need to move on to other teachers to learn more.

The late Satguru Shivaya Subramuniyaswami, the founder of *Hinduism Today* magazine writes in his autobiography, in the April-June 2003 issue of the magazine: "Hinduism is a combination, a collection, of all the teachings and practices of thousands of rishis, gurus, philosophers, mystics and teachers throughout many centuries. Within it are innumerable systems, practices and teachings. If you were to go into them fully, you would find them more complicated than the most complex computer of today. And yet, after my realization of the Self, Hinduism was as simple as kindergarten to me. Hinduism unfolded from the depths of my being. I had found my religion." Note: the word 'rishi' means sage. The similarity to the Islamic word rasul, meaning messenger, is to be noted.

The number of Hindus on earth is now approaching one billion. Unless challenged by those of other faiths, most Hindus would not bother to define what they are or practice--they just live their own way of life. Most people agree that Hindus abide by their scriptures. The Vĕdas are considered the most supreme of all Hindu scriptures, and are considered divine revelation unmodified by man. The word Vĕda is pronounced Vayda, with the "da" pronounced as in the word "the." Part of the Vĕdas is poetic philosophical revelation called the Üpanishads.

I still remember the day I first read the Üpanishads. It was in the United States, several years after leaving India. The reading brought tears into my eyes, and I remember crying out, "Why did no one ever show me these divine scriptures in India?!" Yet most Hindus are oblivious to the wonderful revelations of the Üpanishads. However, most are aware of a magnificent book called the Bhagavad-Gîta, which means "The Song of the Lord." In careful analysis, if you take the essential teachings of the Üpanishads, and reveal them as though spoken by Lord Krishna in the setting of the Great War of ancient India, there you have the Gîta. Taking every utterance of "Me" as spoken by Krishna in this masterpiece, understanding that the "Me" refers to the One that is the universe, and we will understand the teaching of the Bhagavad-Gîta. The problem arises when someone simply takes the "Me" to be a blue skinned god called Krishna, and then they would miss the point entirely. There are Krishna fanatics, just as there are Jesus or Buddha fanatics. They believe that Lord Krishna appeared as an incarnation of a great God called Vishnu; indeed some of them believe, contrary to traditional Hinduism, that Vishnu was but a manifestation of Krishna. They will likely not accept that Krishna was a mythical god. The great sage Vyäsa is said to have "taken dictation" of the Gîta from Lord Krishna. This is one of the ways in which myth is created: a great sage has great inspiration and revelation, and creates a myth to present his or her ideas to the world.

In his book *God: A Brief History* John Bowker writes: "In 1923, the American Journalist H.L.Mencken held a memorial service for the gods, who, as he put it, had "gone down the chute." In his book *Prejudices* he asked: "What has become of Sutekh, once the high god of the whole Nile Valley? What has become of Reseph, Isis, Anath, Ptah, and many others (the list was a page long)?" Then Mencken asked: "Where is the graveyard of dead gods? What lingering mourner waters their mounds? Men labored for generations to build vast temples to them—temples with stones as large as hay-wagons. The business of interpreting their whims occupied thousands of priests, wizards, archdeacons, evangelists, haruspices (diviners who used the entrails of sacrificial animals for their divinations), bishops, and archbishops. To doubt them was to die, usually at the stake. Armies took to the field to defend them against infidels: villages were burned, women and children were butchered, cattle were driven off…They were gods of the highest standing and dignity—gods of civilized peoples—worshiped and believed in by millions. All were theoretically omnipotent, omniscient, and immortal. And all are dead."

Are there any "dead" Hindu Gods? In Vedic times, various gods invoked in prayer such as Varuna, Väyu, Indra, and several others, are only very rarely spoken of or prayed to by most Hindus, though they are still invoked in Vedic ritual performed by Brahmins. So in a way those Gods are still "alive." Hindus are thought to worship countless Gods, though in practice, their prayers are directed to two major Gods: Vishnu and Shiva. The third God of the Hindu trinity, Brahma, is seldom worshiped; there is only one temple in India dedicated to Brahma. For many, Brahma is "dead." However, an essential part of Hindu myth states that the universe blossomed forth from the God Brahma, therefore, for Hinduism, Brahma is intrinsically part of the universe. Indeed, myth has it that a universe appears when Brahma, who rests on a lotus which arises from the god Vishnu's navel, opens his eyes a universe appears, and after four hundred and thirty two thousand years Brahma closes his eyes and the universe dissolves. This cycle goes on indefinitely.

Each "god" is mythical, created in the mind of a sage as a vision. The god is an expansion, a projection, of the sage's consciousness. The god virtually always has various supernatural characteristics, such as multiple arms or heads, and many other symbolic characteristics. The sage reveals this vision to others, and they in turn use that image as a focus of worship. For the worshiper, that image has energy and power; his or her own faith generates that power. It is an extremely personal practice, which no one has the right to ridicule or criticize. Tibetan Buddhism refers to such a deity as a "Yidam." The practitioner is free to create his or her own Yidam, or use existing deities such as Avalōkitĕshwara, the god of infinite compassion.

One of the Üpanishads, the Brihadäranyaka, (as translated by Alistair Shearer) has a way of explaining the nature of these Gods:

Gargi asks Yajnavalkya: "How many dĕvas (gods; Beings of Light) are there?"
Yajnavalkya replies, "As many as are mentioned in the Nīvid, the hymn to all the gods; that is three hundred and three, and three thousand and three." (Three thousand, three hundred and six)
"Yes, but how many dĕvas are there really?"
"Thirty three."
"Yes, but how many dĕvas are there really?"
"Six."
"Yes, but how many dĕvas are there really?"
"Three."
"Yes, but how many dĕvas are there really?"
"Two."
"Yes, but how many dĕvas are there really?"
"One and a half."
"Yes, but how many dĕvas are there really?"
"One."

Gargi asks Yajnavalkya to explain all these numbers, and he does: In fact, said Yajnavalkya, the three thousand three hundred and six, are just thirty-three: the eight Väsus, the eleven Rudras, the twelve Ädityas, Indra and Präjäpati, making thirty-three. The "six" devas, are Agni, Prithivi, Väyu, Antariksha, Äditya and Dyaus. The "three" are the three worlds, earth space and the heavens. Within them the other devas have their being. The "two" devas are simply matter and life. Yajnavalkya then states that the one-and-a-half devas (Adhyardha) is "He who purifies." When questioned about this, he stated "It is because of him that this whole world evolved (adhyardhnot) hence he is called Adhyardha." "And who then is the One God?" asks Gargi. To which he replies: "The Life-Breath, which they call Brahman, or That." The Ūpanishad teaches, very simply, that the various "gods" are just various ways of looking at the composition of the universe. It can be made as complicated, or as simple, as one wishes!

It is simply a matter of Hindu diplomacy that there are various "gods." For a worshipper of Shiva, there is but one transcendent and immanent God, whom the worshipper names Shiva the divine male in the transcendent state, and Shakti, or the Mother, in the immanent manifest state. They are both states of expression of the same entity. This is similar to the positive and negative elements of an electrical circuit. For a worshipper of Vishnu, Lord Vishnu *is* the power of the entire universe; for him, there is not a separate Vishnu or Shiva, there is only Vishnu, with the female element being Lakshmi the Goddess. However, the most important thing about Hinduism has been that each worshipper respects the rights of another to worship in another form. Yes, there have been countless arguments, certainly, but no wars or mass killings over the differences in ideology. This is why Hindus often accept the concept of there being different deities functioning in an orderly manner attending to matters of the universe.

As described above, the origin of these god forms most likely occurred as visions in the minds of mystics thousands of years ago. These visions, or revelations, are of forms that humanity could use as a connection to the Supreme. The gods being worshiped in India today have probably only been worshiped during the past one or two thousand years; the gods spoken of in the Vĕdas are seldom worshiped today. Yet the Vĕdas constantly speak of the unity of the energy of the universe. Creation of form leads to creation of names. The names are known to have divine power, when chanted as Mantra, pronounced "munthra." The word of infinite power and possibility, however, is the word "Om." It is actually "Aum," customarily referred to as Om. Aum is the word. St. John's Gospel states: "In the beginning was the word…" What was this word? The Bible does not explain, because it is considered self-explanatory, and

originally meant the Greek word Logos. In Hinduism, it is simply Aum.
The similarity between Aum and Amen is unmistakable.

At dawn, particularly in Benares, we find people reverently worshipping
the rising sun, often while bathing in the river Ganges. It is so easy
to look down upon sun worship as somewhat primitive, but when we
explore the scriptures, the greater significance of such worship becomes
evident, as revealed in the Ísha Üpanishad:

The face of Truth is hidden by golden light.
Reveal it, O Lord, for my purpose is to know the Truth.
O Lord of light, the knowing one,
Golden guardian, One who nourishes,
Gather together your rays; gather up your brilliance,
That I may behold your most wondrous nature,
The cosmic spirit which is your essence.
For I myself am That!"

In other words, within the sun is the fine and splendid energy of God the
Supreme; the sun is merely a façade, a mirror of the supreme energy.

One of the most important forms of worship in Hinduism is the fire ritual
of offerings given into a sacred fire. It is called Hōma (called Havan in
Hindi). A friend observed the similarity between that word and the word
"homage," or paying respect. The sentiment expressed in this ritual is
actually very profound. All creation is said to be the ultimate sacrifice of
the One, who transformed His energy into all creation. The fire ritual is
an acknowledgement of this sacrifice, in a reverse form. After igniting
the sacred fire, various objects are placed in it as a sacrifice of what is
dear to us, being offered back to the creator. The One is invoked as Agni
(pronounced ugni), god of fire, who consumes all such offerings given
with love. As we were given, so we give back. It is symbolic; we would
not offer up all our belongings such as our home and everything, into
the fire! We must be ready to, however, if required…! Anyhow, there is
a delightful Üpanishad called the Katha, (pronounced cut-ha) in which a
boy called Nachiketas accuses his father of only offering useless objects
in sacrifice! In anger, the father offers Nachiketas, his son, as a sacrifice.
Dutifully, the son Nachiketas proceeds to the abode of the Lord of Death,
where he learns the secrets of immortality. The Lord of Death first offers
him countless wealth, paradise in heaven complete with celestial maidens

and such, but Nachiketas is steadfast: he only wishes the ultimate knowledge. This knowledge is then revealed in the rest of the Üpanishad.

Sacrifice

Sacrifice can be easily misunderstood to be a primitive practice of offering animals and such to God, but in the Hindu tradition, it is much deeper; it is a spiritual practice, referred to as Yajna. This practice originates in the profound sentiment of adoration of God, and also an acknowledgment of the very first sacrifice that ever happened: the process of creation itself, where God sacrificed Himself, and from him came all of creation. God became the primordial man who then was sacrificed into fragments. As fragments of the divine, it is a very deep intuitive desire in each one of us to relate back, to identify with, the source, our origin, our "original self." From this sentiment comes the actual practice of Yajna. How do we reciprocate the primordial act of sacrifice committed by God? The practice can vary enormously, depending on the emotional state or the spiritual state of the practitioner. The simplest and most popular is the practice of "Pooja," or flower offerings. A more advanced practice, one that has been performed for thousands of years, is the "Hōma," or fire offering. This corresponds to, indeed is identical to, the practice of "burnt offerings as described in the Hebrew Bible. All that is precious to us, usually food offerings of rice, butter, and other foods, is given to the fire. It can be just a simple gesture of offering to God what is precious to us, but a more subtle and profound implication, is that we are turning matter back to energy. Just as God, as primordial energy, transformed himself into matter, we acknowledge that process by practicing its reverse: using fire to transform matter into energy. Fire is the medium. In the Hindu tradition, Fire is referred to as Agni, who can also be thought of as the "fire god." However, a more subtle understanding is that Agni is the medium, the messenger, who conveys the thoughts and emotions of the practitioner of the Hōma to the supreme God. Without Agni, there is no Hōma or sacrifice. Agni, therefore, becomes the very core of the practice. He therefore is the "god of the sacrifice."

The fire ritual could only be performed when accompanied by chants of the Vĕdas. Therefore only a Brähmin, or priest, versed in the Vĕdas, could perform it. Perhaps as a reactionary or alternate movement, part of what is called Tantra, arose the practice of Bhakti, or loving devotion. Images of God were created, crafted by master craftsmen and then properly consecrated with extremely elaborate ritual. This consecrated image was then housed in a temple, and there arose the most common form of Hindu worship today. Such an image is referred to as a Moorthi, and many Hindus bristle at the mention of the word "idol." (I personally can't see any difference). The word "Idolater" is very common in Semitic religions, but is a meaningless word in Hinduism. For idols are not God; they are just forms that are used to invoke the presence of the One. Often there are ceremonies that involve immersing such forms in a river or ocean, representing the understanding that the One can never ever be limited to a form that we have created. For convenience, and with daily invocation, temple priests maintain the image in a continuous state of radiance. Many mystics have constantly been apologetic for such actions, but others such as Ramakrishna have taken delight in such expression as only one of many forms of expression.

Many Hindus, however, are uncomfortable with this method. Mahendra Nath Gupta, the author of the book *The Gospel of Sri Ramakrishna* had this conversation with Sri Ramakrishna, one of the greatest saints and teachers of modern India.

M: "But, sir, assuming it is true that God has form, he is surely not identical with the clay image of him?"

Sri Ramakrishna: "Why say that the image is clay? The image is composed of spirit."

M could not understand what was meant by an 'image composed of spirit.' He said, "But those who worship the clay image should be made to understand that the clay image is not God, and that while they are bowing down before the image they must remember that they are worshipping God. They must not worship the clay."

Sri Ramakrishna (sharply): Making others understand- giving them lectures- that's all you Calcutta people think about! You never ask yourselves how *you* can find the truth. Who are *you* to teach others? It is the Lord of the universe who teaches mankind. Will He who has done so much for us fail to bring us to the light? If we need to be taught, He will teach. He knows our inmost thoughts. Supposing it *is* a mistake to worship God in the image—doesn't He know that He alone is being worshipped? He will certainly be pleased by that worship. Why should *you* get a headache over that? It would be better if you struggled to get knowledge and devotion, yourself."

I do believe I have deserved such a chastising on many occasions myself; learning of that episode has had a profound impact on me. Until just a few years ago, I was a rebellious Hindu, often in strong denial of Hindu customs and methods of worship, particularly the worship of images. However, I have found myself returning to my roots as a Hindu in that although my primary practice is that of meditation, I respect image worship when family or friends perform Pooja. The name of the religion, as maintained by most scholars, is "Sanäthana Dharma,' or "Eternal Truth." An appropriate way to describe a Hindu would be to call them 'those that try to explore, and dwell in, the Eternal Truth. There is but one truth; all religions reveal facets of this truth. No one religion can have exclusive claim to the truth, though most do. Hinduism has revealed facet after facet of the truth over the millennia, and states that only the Divine Creator is the absolute truth, everything else, including our opinions, is relative.

The Hidden Teachings of the Moorthi

Perhaps the best and most popular example of the wisdom of image worship is that of Ganesha, the Elephant God. The image of Ganesha consists of that of the head of an elephant on a human body, with a large belly. The myth of Ganesha is that Lord Shiva's consort, the Goddess Pärvathi, was alone and decided to create a boy. She then breathed life into him, and asked him to guard the entrance of their home. Shiva returned, and the boy would not allow him in. Enraged, Shiva cut off the boy's head. Pärvathi was appalled, and full of grief. Therefore, Shiva told his attendants to hurry and bring back the head of the first living being they found. Accordingly, they found an elephant and brought its head back. The head was placed on the boy's body, and thus Ganesha the elephant God was created. The story is a myth. The reality is that the Image of Ganesha is ingeniously devised to convey all kinds of spiritual truths.

Despite a most unusual, indeed seemingly bizarre representation, Ganesha represents a perfect Being. In his book *The Symbolism of Hindu Gods and Rituals* A.Parthasarathy writes: "Ganesha's head is that of an elephant. The large ears denote the ability to hear the scriptures, and the large head represents the ability to understand and retain the knowledge of the scriptures. One tusk is broken, indicating the elimination of being involved in the pairs of opposites, such as pleasure and pain, and so on. The large stomach indicates the ability to "ingest and digest" any problems whatsoever. Ganesha's one leg touches the ground and the other does not, indicating the ability to be part of earthly activity and spiritually connected, at the same time. Ganesha's vāhana, or vehicle, is a rat. This denotes the fact that the superior Being has overcome the characteristics of a rat-like being. The rat denotes greed, but the rat that is part of the iconography of Ganesha sits in a posture of supplication, and awaits permission from Ganesha to partake of the spread of food laid out around Ganesha. Ganesha holds an axe, indicating the ability to destroy desires and attachments. In another hand he holds a rope, with which he binds the devotee to the bliss of his Self. In yet another hand he holds a Lotus indicating spiritual attainment, and the fourth hand holds a sweet rice ball, called Mōdaka, which represents a joyful reward of spiritual seeking."

Every one of the various gods of Hinduism has profound symbolism behind its appearance. Though seemingly human in appearance, they usually have either multiple heads or faces, or multiple arms, indicating a superhuman nature, and also indicating that the god is in all spheres at once.

Moorthi Pooja

Moorthi Pooja, which means 'flower offering to the image of the God,' is probably the most essential aspect of Hindu devotional worship. It is the actual practice of Bhakthi Yoga, or the path of devotion to God. As mentioned above, the image has profound meaning and significance. Another essential aspect of Hindu worship is for the devotee to obtain "Darshan" of and from the Deity. Pooja could be performed at home, with either a Moorthi, or with an icon or just simply a consecrated object such as a coconut placed over a vessel. Temple worship of a divine image, however, is more often referred to as "Darshan." In this practice, it is felt that a consecrated image in a temple has been so transformed by invocations and prayers that part of the actual energy of the one supreme God has been actively drawn into the Image, and God Himself looks out through the eyes of the image, or deity, at the devotee. So the devotee "obtains darshan," allowing him/herself to be seen by the deity while prayerfully looking at the deity. This is also unique to Hinduism, and likely was part of Pagan worship until it was eliminated by the three Semitic religions. This entire practice is very much anathema to those religions, but it is a practice that works. I have most certainly felt the spiritual presence of an enormous power during both Pooja and in temples. I must admit that in many temples I have not felt the "presence." But that was many years ago when I was not spiritually mature enough to feel and sense spiritual presence.

The Microsoft Encarta Dictionary defines "Idol" as "object worshiped as god: something such as a statue or carved image that is worshiped as a god" or a "forbidden object of worship: in monotheistic religions, any object of worship other than the one God." The word is derived from the French 'Idole,' which in turn is derived from the Greek word 'Eidōlon,' or image.

Many apologist Hindu scholars like to state that Hinduism involves the worship of images rather than idols, as though there is any difference whatsoever—there is not. Hinduism has evolved into accepting the worship of idols. It must be clarified that Hindus do not worship an idol or image, they worship a deity represented by the image.

There are many books on Hinduism that explore the practice of image worship, and two of these are outstanding: *The Hindu Vision—Forms of the Formless* by Alistair Shearer, and *Darśan—Seeing the Divine Image in India* by Diana L. Eck, Professor of Religion and Indian Studies at Harvard University. (Darśan is pronounced Darshun) Shearer writes: "Once the sculptor has chosen the deity to be portrayed, he recites the verses from the ancient scriptures—the Vĕdas, Purănas and Shăstras— describing that deity. Then he meditates, waiting in stillness for an image to appear in his mind, which, when it arrives, is drawn rapidly, lest the movement of thought interfere with it. Then a piece of stone that has the right 'tone' is chosen, ritually prepared to be a fit receptacle for the deity, and the light deft touch of hammer and chisel on hard stone rings out like music."

What about the deities themselves? Did they have their own identity in some kind of astral realm, and appear in visions to sages of their own accord, or did sages, by their own minds, conceive the deities as focuses of divine energy that would benefit the masses? It is quite clear to me that the latter has been the case. Shearer writes: "'But are the deities real' asks the mind. To which the answer is that there are any number of different 'realities' within the relative universe; only the unbounded

140

Consciousness, in which they all inhere, is reality." He continues: "And are the deities projections of the mind or objectively outside us?' The answer is: both—it depends on our viewpoint." However, it can be noted that Shearer has found it difficult to have a definitive answer for the questions he has posed. As he has described above, sages in deep meditation conceive images of deities in their mind's eye, which they then express as an image. The image is then consecrated and worshiped, and daily worship maintains divine energy in the image. The image is an expansion of the seer's consciousness, or indeed it can be said that the sage transforms his own limited form into a more vast form, and creates and object of worship for others. Others are meant to worship the form initially, but soon ought to expand their own consciousness into that form as the sage originally did; a vast majority of people, however, limit themselves to the first step.

Does this practice work? For hundreds of millions of Hindus, it works well enough to given them great comfort and consolation. For them the deities have such spiritual energy that they are worthy of worship, worthy of supplication to. For a Hindu, the deity is a source of solace, of inspiration, and guidance. I believe that the essence of religion is to have a superhuman figure deep within the worshiper's psyche, a figure that is a mentor, guide, and savior. Such a figure may have an anthropomorphic representation (an idol) or it may be an object of veneration, but such a figure provides support and solace. Humans do crave objects of devotion, even adherents of so-called monotheistic religions that seemingly abhor idols. For Muslims, the Ka'bah itself, and various tombs of saints, are objects of devotion. For Christians, the cross itself serves as an idol. It could be argued, of course, that the cross is only an icon, but for a Christian it represents 'God who once was on Earth.' As far as I am concerned, a cross is an idol. An image of the Madonna is an idol. Therefore, there is hardly any religion in the world that is free of idol worship. These objects or focuses of worship are not any "superior" to idols simply because they are not anthropomorphic.

What is important is that there *is* a great power/energy pervading the earth, the universe, our bodies, and our minds. This energy can, by our own minds, be focused into us to guide, support, and invigorate us, give us courage, strength, and resolve. This focusing is what prayer is all about. The mechanism of the practice does not matter. To bring in that Universal Spirit within us is what matters. The means is not the end. The goal is to be empowered, in-powered, by God.

Despite its extremely sophisticated philosophical background and understanding, Hinduism, like other religions, has sadly degenerated into a "Give me, God!" religion, rather than a "Give me God" religion. Prayers for relief at temples or shrines are customarily done with prayer offerings, with the attitude that you don't get something for nothing. It does not surprise me that this approach has spread into a way of life where anything requested of an officer of government is accompanied by a "donation." Call it that or bribery, it is the absolute antithesis to the most profound teaching of the Gita, where all actions must be performed in a selfless manner. We must sympathize with the fact, however, that officers of the Government of India are severely underpaid. No can possibly live on their salary. Therefore, it has become a matter of being paid a fee for service. However, society has taken it for granted now, and does not stop to realize that such a way of function can only serve those who can afford payment. The poor therefore will be denied any service. Unless Indian society finds a way to properly compensate every official in keeping with the cost of living, bribery will continue to be the norm.

I doubt that I would have found the spiritual path that I have within the confines of contemporary Hinduism as customarily practiced. Just try discussing the Üpanishads or such at a Hindu social gathering, and you will be met by sympathetic smiles, or perhaps be dismissed as an eccentric or one destined for sannyäs, the final state of renunciation. Spirituality is set aside for that äshrama, or stage of life. The grihastha, or householder stage of life, is devoted to the duties of everyday life, and does include enjoyment of life and the senses, accumulation of wealth, and such earthly pursuits. The Dharma, or proper way of being, would be to continue all the excellent behavioral characteristics learned in the brahmachärya, or student stage of life, into the next stage. This however is commonly forgotten. In the grihastha life of today, anything goes. Artha, or accumulation of wealth, is pushed to the limit. Any means can be justified. Forgotten is the ancient teaching that any form of cheating or lying in business practice is very much against the Dharma. It is no wonder that Rabindranath Tagore cried out, in his Nobel prize-winning book *Geetanjali*:

Where the mind is without fear and the head is held high,
Where knowledge is free;
Where the world has not been broken up into fragments by narrow
domestic walls;
Where words come out from the depth of truth;

Where tireless striving stretches its arms towards perfection
Where the clear stream of reason has not
Lost its way into the dreary desert sand of dead habit;
Where the mind is led forward by Thee into ever-widening thought and
action;
Into that heaven of freedom, my Father, let my country awake.

The "narrow domestic walls" brings to mind the most brutal part of
Hinduism, the all-pervasive caste system. A religion which keeps three
hundred million people in a veritable prison of untouchability is to be
derided most severely. However much one tries to explain away the
ancient idea of specialization of duty, the fact remains that there is severe
oppression of the lower castes, particularly the "untouchables." The
entire idea has been abhorrent to me ever since childhood and I never
did cherish the fact of being Brahmin by birth. The fact that the majority
lower castes now oppress the Brahmins by minimizing their ability to
obtain University admissions and government jobs does not remove the
oppression of the untouchables which Brahmins continue to practice.
The Buddha, in the Dhammapada, stated the ideal characteristics of a
Brahmin, clarifying that it is spiritual status, rather than privilege of
birth, that decides the caste status of an individual. Here is an excerpt
taken from the book *The teachings of the Compassionate Buddha* by
E.A.Burtt:

"I do not call a man a brahmana because of his origin or his mother. He
is indeed arrogant, and he is wealthy; but the poor who is free from all
attachments, him I call indeed a brahmana.
Him I call indeed a brahmana who, after cutting all fetters, never
trembles, and is free from bonds and is unshackled.
Him I call indeed a brahmana who, after cutting the strap and the thong,
the rope with all that pertains to it, has destroyed all obstacles and is
awakened.
Him I call indeed a brahmana who, though he has committed no offense,
endures reproach, stripes, and bonds; who has endurance as his force
and strength for his army.
Him I call indeed a brahmana, who is free from anger, is dutiful,
virtuous, and without appetites, who is subdued and has received his last
body.
Him I call indeed a brahmana who does not cling to sensual pleasures,
like water on a lotus leaf, like a mustard seed on the point of a needle.

*Him I call indeed a brahmana who, even here, knows the end of his own
suffering, has put down his burden and is unshackled.
Him I call indeed a brahmana whose knowledge is deep, who possesses
wisdom, who knows the right way and the wrong, and has attained the
highest end. "*

Hindus must remember that the most essential, vital, crucial part of being
Hindu is that we bear the burden of our karma, of our actions. Every life
is recorded as on a long videotape that cannot be erased. Unfortunately,
it is also a videotape that stays fully open and stretched out, not wound
up and concealed; it is visible to the One at all times! You just don't
go to a priest, beg and receive forgiveness for your actions. Actions
that are not part of Dharma are bad karma. Dharma involves kindness
and consideration for all living beings. It consists of absence of greed,
covetousness, lying, cheating, and deceit. It consists of knowing that all
our actions affect not only ourselves, but also all those around us. The
sage Pathanjali taught us the Yamas, (referred to as abstinences, though
some of the terms are written in a positive usage): Satya (adherence
to the truth) Ahimsa (non-violence) Asteya (abstaining from stealing)
Aparigraha (non-covetousness), and Brahmacharya (usually translated
as abstaining from sexual misconduct). He also taught the Niyamas, or
observances, which are Saucha (purity) Santosha (joyful contentment)
Tapas (austerity) Svädhyäya (learning of scriptures) and finally Îshwara-
pränidhänäni (submission of our entire being to God). These are the
building blocks of spirituality, but sadly, Hinduism has found a way
of Bhakti, "devotion" to God that has forgotten these building blocks.
Bhakti can be like white paint that is used to cover up corroding, rusting
metal beneath; the paint will always flake off. The rusting karma beneath
eventually reveals itself. Devotional religion is only of value if that
devotion allows the Divine to cleanse our minds and hearts of egotism,
greed, hate, and other base characteristics.

The Ätman, or Soul

One of the subjects of a raging controversy in ancient India was the
concept of "Atman," or Soul. Six major schools of philosophy emerged
at the time, all of them trying to explore, evaluate, and explain the very
nature of our beings. The most widely studied schools of thought in India
today are those of Vĕdanta and Yoga.

Vĕdanta comprises of 108 well known Ũpanishads, of which about ten are the principal ones, and probably several others as well. The word Ũpanishad refers to a teaching, a lesson, learned at the feet of a Master. Listening to a chant from even one Ũpanishad, and learning the translation, is an incredibly moving experience. We need to explore more than one translation, as Sanskrit is easily translated in so many ways! Many of the Ũpanishads were preceded by an invocation. Here is one:

That, the Infinite Being, is full and complete.
This, all of visible creation, is full and complete.
All of This, is derived from That.
Having so derived,
All that remains is fullness and completeness.
Aum, let there be peace, peace, peace.

The most popular of all the Ũpanishads is the Ȋsha. The word Ȋsha, short for Ȋshvara, refers to "The Supreme Lord," the only Reality there is. Even the very first verse strikes at our human folly:

"Ȋsha, the Supreme Lord, resides in every part
Of this ever-changing universe.
Follow the pure path of renunciation,
Do not lust after anyone's wealth."

There is but one message to be obtained from the Ũpanishads, and that is: There is only one all- pervading force in the universe. This force is called Brahman, meaning the Mind from which all arises. All that we see, all that we do not see, consists of the energy of Brahman. Our body, our living energy, mind, everything. Therefore, in essence, we are immortal. In the Bhagavad-Gȋta, a later work that brings the various schools of thought together in one approach, Krishna says to Arjuna: "There never was a time that you, or I, or all these people you see here, did not exist. And there never will be a time that we do not exist."

The Ũpanishads and the Bhagavad-Gȋta acknowledge that the body is frail, will fall away, and perish, but the inner being lives on. This "inner being" was stated to be immortal. It was called the "Atman." Many schools of thought then arose, trying to discuss whether Atman is the same as Brahman, or separate, and also discussions on how to merge the two, thus leading to absolute immortality.

The Buddha, the great Hindu reformer and sage, then made his great contribution. He meditated to the highest possible levels of meditative achievement, and stated that everything that can be seen, felt, perceived, or conceived of, is transient and impermanent. This constitutes the "great doubt" that seemingly casts a huge shadow on the "great faith," the Üpanishadic concept of everything being immortal. Yet, there is a way to reconcile the two; the Taittiriya Üpanishad and Tantra provide the answer.

Before we get to that, let us remember that even the Buddha once said: "There is, O Bhikkus, an unborn, unoriginated, unmade, and unconditioned. Were there not the unborn, unoriginated, unmade, and unconditioned, there could be no escape for the born, originated, made, and conditioned." So just what is this unborn?

The Taittiriya Upanishad and Tantra describe the various layers, or sheaths, of energy and intelligence of which we living beings are comprised of. Easily visible is the physical body. Inner to that is the energy body, inner to that is the thinking mind sheath, and deeper still is the sheath of intelligence, also called "the Knower, or Seer." The Seer is our connection to our innermost layer or Sheath, which actually is the Infinite Being or Cosmic Intelligence. This is the energy that pervades me, you, others, all living things, all non-living things. What, then, do we call the "Atman?" It would be a misunderstanding to call it "mine" or "yours." We do not own it, It owns us. Therefore "we" as we know ourselves, are not immortal. The mind and energy body survive death, are subject to a multitude of possibilities such as life in heavenly or hellish realms, or being merged with the mind body complex of a newly formed embryo in "reincarnation." After such reincarnation, aside from flashes of memory and mental predispositions or cravings, there is no permanent identity to the mind/energy body. How permanent and unchanging is sodium chloride? Just try adding some calcium compound and see! One could argue that the element sodium is immortal and indestructible, but then have you ever seen freestanding sodium in nature? It is ever in flux, changing from chloride to sulfate to something else. Such is the case also with the physical body, and mind/energy body. They constantly interact. "I" likely consist of everything that I have learned in this life, into which has been blended the "I" of another being, so there is no longer a "Constant I."

Therefore, there is no need for either dire pessimism, or ebullient optimism; they both must be balanced into a deep understanding of the nature of things. Once understood, then the truth of the Buddha's teachings can be discovered to be only a part of Universal Truth. The teachings of the Üpanishads are another part. All fragments of understanding. The day we learn the fullness, is the day we abandon holding to doctrine that we were told or taught. That is the day we learn that all of creation, in every impermanent moment, is in a constant state of goodness, fullness, beauty, and splendor.

The many facets of Yoga

In Hinduism, any practice that attempts to lead one towards God is an aspect of Yoga. Indeed, Hinduism could be said to a collection of various Yogic practices. The Oxford Paperback Encyclopedia defines Yoga as (Sanskrit, 'yoking', 'union'): "Any form of religious activity, particularly within Hinduism, designed to harness the practitioner to the knowledge of the divine." Yoga is a general term, referring to ways and means of experiencing God's presence, but it has several facets. Jnana Yoga, which is similar to the word Gnosis, refers to the facet of Yoga dealing with the first-hand experience of God. Raja Yoga, which literally means the Royal Path, is the actual Classical Yoga codified by the Sage Pathanjali, describing an eight-fold path of attaining Samadhi, or union with God. Bhakthi Yoga is the path of devotion, and Mantra Yoga is the practice of the use of various Manthras (holy syllables) to attain oneness with God. Hatha Yoga is the best known of Yogic arts in the West, the exercise form. The most pragmatic of all, however, is Karma Yoga, the path of selfless living.

Jnäna Yoga is the Yoga practice taught particularly in the Üpanishads, part of the Hindu canon of scripture called the Vĕdas, or God-revealed Knowledge. Jnana Yoga of the Üpanishads goes into very great detail explaining the nature of God and the universe. There is only one force/power in the universe, and S/he is called Brahman, pronounced Brhmn, a word with no vowels, as is the word YHVH. Brahman performed the ultimate sacrifice, in which he sacrificed Himself and transformed Himself into the visible universe. He converted himself into a golden egg, from which all matter was derived. Compare this idea with that of the Big Bang, when a golden dot expanded into the entire universe. Yet, no matter how huge the universe, Brahman remains a hands-breadth larger than it! Other traditions say that only one-quarter of Brahman constitutes the visible universe.

The Üpanishads are the most sacred of Hindu scriptures. The German philosopher Schopenhauer said: "In the whole world there is no such study so beneficial and as elevating as that of the Üpanishads. It has been the solace of my life; it will be the solace of my death." There are perhaps two hundred Üpanishads, or "that which is learned at the feet of the teacher." Of these, ten to thirteen are the principal Üpanishads. The focus of the Üpanishads is the Ätman (pronounced Aathmun), the part of the Supreme one God, Brahman, which exists and gives life to each living creature. There is, however, essentially no difference between the Atman and Brahman. If you immerse a sponge in water, there is water in and all around the sponge. The water within the sponge is the same as without, and it is in continuity with the water outside. In the same way Atman and Brahman are contiguous, continuous, and the same. From the Atman arises the Mind, and also arises the physical body, which is immersed in, and surrounded by, life energy called Präna, the energy component of the Atman. Präna is called Chi by the Chinese.

The Mündaka Üpanishad teaches that there is the lower knowledge, consisting of the four Vĕdas, and the sciences, including pronunciation, ritual, grammar, etymology, meter and astrology. The higher is that through which the Eternal is directly experienced. This Eternal is Brahman, the Supreme One God. It continues: "That which cannot be seen and is beyond thought, which is without cause, or parts, which is beyond perception or action, which is unchanging, all-pervading, omnipresent, subtler than the subtlest, that is the eternal, which the wise know to be source of all. Just as a spider spins forth its thread and draws it in again, the whole of creation is woven from Brahman and unto it returns. Just as plants are rooted in the earth, all beings are supported by Brahman. Just as hair grows from a person's head, so does everything rise from Brahman."

The Îsha Üpanishad teaches: "All of what exists in this changing universe is enveloped by the Lord. Reveal the greatness of the Atman by renunciation. Do not lust after anyone's wealth." The Üpanishad further teaches: "The Supreme Lord pervades all--He who is radiant, bodiless, invulnerable, devoid of sinews, pure, untouched by evil. He is the Seer, the Thinker, who is all pervading and Self-existent. Those who remain ignorant enter a blind darkness, but those dedicated only to world knowledge enter into an even greater darkness. One who knows knowledge and ignorance together and side-by-side, attains life eternal. Those who worship the unmanifest alone are in darkness and those who delight only in the manifest are in a greater darkness; one who understands the unmanifest and the manifest together, crosses death through the unmanifest and attains life eternal through the manifest." The Üpanishad then addresses the sun: "The face of truth is covered by a golden disc (the sun). Unveil it, O sun, so that I may see it; gather your rays, withdraw your light, so I can see, through your grace, that truly brilliant form of yours. For it I who dwells there." The teacher of the Üpanishad refers to his inner Self, which is part of the Supreme Lord, which is also the power and energy that is at the core of the sun.

The Üpanishads teach unity: that there is only one reality in the universe, which *is* the universe; that is God, Brahman. He pervades all, and is all. Like flowers arising from a tree, all of matter and life sprouts forth from Brahman. Therefore all of what is visible and even invisible is all connected; all part of a greater One. The One can be represented by the three-part syllable Aum, (Aa-Oo-Mm) simply pronounced as Om. Many scholars have remarked upon the word Amen as being derived from the root Aum. Amen is an assertive word, and Aum asserts the unity of all. The Üpanishads and the syllable Aum must be used as a great bow, with our entire selves as the arrow, and the target is the supreme Brahman. The Mündaka Üpanishad advises: "Meditate with the mantra Aum as your bow, consciousness the arrow, and Brahman the target. Free from the distractions of the senses, take aim, release the mind, let it fly with Brahman, and be one with It, as the arrow becomes one with the target."

Manthra Yoga refers to the practice of repetitious use of holy syllables or phrases to help steady the mind in its attempt to be one with God. The primordial root syllable, as described above, is Aum. This word is also used in conjunction with countless other phrases, usually used to describe attributes of God. One example is Om Namō Näräyana, which means 'I bow to the One who is the Lord of all people.' Such words are mostly secular, but the Supreme Court of New Jersey declared that Manthras are part of Hinduism, and could not be used in the school system as desired by the teachers of Transcendental Meditation. The desert fathers of Christianity used phrases such as 'Maranatha' meaning 'Come, Lord,' and extended sentences such as "Jesus Christ, son of God, have mercy upon me a sinner" in endless repetition to attain the same result as manthra Yoga. One simple manthra that I have found will work well for Christians is 'Yĕsu' with 'Ye' uttered in the mind on breathing in and 'Su' on breathing out.

Rāja Yoga gives further advice on how the attain the Eternal One God, called Îshvara in the Yoga Sutras of Pathanjali. It teaches, first of all, ethical principles. Yamas, or 'Abstinences' are five: Avoidance of harm or injury, truthfulness, avoidance of stealing, sexual restraint, and non-covetousness. The Niyamas, or 'Observances,' are: purity, contentment, austerity, study of scriptures, and total devotion/dedication to God. The next two limbs of Raja Yoga are methods of posture (Äsana) and breath management, (Pränäyäma). These relate more to the practice of physical Yoga, but are included within the eight limbs, because the development of physical purity is an essential prerequisite to spiritual purity. Finally, a four-part approach to meditation: Pratyähära, or withdrawal of the Senses from the outer world, Dhärana or concentration, deepening into Dhyäna or deep meditation, and finally attaining samädhi, or full absorption into the object of concentration.

Pathanjali offers a variety of methods of attaining concentration and samädhi. It even includes meditation on the heart of a Spiritual Master, or Guru. For a Christian, this would mean to meditate on the heart of Jesus. A variety of objects could be chosen as objects of concentration, as no matter what object is chosen, that object contains the essence of God within it. Objects holy to one's own religion could be used.

Shamatha meditation of Theravada Buddhism uses the breath as the object of concentration. However, I have found that the learning of mindfulness is very appropriate before learning the practice of concentrative meditation. This is simply because the mind is prone to wander even after just seconds of attempted concentration, and mindfulness teaches us to be aware of thoughts as they arise and disappear. As thoughts get sparse with mindfulness practice, then the mind is able to attain very significant progress in the practice of concentrative meditation. Thoughts cannot be forcefully suppressed; they can only be observed, at which time the development of higher consciousness, leads to thought-free awareness. Buddhism and Yoga therefore are not mutually exclusive, and indeed work extremely and desirably well together. This subject is discussed in detail in the chapter "A Way Inward."

Bhakthi Yoga or the Yoga of devotion: this is the most popular form of Hindu religious/spiritual practice today. In everyday practice, it consists of devotional songs and chants called bhajans, sung along with flower offerings to a chosen deity. Bhakthi consists essentially of prapatthi (submission) to God. It originated with the teachings of the Bhagavad-Gita, one of the most well known of Hindu scriptures. Indeed, long before Muhammad recited in the Qur'an the need for submission to God, Hindus had been practicing it. The Gita, as it is known in short, consists of eighteen chapters. The background is the epic story of the Mahabhäratha, which is a very long epic, longer than the Iliad and Odyssey combined; the Gita is part of the Mahabharätha, though often thought to have been skillfully interpolated within it. Devout Hindus take the Gîta literally as actually something that transpired in history, but truly the Gîta must be taken as a play written by a sage who wished to convey his sublime ideas to the world, and made them to be the words spoken by a God-man, Krishna. In the Gîta, the supreme way to attain oneness with God is by complete surrender, in deep devotion. Readers of the Gita could easily and erroneously conclude that Krishna wanted people to surrender to him as the best way to attain salvation. However, deep understanding of the Gîta leads to a different conclusion: surrender to the supreme one God, Brahman, or in practice, to surrender to the Atman within us, is the easiest and most effective way of attaining salvation, enlightenment, and supreme wisdom and the ultimate knowledge. It is this state which allows God's grace to effortlessly flow into us in its fullest. It has taken me years to realize that whether it is the practice of surrender to the supreme Brahman in Hinduism, or to Allah in Islam as practiced by Muslims, particularly their Sufis, or of the practice of surrender and letting-go in Zen meditation, the actual mechanism in all these practices is the same; the result is the same. The ultimate experience cannot be different for all these people, because the ultimate reality is the same for all, no matter what their religious practice.

During Vedic times, Hinduism did not use consecrated images as the focus of devotion, but the practice became popular over the past thousand years or more. Commonly used are images of Vishnu and Shiva, gods of Hinduism. Moorthi Pooja was discussed earlier. Using elaborate ritual, the energy of the one God is invoked and invited into a consecrated image and sustained there by constant ritual, and that energy is allowed to radiate on to worshipful onlookers, called bhakthas, or devotees. This is the essence of the practice of idolatry, ridiculed by the Semitic religions of Judaism, Christianity and Islam. For Hinduism and

Paganism, however, the use of consecrated images either in temples or in the home, is a practical and easily visible way of bringing God's power and energy into their lives. It gives them a 'focus' to concentrate their minds and spirits.

Hatha Yoga: Finally, we come to the Yoga of physical effort. Hatha very simply means forceful effort, but can also mean a balance of rest and effort with two components, 'ha' and 'tha' which are complementary forces of power and submission. One could define Hatha Yoga in many ways, but mine is: Hatha Yoga is an exercise form consisting of a series of poses promoting extended stretching, held in a state of great steadiness, assisted by deep relaxation, and powered by deep breathing. Practitioners very quickly learn that the practice helps them develop a calm and steady mind, and powerful and strong bodies. Hatha Yoga helps endurance and is very aerobic. Accomplished practitioners develop become very agile and lithe. The flexibility that results is in great contrast to the very significant decrease in muscle flexibility that is the result of the usual practice of what is called aerobic exercise. Indeed, the stretching that most physical education instructors teach at the end of an aerobic exercise session is only a simple form of Yoga practice. As muscles stretch and extend, there is a progressive decrease in the firing of what are called proprioceptors, which are "sense organs" deep in the muscles. As their activity diminishes, the central nervous system is allowed to relax more because increased firing of these sensors causes heightened tension in the central nervous system. In addition to allowing more grace in movement, Hatha Yoga promotes a physical state that is very conducive to meditation. This then, is the most valuable aspect of Hatha Yoga. The practice is also accompanied by powerful breathing techniques called Pranayama, which is best taught by an experienced instructor. These methods, similar to that of Chi Kung, a Chinese yogic art form, allow the breath to activate and manipulate the vital energy of the body, referred to as Präna, or Chi in Chinese. Like water in Jell-O, our body is permeated by living energy. We may not easily believe in the presence of this energy, but yogic adepts, Indian and Chinese, have demonstrated the power of this energy in various martial arts forms as well as demonstrations of super-human strength and achievement. Yogic practice is now being accepted worldwide as a very effective, perhaps the most effective way, of maintaining health, energy, and to slow the aging process.

Combining paths: There are therefore a variety of Yogic practices, designed to suit just about every temperament or stage in life. A practical and simple way of life is to practice **Karma Yoga,** or the practice of selfless service to the earth and all that lives in it. A mind and body suffused with the energy of God has no more to attain than to dedicate itself to activity in life free of desire and selfishness. Selfless loving service is the end result of all the practices above. An attempt can be made to practice this from the very start, but such efforts are extremely likely to be frustrated when the egoistic self-centered mind thwarts such efforts. Meditative and devotional practices that allow the inner spirit, the Ätman, to prevail, make it an 'effortless effort' to practice selfless service. It then becomes meditation in motion, and is effort without effort as extolled by the Chinese Tao Te Ching and by the Buddha in his teaching of Mindfulness. There are very many religions, but humanity is one. And the goal of humanity, truly, should also be one: to allow the Inner Greatness to prevail over the Outer Smallness.

Chapter IV of the Bhagavad-Gîta called the 'Yoga of renunciation of action with knowledge' says: "Even the wise are at a loss to know what action is and what is inaction. Therefore, I will expound to you the truth about action, knowing which you will be free from its binding nature. He who sees inaction in action, and action in inaction, is wise among men; he is a Yogi who has accomplished all action. He whose undertakings are free from desire, whose actions are burnt up by the fire of wisdom; the wise call such a one a man of learning." 'Inaction-in-action' is virtually the same as 'Wu-Wei' of the Chinese Taoist tradition and constitutes the highest achievement in the art of living. It is difficult to explain, and is explored thoroughly in the chapter *A Way of Being*: truly, the result is a life free from stress and strain.

Such a person manifests his or her attainment in the following manner: (Gîta XVI: 1-3): Fearlessness, purity of heart, steadfastness in knowledge and Yoga, also giving of charity, control of the senses, worship and sacrifice, study of the scriptures, austerity and straightforwardness. 2. Harmlessness, truthfulness, absence of anger, renunciation, tranquility of mind, abstaining from malicious talk, compassion to all creatures, absence of desire, gentleness, modesty, absence of fickleness. 3. Splendor, forgiveness, fortitude, purity, absence of malice, absence of pride—these are the qualities of those endowed with divine virtues.

The Tao Te Ching states:
"The Sage manages his affairs without ado,
And spreads his teaching without talking.
He denies nothing to the teeming things.
He rears them, but lays no claim to them.
He does his work, but sets no store by it.
He accomplishes his task, but does not dwell upon it.
And yet it is just because he does not dwell on it
that nobody can ever take it away from him"

—Tao Te Ching, Chapter 2. (Trans. John C.H.Wu)

And that statement of the Tao appropriately summarizes the characteristic of the sage who has attained to karma sannyäsa Yoga, the 'Renunciation of action with knowledge.'

CHAPTER SIX:
ANCIENT TREASURES: THE TAO, VEDÄNTA AND THE BHAGAVAD-GÎTA

Take a stone and tie a two-foot long piece of string to it. Then twirl the stone around. See how little effort it takes to make the stone fly at a most dizzying speed; your hand seems to move hardly at all, yet the stone flies. In the same way, just imagine an incredible energy or force beneath all that can be seen and unseen: a force behind and beneath the entire universe, giving the power for the sun to shine, the planets to revolve, the universe to expand. An understanding of this will help us understand the teaching of the Tao Te Ching. This force was called the Tao by Taoists. The nature of the Tao was revealed in the most magnificent of spiritual revelations, the Tao Te Ching. Lao Tzu, the author of the Tao, is said to have lived around 500 BCE. It is quite likely the name is a mythical one; no one really knows. Legend has it that he wrote the verses of the Tao Te Ching and gave them to the gatekeeper at one of the western gates of China, and then left, never to be heard from again. As I have written elsewhere in this book, it does not matter what the author's name was; the message is divine, pointing to the divinity of our inner nature: Lao Tzu simply called it the Tao. Tao is Thou!

It was several hundreds of years prior to this that the Vedänta, "the culmination of the Vĕdas," was written in India. Vedänta consists of profound teachings called the Üpanishads, which referred to the Supreme One from whom the universe arose, and who *is* the universe: Brahman. Scholars believe that they were written around 800 BCE at the latest. In careful analysis of both these lines of thought, there is incredible similarity. One could easily use the word "Tao" instead of the word "Brahman" interchangeably in these philosophical masterpieces. I interpret the word "Tao" to be the one mind and energy of the universe. It is given various characteristics in the Tao Te Ching. Its flow and nature is compared to water, which though supremely yielding, is yet incredibly powerful. It is compared to a child, who can "cry all day without straining, so perfect is his harmony; so magically does he blend with this world."

If you have ever read the Tao Te Ching and set it aside as something you cannot fathom, please take heart. It reverberates with the resonance of the deepest mysticism, and I believe that it is one of the most wonderful of revelations that ever was written. Its essential teaching is that *just beneath the surface of all that can be seen and felt, is the undercurrent of the power of the Tao*. The Tao is energy, a force, *the* force. All that is, is the Tao. The Îsha Üpanishad teaches "Îsha väsyam idam sarvam," which means that Îsha, the Lord, resides in all that is around us. Take any of these words, such as Lord, or God, and use it in substitution for the word Tao and see how it feels when you read the Tao again. One can only marvel at Lao Tzu's wisdom, however, when he chose simply to call it "Tao," or "The Way." "The name that can be named is not the eternal name." This also is unmistakably similar to the teaching of the Old Testament, God cannot be described by anything other than "I am that I am": eternally present. The Tao Te Ching states simply as a matter of fact: (translated by Stephen Mitchell) "Every being in the universe is an expression of the Tao. It springs into existence, unconscious, perfect, free, takes on a physical body, and lets circumstances complete it. That is why every being spontaneously honors the Tao." Worship of nature, therefore, came naturally to earthy religions of old. All that is visible, heard, and sensed, is worthy of worship. The heavens are worthy of worship, as is the Earth with all that is in it.

I would urge the reader to read at least two different translations of both the Tao Te Ching and the Üpanishads. If at first they seem exotic, hard to comprehend, or speak of concepts that just cannot be understood, do not give up. For they hold in them truth that will endure for all time. Having twirled the stone on the string, you can identify with this excerpt from the Îsha Üpanishad: "The Atman or Self is One. Unmoving, it moves swifter than thought. The senses do not overtake it, it for always precedes them. Remaining still, it outpaces all that can run." Brahman is the mind and energy of the universe, and the part that pervades a living being, is its Atman. Similarly, "Tao does not act, yet is the root of all action. Tao does not move, yet it is the source of all creation."

The Tao and the Üpanishads have been an incredible source of enlightenment for me. Without them, the teachings of Buddhism would not have made any sense whatsoever. Stand on the bank of a raging river and sense its power. Let your feet be in the powerful current. You feel the incredible energy of movement, yet you are still. Deep in meditation, this same duality can be felt; deep stillness from which all activity arises. The stillness is the Tao, or Brahman, and activity is all that is manifest.

Here's a poem that I wrote quite some time ago, inspired by the Üpanishads. The poem is somewhat childish, but the essential thing in spirituality is the need to see things as a child anyhow, as I wrote in this poem back in April 1994:

Life's a bowlful of Jell-O!

There once was a bowlful of Jell-O,
Bright lively green it was.
Scoffed when told it was mostly water,
"What, me? Full bodied and firm,
Bouncy and green- impossible!"

Well, dear reader, as water is in Jell-O,
Hidden and without identity,
Is the Spirit in our beings;
We know It not, or would rather not know It.

The Spirit is real, yet so is our existence.
As the Jell-O crystals hold the water,
We sustain the Spirit.
Hidden from view yet the basis of strength;
Formless and fluid, yet
The firmament of form.
We are the instruments of His work,
The bearers of His flame.

Tantra, another Indian philosophical system, gives the name Shakti (pronounced shuckthi) to this manifest power, and the stillness is Shiva. Indeed, the word Shakti means power or energy. It is considered feminine. Tantra, like the Tao, understands the unity of the seeming duality: good and evil, dark and light, male and female, heaven and earth. "As nameless, it is the origin of all things; As Named, it is the mother of all things." Many people have considered Tantra to be a dark practice, but little do they know. The teaching of Tantra is that unless you have experienced sensuality you cannot understand transcending it. You cannot be of the world unless completely part of all that it comprises. You cannot meditate in the forest and yet know how to take care of a crying child. The Îsha Üpanishad says: "Worship of the body alone leads to one result, worship of the spirit leads to another. So we have heard from the wise. They who worship both the body and the spirit, by the body overcome death, and by the spirit achieve immortality." This statement, though from the Üpanishads, is also the teaching of Tantra.

As I had mentioned above, unless one discovers the inner peace, stillness and power that is the essence of each one of us, the magnificence and beauty of the Tao or the Üpanishads cannot be appreciated. After which, one can truly sympathize with the Îsha Üpanishad again: "Life in the world alone leads to one result, meditation alone leads to another. So we have heard from the wise. They who devote themselves both to life in the world and to meditation, by life in the world overcome death and by meditation overcome immortality."

Another immortal masterpiece of Indian origin is the Bhagavad-Gîta, or "Song of the Lord." Although believed by most Hindus to be based on historical fact, the Gita is spiritual fiction. The setting is the mythical battlefield of Kürükshĕtra in ancient India. Two armies are set for great battle, the Pändavas and the Kauravas. They are cousins, and the Kauravas have cheated the Pändavas out of their land. This was therefore a war waged by the Pändavas for justice. Arjuna, the warrior hero of the Pändavas, is despondent, as he does not wish to fight his cousins. Krishna, considered by Hindus to be a manifestation of the great God Vishnu, volunteers to be his charioteer. Krishna consoles and teaches Arjuna. Entire volumes have been written in translation and interpretation of this wonderful work. Take the wisdom of the Üpanishads, and have Krishna speak it on the battlefield, and there you have the Gîta. However, in any passage in which Krishna says "Aham," which means "Me," we must think of the One God/Energy of the universe. If we try to interpret the "Me" as referring to Krishna, or to Vishnu, then we will not fully realize the meaning of the teachings in the Gîta. The "Me" refers to the mind/energy of the universe seemingly speaking through a person, in this case Krishna. The Gîta consists of eighteen chapters. Apart from the first chapter which describes the stage where the play is enacted, the other seventeen chapters each have a discourse on an aspect of Yoga, or the ways of attaining God. Krishna starts with the Yoga of knowledge, then the Yoga of action, and then renunciation. He then discusses meditation, knowledge and wisdom and describes the Supreme One. He then discards his earthly form and reveals to Arjuna his cosmic form, in which the entire universe is revealed to Arjuna. Krishna then discusses the way of simple devotion to Krishna in whom the Universal Spirit is condensed, and finally discusses true renunciation. The Gîta may be somewhat confusing at first, in that in each chapter, a particular form of Yoga is discussed. Sometimes it appears that Krishna favors one aspect of Yoga to another. According to the Gîta, devotion to God seems to be the most favored, as well as the simplest way of attaining God. The Gîta reveals the mechanism of deity worship. The infinite One can, in the devotee's mind, focused into a limited form. Whether the form is Krishna or Christ, the result is one and the same. Devotion to a deity stabilizes the mind and gives it direction and strength. The fact that these deities are not historical does not matter. For devotees, in actual practice, the deities become absolutely real, and they will furiously object to any questioning as to whether their deities have historical validity. Interestingly, I sincerely believe that even realizing that they are not historical entities does not take away from the mystical power that these deities have.

One of the key teachings of the Gîta that is most difficult to understand is that of "freedom from attachment to the fruits of action." Very few people have been able to grasp this. Most people seem to think that it simply means we ought not to do anything for a reward. Sounds magnanimous, but how many people can afford to work forty hours a week for nothing?

It is the "fruits of action" rather than "action" that has caused all the confusion. Once we understand the Tao, then the teaching of the Gîta becomes as clear as daylight. Transcending all action is the Way. You sit by the river, your feet are in it, but you are not carried away by it. It is important to realize that all these great works of literature are all trying to point to us a way of being. They are set in various times and places, but their essential message is the same: we need to act in a manner of 'actionless' action, or in other words, act in such a mindful manner that we transcend action at every moment. It is in such a state that the Gîta says that we will not be bound by action or its results. A way of looking at it would be to think that all actions generated in such a state are generated by a greater mind and will than our own, and therefore we are not responsible for the consequences. The way of learning this is by learning mindfulness as taught by the Buddha discussed in much more detail in another chapter, called "A Way within." The Gîta's way of describing this process is slightly different than that of the Buddha (Verse V: 8-9): "I do nothing at all," thus would the enlightened knower of truth think, while seeing, hearing, touching smelling, eating, going, sleeping, breathing, speaking, letting go, seizing, opening and closing the eyes— convinced that only the senses are in the realm of the sense-objects." This would equate with mindfulness in Buddhist terms, being one with Tao in Taoist terms, and just simply being, in Zen terms. Though, of course, the person would not "think of not doing," but would simply practice non-doing. Zen teachers often advise "think of non-thinking," but in my experience that advice is quite misleading, and in a way self-contradictory.

Krishna continues in verses V: 10-12: "He who performs actions, offering them to the Supreme, abandoning attachment, is not tainted by sin, just as a lotus leaf remains unaffected by the water on it. Having abandoned attachment, he performs actions merely by the body, mind, intellect and senses, for the purification of the lower self, the ego. Such an enlightened one, having abandoned the fruits of action, attains eternal peace; the unilluminated one, impelled by desire and attached to the fruit, is bound." The Tao similarly states (Chapter 1): "Free from desire, you realize the mystery. Caught in desire, you see only the manifestations."

Verses IV: 18-20 also explain: "He who recognizes inaction in action and action in inaction is wise among men; he is a yogi and a true performer of all actions. He whose activity is devoid of desires and purposes, and whose actions have been burnt by the fire of inner knowledge, him the wise call a sage. Having abandoned attachment to the fruits of action, ever content, depending on nothing, he does not do anything, though engaged in actions." The Tao, similarly, in Chapter 3, states: "Practice non-doing, and everything will fall into place."

Ultimately, Krishna tells Arjuna, complete and absolute devotion to God is what leads to an actionless state (Chapter XII: 8-20): "Therefore, fix your mind one Me alone, let your intellect dwell in Me. Without a doubt, you shall then live in Me alone. If you are unable to so fix your mind on Me, try abhyäsa (which means to practice again and again). If you are unable to practice, just be intent on doing actions for My sake; even by performing actions for My sake, you shall attain perfection. Taking refuge in Me, self-controlled, renounce the fruits of all actions. Superior to just practice is the attaining of inner Knowledge; superior to such Knowledge is meditation; superior to meditation is renunciation of the fruits of action—peace immediately follows renunciation." To repeat, renunciation is not to abandon our activity; it is the art of 'non-doing in the midst of doing.' Also, the "Me" may again and again cause questions. Does one dedicate one's life to the infinite formless cosmic One, or to Krishna? As mentioned above, if we condense the universe into one single form of a preferred deity, which is the essence not only of Hinduism but that of Gnostic Christianity, it is so simple, yet effective a practice.

Verses XII: 13-14 continue: "He who hates no creature, who is friendly and compassionate to all, who is free from attachment and egoism, balanced in pleasure and pain, and forgiving, ever content, steady in meditation, self-controlled, possessed of firm conviction, with mind and intellect dedicated to Me, such a devotee is dear to Me."

Verses XII: 15-16 further describe desirable qualities in a human being: "He who does not cause agitation to the world, and who cannot be agitated by the world, who is freed from joy, envy, fear, and anxiety—he is dear to Me. He who is free from wants; pure, alert, unconcerned, untroubled, renouncing all activity—he who is thus devoted to Me, is dear to Me."

Verses XII: 17-20 conclude with further characteristics of the life of one who has attained transcendence: "He who neither rejoices, nor hates; neither grieves nor desires; such a one who transcends good and evil, that one who is full of devotion, is dear to Me. He who is the same to friend or foe, and also in honor and dishonor, who is the same in cold and heat and in pleasure and pain, who is free from attachment; to whom criticism and praise are equal, who is silent, content with anything, homeless, steady-minded, full of devotion—that man is dear to Me.

They, indeed, who follow this immortal Dharma (law of life) as described above, endowed with faith, regarding Me as their supreme goal, such devotees are exceedingly dear to Me."

The Gîta, therefore, is a teaching combining all teachings. It allows for people to be at any stage of spiritual development, though it encourages them onward and upward. It seemingly teaches that all paths lead to God, but the greatest teaching in the Gîta is that we are already on the path; indeed there is no path to take as we have already arrived at our destination. To know that we have arrived is the supreme knowledge; to then continue to travel without traveling, is the Way, the Tao, of the wise.

Just as in the Üpanishads, the Tao states: "The Tao is called the Great Mother: empty yet inexhaustible, it gives birth to infinite worlds. It is always present within you. You can use it any way you want. It is like a well; used but never used up. It is like a bellows: empty yet infinitely capable. The more you use it, the more it produces; the more you talk of it, the less you understand. It is like the eternal void: filled with infinite possibilities. It is hidden but always present. I don't know who gave birth to it: it is older than God." The Katha Üpanishad states: "The Supreme, whose symbol is Aum, is the omniscient Lord. He is not born. He does not die. He is neither cause nor effect. This Ancient One is unborn, imperishable and eternal: even if the body is destroyed, he is not killed." The Tao, similarly, says (Chapter 7): "The Tao is infinite, eternal. Why is it eternal? It was never born; thus it can never die. Why is it infinite? It has no desires for itself; thus it is present for all beings." And perhaps the greatest feature of the Tao is: (Chapter 8): "The supreme good is like water, which nourishes all things without trying to. It is content with the low places that people look down on. Thus it is like the Tao."

As can be clearly seen, the teaching of these ancient treasures is very similar. They have to be: there is no separate truth for people following different religions. These ancient classics should be used to cleanse our minds of limitation to limited thinking and egotism.

CHAPTER SEVEN:
YOGA: A TOUCH OF CHI

The yoga practice of physical exercise is called Hatha Yoga. The word is actually pronounced hut-ha, with an aspirated "t" said with the tongue rolled back on the palate. That particular sound of the consonant "t" is unique to Sanskrit derived languages. Anyhow, try expressing the words Ha. Ha! Hahh!!! See if you can feel some power expressed through the word. And then you get to know the origin of the "Ha" part of the hatha. The remaining half, the 'tha,' represents the extreme opposite, total giving, relaxing, and letting go. That is the essence of hatha yoga. When in a particular yogic posture, you must use great effort to maintain the pose, all the time with deep relaxation and letting go. Then you find the right balance of tension and relaxation. A few breaths later, you just became able to open up the posture another inch, and a few months of such practice later, you just cannot imagine you could *ever* get into such a pose! However, the word hatha has been translated as "force" which is misleading. Brute force never did accomplish anything in hatha yoga, except perhaps to tear a muscle or tendon! Yoga can be said to be the practice of achieving a "butter body, water mind."

Hatha yoga could perhaps be defined as a practice consisting of the body performing a series of postures, usually in a particular sequence, aided by deep relaxation, energized by deep breathing, and guided by deep awareness. I wish someone could come up with a Sanskrit phrase that says "energy activating, deeply centering, muscle and tissue stretching, aerobic practice." There is just no exercise practice like yoga; nothing as powerfully effective, and indeed nothing so potentially harmful. I have found that I had to combine the knowledge and understanding of Chinese yoga, also called Chi Gung, and blend it into Indian hatha yoga practice. Chi Gung never involves any kind of rigidity, and particularly avoids holding the knees straight while doing standing forward bends. Chi Gung also helps us with the management of the breath, and teaches us the art of letting go into a deeply relaxed state, as well as maintenance of awareness throughout.

Learning yoga is a time consuming practice. For me, it has taken several teachers, videos, numerous books, lectures, workshops, and some years of practice to get a feel of what it really involves. And the learning process was somewhat painful, involving a damaged facet joint in the back from brisk standing forward bends, damage to a rotator cuff in a shoulder from too vigorous a "sun salutation," and a torn adductor muscle in my left thigh from vigorously swinging into the Triangle pose; all from overly enthusiastic Ashtänga Yoga practice performed without warming up. This term refers to a school of Hatha Yoga called "Ashtänga Yoga" where the practitioners work up a sweat and maintain that heated body state during the entire practice. Learning Ashtänga yoga is quite a feat. It requires dedicated daily practice and is thought by many experts to be the classic form of the art. Ashtänga yoga involves a series of movements called "Sun salutations." You start standing and stretching the arms up to the sky, and then perform a forward swing-fold with the arms still stretched out, till your hands reach your feet. This swing fold is so graceful to watch when performed by an expert, but can be disastrous to the lumbar spine. Let me explain:

Lie on your back with knees bent. Then bring your hands behind your thighs for support, and bring your knees toward your chest. Only as far as you can, maintaining comfort. Now, gently straighten your knees. Now your body has formed an angle, with the tailbone being at the angle. How acute an angle can you form? 90 degrees? 60? A little more? Now, imagine yourself holding this angle, except you are on your feet. Now—to close the gap between the hands and feet, bending at the spine is the only way, is it not? Such a forward bend is called ventral flexion, and develops a great deal of pressure on the lumbar discs. When we are young, the body can handle this quite well, but as we get older the body is nowhere as forgiving. I believe I would not have learned this had I not been around forty five years old when I started learning yoga! Yoga masters do forward bends, whether standing or sitting, by developing enormous flexibility of their hamstrings. The actual forward bending of the lumbar spine and the resultant pressure on the lumbar discs is minimized. Forward bends are considered to be very invigorating and are an essential part of yoga practice. However, we must be aware of the extent to which our hamstrings are flexible, before we get into forward bends.

Sam Dworkis has written a wonderful book called *Ex-Tension*, and another valuable book is called *The Stark Reality of Stretching*. I believe yoga students ought to read such books before getting into yoga. The authors teach the right way to stretch, and the dangers of forward bends with the knees straight. And once learned properly, you obtain the best results with minimum strain and injury.

One other significant injury I suffered during Yoga practice was to my left knee. I had been practicing a Yoga posture called Pärshvottanäsana, a standing posture where one leg is extended and the practitioner does a forward bend from the waist. After a few weeks, I developed a painful cystic degeneration of my left knee cartilage. My uncle, an orthopedist, had to use a wide bore needle to drain the thick cyst fluid, which consisted of degenerated cartilage material. I had never had such a problem before, and it did not recur after I stopped practicing that particular Yoga posture. Indeed, in twenty five years of Internal Medicine practice, I have never seen a patient with such a problem. My theory is that the posture causes such a great accumulation of pränic energy in the knee that it actually melted down the cartilage. Alternatively, the steady static pressure on the knee was so intense that it simply just melted down the cartilage. In any case, this episode shows the actual destructive power of yoga practice. The idea of a "double edged sword" comes to mind. Anyhow, the posture can be done kneeling, without generating the excessive pressure on the knee described above, which I have practiced safely. There are many Yoga postures, particularly standing and sitting forward bends, which are more hazardous than helpful; they involve continuous pressure on joints, which certainly can cause problems.

I would recommend the reader to look at a book called *Essential Stretching* by Michelle Lemay. The author shows a movement where you gently flow in and out of a posture, and calls such a flow an "oscillation." The book reveals numerous such postures, many of them reminiscent of yoga postures. The author is really teaching a series of dynamic stretches in contrast to the static stretches of yoga. T.K.V. Dësikächär, a great Indian Yoga teacher, explains in his book *The Heart of Yoga* that many postures must be followed by counter-postures, which he calls *pratikriyäsanas,* in order to neutralize the potentially harmful effect of a posture. As far as I know, he is the first teacher to have taught this important concept; flowing from a posture into a counter-posture is called a *vinyäsa.* I have personally found that if you go into a pose gently and only as deeply as the body will permit, following gently into the counter-pose, again only as deeply as the body will allow (I have discovered many counter-poses which are somewhat different from the ones that Dësikächär teaches; you can find your own, too!) and repeat this several times, it warms up the body very nicely and makes for a powerful practice. Holding a pose longer than a few breaths does not seem to be beneficial, and indeed may cause the kind of injuries that I described

165

above. Some of these flows have been illustrated in books on Chi Kung, which is not surprising; after all, these yogic practices are ancient, and could well have been discovered simultaneously in India and China. One other way is to get into a pose, but only say 30-50% of the full depth of it, then come out of it, guided by the breath. Repeating this maneuver, but slowly deepening the stretch every time, will find that after a few breaths, we can achieve a little more each time. Or, if a pose is held steadily, with deepening relaxation and with breath energy, one can go a little deeper and a little deeper into the pose. After 5-6 breaths, it is best to ease out of the posture.

A deeper understanding of the secret of Hatha Yoga came suddenly one day. There I was on my back, legs up in the air, puffing away and trying to hold a pose, and I felt this amazing fire like warmth in the abdomen spreading outwards. I found I could mentally direct this warmth to the limbs doing the work, helping them relax and become more energized, bathing them in healing warmth. It is when I combined Chinese Chi-Gung and yoga that I developed this most fulfilling practice. This warmth is generated by what can only be described as "fire breath." You must learn perineal muscle contraction, referred to as the moola bandha. This is the Kegel exercise taught by physicians, and it is effective for men and women. With this contraction maintained, breathe out using the abdominal muscles. This pushes the diaphragm up. At this point inspiration starts using the chest, and then the inspiration continues into the abdomen with the diaphragm moving down. During inspiration, the perineal muscles stay contracted and the lower abdominal muscles are tight. Pressure now develops in the mid and lower abdomen! This pressure, just like in an automobile engine, helps develop enormous amount of energy. It is this energy activation that is the heart of any yoga practice, whether Chinese or Indian. This energy can be allowed to flow into the chest, neck, head, and extremities. It is energy that in India is called "präna," and in China is called "Chi." In India it is taught that the entire universe is nothing but präna in various forms. The body is präna in high density, mind energy is pränic energy that has a purpose, and between the mind and the body is a great buffer of floating präna. It is this floating präna that is activated by breath manipulation, and utilized to produce seemingly impossible yogic feats such as allowing an elephant to walk on the body, or breaking a wooden plank with a blow of the hand. Combine this fire breath and deep meditative awareness during practice and one has a combination that leads to supreme success in yoga. A more relaxing alternative is to contract the pelvic and abdominal muscles while breathing out, and relaxing them while breathing in.

Learning to develop this "fire-breath" is no easy task. I have found two superb books describing Chi and its activation, one called *Iron Shirt Chi-Gung I* by Mantak Chia, and *Back Pain* by Dr. Jwing-Ming Yang. *The Complete Book of Chinese Health and Healing* by Daniel Reid also has a great deal of information. Such a manipulation of Chi is called "Pränäyäma" in India. Interestingly, no book on pränäyäma I have read has been as effective as the Chinese texts on Chi Gung that I mention above. Once you discover fire breath, yoga practice is transformed forever. Indeed there can never be truly effective yoga practice without it.

Deep diaphragmatic breathing without implementing any pressure modification, has great value by itself. I call this "deep belly breath," in contrast to relaxed easy diaphragmatic breathing which I call "baby belly breath." The latter is extremely valuable during meditation, and has been described in the chapter "A Way Inward." Deep belly breathing is a technique I have personally found to be valuable in the management of acid reflux and heartburn, and I have taught it to several people who have also found great benefit. The technique is also valuable in the management of constipation and colonic disturbances such as irritable colon syndrome. By activating the lower lobes of the lungs, it also helps increase athletic performance.

Of the various Buddhist traditions, only Tibetan Buddhism, which is actually a blend of Tantra and Buddhism, gives importance to Hatha Yoga. The Buddha's life history mentions that he tried various ascetic practices and gave them up as unprofitable. It is quite likely that he just did not have the right yoga masters to show him the inner secrets. The "ha" without the "tha" in yoga is most likely to lead to depleted energy, muscle strain or injury, fatigue, and even sickness. The proper practice of Hatha Yoga ought to give a feeling of well-being, energy, restful sleep, and prevention of illness. Can advanced pränäyäma under the guidance of a master lead to super conscious states? Quite possibly so. For most of us, however, Hatha Yoga is best used to improve flexibility and strength, and help develop grace, poise, and balance. There are millions of yoga practitioners in the world today. They must be continuing the practice because it makes them feel better. Indeed, Hatha Yoga also helps develop tranquility of mind as well. And that is also a major part of feeling well. "Churning mind causes burning body." Imagine a horse and rider storming by you at break-neck speed. Either the rider is crazy, or the horse is! Equate that with the body and mind. Meditation will help soothe the rider, and Hatha Yoga calms the horse! Both are usually taught together in most yoga classes. One cannot effectively do one without the other.

Imagine you want to make some dough. Kneading is an essential part of the job. To get the dough into the right shape, you push and knead in various directions. The physical practice of yoga also involves stretching in various directions, in the numerous poses. Every pose, combined with fire breath, moves healing energy in ways that some other pose may not. Therefore as you practice, you discover the value of learning many poses. And eventually you even come up with your own that no one ever taught you! And you find that some are more beneficial to you than others. A fellow student may find that some other poses are more valuable. Each one of us is different.

Hatha Yoga is one of those "do it and you'll find the value" exercises. There is no way on earth to read a book and decide whether it's going to be of value. Explore it, and mark my words: you will never leave the practice once you discover it. And it does not have to be the mainstay of spiritual practice either. Indeed, Hatha Yoga is only a stepping-stone, a way of helping us develop a strong constitution that helps our being to be prepared for higher levels of spirituality.

Once we feel the inner peace that can be discovered with Hatha Yoga, we will find it easy to resonate with the words of the *Tao Te Ching* as translated by Stephen Mitchell:

Close your mouth, block off your senses,
Blunt your sharpness, untie your knots,
Soften your glare, settle your dust.
This is the primal identity.

The Taoist principle of "non-doing" has immense value when applied into our daily lives. "Non-doing" is a seemingly difficult principle to understand, but once understood, its value and meaning can be easily grasped. It really means doing anything with the least effort. And even that is not adequate. Not until we get into awareness, meditation, yoga and similar disciples, do we realize just how much inner tension goes into our lives. We go to bed to obtain restful sleep, yet wake up full of aches and pains and feel tired. This is because we sleep in a state of tension.

Tension levels are governed by the autonomic nervous system and the extra-pyramidal nervous system, parts of our nervous system that are usually beyond our control. It is not only possible, but essential, that we make a deep seated effort to relax consciously that the deeper parts of the nervous system start behaving accordingly. Subconscious worries and concerns are probably a major factor causing the nervous system to always be in a state of high alert, non-relaxed, and therefore full of tension.

This state of tension affects most muscles of the body, particularly what yoga experts love to call "core muscles," those of the low back, abdomen, which are important muscles governing our upright posture. A constant state of high tension in this area results in chronic low back pain, digestive urinary and sexual disorders. Trunk muscles that are tense jam the vertebrae against each other, resulting in degenerative arthritis and disc disease. Taoist principles state that a high level of tension in an area of the body displaces life-giving energy from the area, causing disease. As I have mentioned above, this energy is called Chi by the Chinese and Präna in the Indian tradition. Even if we do not believe that such a thing called Chi exists, it is extremely easy to see that vertebrae and discs, subjected to excessive pressure on a constant basis, will degenerate because of lack of circulation. Microcirculation is seriously impaired by constant pressure, as any nurse who has tried to treat bedsores in elderly people, knows.

It is extremely difficult to become aware of the state of tension we are in. It becomes an automatic thing, and only the knowledge of the phenomenon can help us. A yoga teacher once pointed out that I was holding my left shoulder up higher than my right. For a few days, I tried to consciously bring it down, but it caused discomfort; my shoulder had become "comfortable" in an abnormal state. I later discovered that improper sleep posture had caused inflammation of the sterno-clavicular joint, the joint that connects the collarbone to the sternum or breastbone and the surrounding muscles and ligaments. Lifting the shoulder up relieved this discomfort so it had become a habit and I was not even aware of it.

169

Learning to sit or stand or even fall asleep in a relaxed manner often feels strange and may indeed be uncomfortable initially, just as my shoulder was. But to not correct improper posture, is to perpetuate the underlying imbalances that over a few years are sure to cause degenerative disease. I cannot help but feel that the disease fibromyalgia has its origins in this manner. It is known that people suffering this disorder have inadequate restful sleep. But to place them on sleeping pills would be poor practice. Elimination of the tension that they are taking to their sleep with them is one of the ways of providing relief; daily exercise which warms up the entire body is the other.

To start learning Taoist ways of low effort activity, let us first sit on a chair and then lift a leg up. Try to be aware of how much tension is developed in the entire body by just simply trying to lift a leg. Relax the entire body, and just focus on the movement of the leg only. It may seem to be strange and feel like it is quite an effort at first. But with consistent practice, we can and will find that we will achieve the same movement with much less generalized tension, and also achieve the same result with less effort. Indeed, the movement becomes more efficient, with more achieved with less general wear and tear.

I don't think there is any hope for arthritis and other degenerative processes unless we learn this principle. Dying tissues bring in white cells that result in inflammation. At this time, the use of anti-inflammatory drugs is the mainstay of arthritis care. It is supposed to be "scientific." I cannot think of anything less scientific than the ignorance of disorders in muscular tension and balance. It is like driving a car with its brake and accelerator pedals depressed at the same time. On the one hand you destroy your bone and cartilage with inordinately high muscular tension and then you make a feeble effort to "clean up" the inflammation that results with drugs. A scientific study showed that teaching older people Tai Chi significantly lowered their rate of falls and injury. Tai Chi involves use of deep relaxation and "low-effort" in the course of a variety of slow dance like movements.

Hatha Yoga tries to teach its practitioners ways of attaining and holding numerous poses. Unlike texts on Taoist Yoga, Hatha Yoga texts seldom emphasize the need for deep relaxation during the practice. They are more concerned with proper alignment. The problem is, without relaxation, proper alignment is forced, not something that comes naturally. One can "do yoga" for years and only have back and other muscle strains and tears as the end result. I imagine that the dropout rate from yoga classes is significant, because of the seemingly impossible task of achieving the accomplishment level the teacher displays. There are numerous videos demonstrating yoga practice available. Many of them display the result of between twenty to thirty years of daily, dedicated practice, make it appear effortless and do not emphasize that these videos display the supreme achievement in yoga. The "Sun Salutation" is a good example. I am convinced that it is not a series for beginners, but one for adepts. A standing forward bend is an important part of the series, and it takes years of proper practice to achieve a "low-effort" forward bend. It is sad that every physical therapist is trained to teach people not to bend forward without bending their knees first, and yoga teachers are teaching the opposite. Standing forward bends have had an awful damaging effect on my low back, giving me a year or two of back pain from which I have recovered using a blend of Indian and Chinese Yoga styles. Indeed, we are seeing yoga studios offering 'Chi-Yoga.' Performing the Sun Salutation as a warm up practice first thing in the morning is, in my view, just asking for trouble! There are numerous moves and postures done supine that could be used to warm up the lower extremities and low back before attempting anything like the Sun Salutation.

In summary, dear reader, if you plan to explore Yoga, I would caution you very strongly to avoid forward bends in a manner that would put strain on your lumbar discs. If done standing, make sure your knees are adequately bent to allow stretching of the back muscles without excessive disc pressure. Forward bends performed while sitting are even more difficult to do, and are very likely to strain our discs greatly. They must only be attempted under the direct supervision of someone who has had years of experience in Yoga. Too many Yoga teachers in their twenties have learned Yoga for 3-4 years preceded by proficiency in ballet or gymnastics; their manner of teaching may well be quite hazardous to your body. Make sure you are thoroughly warmed up, and avoid rapid jerky movements. Listen to your body. If something hurts, back off immediately. Go into each pose very slowly and relax deeper and deeper into the pose, using the breath and your inner consciousness to guide you, listening to the body every second. And contrary to popular view, no pain is all gain.

I have developed a routine which blends Hatha Yoga, Chi Kung and Pilates, in which I flow in and out of a series of postures and counter-postures. I start with some flows lying supine, then a few sitting up, following which I do some kneeling, then prone, then kneeling again, and then finally standing. It can vary anywhere from a half-hour to an hour. I have found it perfectly safe, very calming, yet powerful. I have taught it to some of my patients and friends, even to people with back problems, and have found it to be safe.

To repeat myself one more time: Unless you born with mile-long hamstrings, avoid or be very careful with traditional yoga postures involving forward bends; you could hurt your back. Also, make sure you warm up thoroughly before doing any form of yoga. Avoid using the "sun salutation" as a warm-up routine.

CHAPTER EIGHT:
ALL BUDDHAS, NO BUDDHISTS

In this book, I mostly refer to the Buddha as though he was a historical person as is traditionally done, though it is very likely the "Buddha" was a mythical being, just as Krishna or Jesus. This approach makes relaying the message much easier, and I have taken care to avoid any mythical overtones pertaining to the life of the Buddha. The sage who conceived the character of the Buddha, just as the mystics who spoke through the character of Jesus or Krishna or Lao-Tzu, was indeed a great teacher: The Buddha taught us not only to think for ourselves, but that within us are all the answers we are looking for. It does not matter whether we think of a person called the Buddha as having taught something, or realize that a sage using the character of the Buddha did the teaching. *Somebody* taught what is attributed to the Buddha, and surely that person was a Buddha! Myth always blends story with teaching; some of the most powerful spiritual teachings have been blended into most fascinating "biographies." We need to use the teaching to awaken ourselves. But many Buddhists seem to limit their knowledge to Buddhism; some of them elevate the Buddha to a god-like being, and try to interpret their entire understanding of life based on the Buddha's teachings. Indeed, Buddha becomes the deity they have to surrender to in order to reach heaven. According to Theravāda writings, the Buddha never did claim to be a god, only an enlightened one; it is said that Mahāyāna transformed Buddha into a deity. Vajrayāna, the path of Tibetan Buddhism, teaches that these deities are simply just projections of our own consciousness. The mythical nature of the Buddha is becoming clear to many scholars. Acharya S., in her forthcoming book *Suns of God: Krishna, Buddha and Christ* discusses the idea that these "divine beings" are all solar gods. Her website www.truthbeknown.com provides a great deal of information. The mythology of all these gods is similar; these "gods" actually represent the wisdom consciousness within each one of us, and are pointers to that inner wisdom. True wisdom is to understand the teaching, and not obsess with the "teacher" as a god. Perhaps the myth is relatively simple to begin with, and then becomes more and more convoluted over time. People have got to the point of accusing those of another religion of following a myth while they follow the "true" religion based on history. This explains the most frantic search for Noah's Ark and various relics such as bones and teeth. Each one of us takes the attitude of "They

worship a mythical god; we worship the real one." It will be a great day
for humanity when we *all* realize that it's *all* myth.

Buddhists see suffering;
Buddha sees joy and sorrow,
   Ups and downs,
      Pleasure and pain,
         Gain and loss,
            Life and death,
               One with the other.

Buddhists see impermanence.
   Buddha sees dynamic, ceaseless change.
      Buddhists see what is, thinking of what it will not be;
         Buddha sees it as it is now,
            and when tomorrow comes,
               will see it as it will be, or perhaps not be.

To be a Buddhist does not necessarily make you a Buddha; a Buddha
does not necessarily have to be a Buddhist. It is *"Being nobody, going
nowhere,"* as the title of a book by Ayya Khema states. To narrow our
understanding of life down to the Four Noble Truths and the Noble
Eightfold path is to see life through a tube. The Noble Eightfold path
provides a superb way of understanding the dissatisfaction that we have
in life or with life, but there is so much more to learn and understand
than that. Even the Buddha himself stated so clearly that what he had
spoken was equivalent to a handful of leaves, when a large of forest of
leaves lay behind him unspoken of. Robert Mitchell relates, in his book
The Buddha His Life Retold: "The next day the Tathagata took up a
handful of Simsapa leaves and said to the monks who were present in the
grove: "Now what do you think, O monks? Which are the more, these
few Simsapa leaves that I hold in my hand, or those that are in this entire
Simsapa grove?" "Few in number, Lord, are those Simsapa leaves that
are in the hand of the Perfect One; far greater in number are those in this
entire Simsapa grove." "Just so, monks, those things which I know by
my super-knowledge, and have not revealed, are greater by far in number
than those things which I have revealed. And why, monks, have I not
revealed them? Because, O monks, they are not conducive to welfare,
to cessation, to calm, to Nirvana. That is why I have not revealed them.
But what have I revealed? Suffering and the extinction of suffering.
Therefore, O monks, exert yourselves diligently to realize pain, pain's

origin, pain's ending, and the path to pain's ending. Build yourselves a raft of Dharma for crossing the current of life and death to yonder shore of immortality."

That is exactly it. Why try to interpret our understanding of everything through the Four Truths, or Eight Truths, or Eight Thousand? Why just focus on the trees and miss the forest? Truth is one; its facets are many.

Once we really understand the Buddha's teachings, we understand why he spent a great deal of time trying to decide whether to teach at all. What he revealed is so profound, that it far exceeds the Four Noble Truths and the Noble Eightfold path. Some years ago, if someone had approached me and said: "you are suffering and that is because you are full of craving, and the way out of your suffering is to be rid of your craving," I'd probably have politely asked them to preach someplace else! Since then, I have understood how very difficult it is to understand Buddhism.

To take refuge in the Buddha, and the Dharma his teachings, is something that must be done only until the day we obtain deep understanding. There was once a time when I finally decided to 'take refuge' in the Buddha and the Dharma. As a child sits happily back in its mother's lap, I took a breath, let myself go, and surrendered myself to the Buddha. However, the Buddha disappeared, only to be replaced by a brilliant clear energy that seemed everywhere. The Buddha was nowhere to be seen, heard or felt. I suddenly realized that Buddha was nothing but my inner, greater, consciousness: pure energy, pure bliss, radiating nothing but positive energy outward. The energy that radiated was nothing but the Dharma, which translated "all that there is, with one uniform Law." There was no need for questions, as it was just there. This energy poured over all things and beings. It surrounded suffering beings that reveled in sensuality and reviled against the shriveled and crippled. It also poured over part-Buddhas who reviled against sensuality, and who reveled in a display of compassion over the suffering of the shriveled and crippled. It finally also poured over fully realized Buddhas who neither reveled nor reviled over either extremes. It did not pour over or around such Buddhas; it seemed to pour right through them.

Following that experience, the laws of the world seemed clear and uniform to all, sparing no one, no matter of what race or religion. The wonderful old saying "Gäthe, gäthe, paragäthe, parasamgäthe, bodhi sväha" seemed to manifest its meaning so clearly. To me it translated to 'dissolving, dissolving, and further dissolving into pure light and consciousness, which then pours forth over all that is.' 'Sväha' is the syllable uttered during the pouring of libation offering during Hindu sacrificial ritual. The Buddha energy seemed neither caught up in impermanence, nor was it discerned as a fixed entity, permanent and unchanging. A sailboat gently caught up in the wind represents the state of samsära, or life, and its inability to turn around and see its source of energy, its Nirvana, seems natural: for to turn around would be to make it just collapse in the water. Some things are sensed, but never seen! It is so ironical that it is just impossible to see, feel, touch or describe our essential source of energy, light and consciousness. We cannot become aware of our greater consciousness; it simply is. Much poetic description of this energy was made in the Üpanishads of ancient India, but once the charm of the poetry has faded, nothing remains, no lasting impression, no personal experience....yet once experienced it transforms us for ever. It is, however, beyond description itself.

So to take refuge in the Buddha is to take refuge in the guiding light of our own inner consciousness. The Buddha said: "Be lamps unto yourselves," a most important piece of mystical advice. To take refuge in the Dharma is to intuitively know the nature of our beings, and act accordingly. To take refuge in the Sangha is to humbly bow to the countless wonderful sages and teachers who brought the teachings of Buddhism to us unaltered over the centuries, for without them we would not have meditation methods unique to Buddhism. Seldom can one see so much offered in the way of valued teaching, for so little as a bowlful of sustenance. May such beings always be blessed with health and long life so that they may continue their good work. Still, birds must fly from the nest once full grown. The Sangha of Buddhas points the way; it gently directs. But neither the Buddha, nor the Sangha is the destination! Our inner understanding, our enlightenment, and salvation from suffering, is the destination. And that is the true Dharma, not a Dharma limited to a religion.

The Buddha clearly defined his own nature, and also taught us to identify ourselves with that same nature. The Buddha was meditating under a banyan tree, when a Brahmin called Drōna came up to him. Drōna asked the Buddha if he was a god, or a celestial being such as a Gändharva or Yaksha. The Buddha said he was not any of those; he stated he was not a mere human being either. Drōna was puzzled and asked the Buddha what he was. As the book *The Buddha His Life Retold* by Robert Allen Mitchell clarifies:

"Those tendencies which would have made me a god, or a non-human being, or a human being," explained the Perfect One, "have been thoroughly given up, completely rooted out, like the stump of a palm tree, and are incapable of reappearing."

"O Brahmin, just as a lotus, born in the water, grown up in the water, raises itself above the water and stands there without being polluted by the water—in the same way, O Brahmin, though I was born in the world and grew up in the world, did I transcend the world; and having transcended the world, I live as one who is not polluted by the world. As *Buddha* should you know me, O Brahmin!"

The act of "having transcended the world and living as one who is not polluted by the world" consists of the act of living a mindful life, a life of awareness.

I will talk more about the most wonderful path of understanding, the art of mindfulness, later on in more detail, and will also frequently refer to the teachings of the Buddha wherever appropriate. Some of the Buddha's ways and teachings are not, in my view, practical ways of living today. For instance, I am uneasy about someone having to live the life of a monk, at the mercy of others. Each one of us must live in harmony with people of all faiths, all walks of life. To create a monastery is to perpetuate religious difference. To live the life of a monk is to depend on others for food and other sustenance. I believe that we each must fend for ourselves. The Dharma could still be upheld. There ought not to be a separate Dharma for a monk and a separate Dharma for you and me. Overall, however, the way of the Buddhas plays a major role in helping define, or guide, a Way of Being for us all.

The Buddha and his teaching of Anäta, or No-Soul

In Hinduism, the word Ätman refers to the immortal soul. Buddhism believes in the concept of Anättha, or without Ätman. The Buddha was once approached by an ascetic called Vacchagotra. The latter wanted to know something about the Ätman, or soul, but the Buddha declined to say anything. Änanda, the Buddha's disciple, asked him why he did not give an answer to the ascetic. The Buddha said that if he had said the soul does exist, he would have been saying that there is a permanent entity called the Ätman, whereas if he had said that the soul did not exist, he would have sounded like a nihilist. The Buddha said "If I had replied, 'No, the soul does not exist,' then that would have increased the bewilderment of Vacchagotra the wanderer, already bewildered. For he would have said, 'Formerly I had a soul, but now I have a soul no more.'"

One other episode documented in Robert Allen Mitchell's book *The Buddha His Life Retold* further reveals the purpose of the Buddha's teaching: "One day the monk Malunkyapütra sat apart from his fellows, thinking: "There are certain things the Perfect One has left unexplained, certain views the Perfect One has not expounded. I am not pleased by his failure to explain them. I, myself, will therefore approach the Perfect One and say to him: 'If the Perfect One will explain the truth of these things to me, then I will follow the religious life under the Perfect One. But if the Perfect One refuses to explain them to me, then I will give up the training and go back to the lower life of the world.'" So Malunkyapütra, rising from his solitude in the late afternoon, entered the Simsapa grove and drew near to the Perfect One, seating himself at one side."

Malunkyapütra demanded to know whether the world is temporary or eternal, whether the world is finite or infinite. He also wanted clarification on whether an Arhat (enlightened one) is beyond death or not. "If the Perfect One will declare these things to me," continued Malunkyapütra, "I will continue in the holy life; but if he does not, I will give it up and return to the lower life of the world."

"Now, Malunkyapütra," replied the Buddha, did I say to you, "Come, Malunkyapütra, follow the religious life under me and I will declare to you, "Eternal is the world" or "Temporary is the world,' and so forth?" "No, Lord, you did not." "And did you, Malunkyapütra, say to me, "Lord, I will follow the religious life under the Perfect One, and the Perfect One will declare to me, "Eternal is the world" or "Temporary is the world,' and so forth?"

"No, Lord, I did not." "That being the case, foolish man, who are you to find fault? He who asks the questions you have asked, Malunkyapütra, would surely come to the end of his days before those questions of his would be answered by the Tathagata! Pay close attention, Malunkyapütra. Suppose a man were pierced by an arrow well steeped in poison, and his relatives were to summon a physician, a surgeon. Then suppose the man says: "I will not have this arrow pulled out until I know something about the man who shot the arrow, both his name and his clan, whether he be tall or short or of middle stature, whether he be a black man or swarthy or fair, whether he be of such and such a village or suburb or town. I will not have this arrow pulled out until I know something about the bow, by whom it was made, and whether it be a longbow or crossbow. I will not have this arrow pulled out until I am told something about the bowstring that drove the arrow, whether it was made of creeper, reed, tendon, or of hemp or sap-tree; till I know of the arrow by which I have been pierced, whether it be a reed shaft or fashioned from a sapling; till I know of the feathers of it" and so on. Well, Malunkyapūtra, that man would die, but still the matter would not be found out by him. Just so, Malunkyapūtra, he who should ask the ontological questions you have asked would come to the end of his days before those questions of his would be answered by the Tathagāta!" The monk Malunkyapūtra was satisfied with what the Buddha said.

The exchange between a student and the master reveals the great difficulty in teaching what is near impossible to teach. Some of these ideas are very difficult to express. Hindus believe in an immortal soul, which they refer to as the Atman. The Buddha apparently taught that everything is without a soul, which is the concept of "Anäta," meaning "without-Ätman." So how do we reconcile the differences in the two teachings? Let us look at things this way. Suppose a sage "sees" that all what he sees is impermanent. Yet, the "Seer" within the sage, *that* which sees the impermanent, is *not* impermanent, or it will not be able to see the impermanence of all around it. Therefore the Seer, called in Hinduism the Atman, or Soul, is able to see and comprehend the impermanence of all that exists. However, only a sage, who comprehends in this way, can understand this. Otherwise, most of us would just sit and argue that "all is impermanent" and argue further as to whether there is a soul or not, and whether *it too* is impermanent.

The word 'Ätman' is often referred to by the word 'Self' by many scholars. Walpola Rahula, in his book *What the Buddha Taught* quotes the Buddha as saying: "When he reflects unwisely in this way, one of the six false views arises in him:

1. I have a Self: this view arises in him as true and real.
2. I have no Self: this view arises in him as true and real.

3. By Self I perceive Self: this view arises in him as true and real.
4. By Self I perceive non-self: this view arises in him as true and real.
5. By non-self I perceive Self: this view arises in him as true and real.
6. Or a wrong view arises in him as follows: This my Self, which speaks and feels, which experiences the fruits of good and bad actions now here and now there, this Self is permanent, stable, everlasting, unchanging, remaining the same for ever and ever.

This, Bhikkus, (renunciate monks) is what is called becoming enmeshed in views; a jungle of views; a wilderness of views; scuffling in views, the agitation (struggle) of views, the fetter of views. Bhikkus, the uninstructed ordinary man fettered by the fetters of views, does not liberate himself from birth, aging and death, from sorrows, lamentations, pains, grief, despair; I say that he does not liberate himself from suffering."

That is exactly the point. The view "I have a soul" is just a thought, a view. A sage who has known the nature of his inner being finds it extremely difficult to express to an ordinary person as to the nature of this inner being. It cannot properly be described as an object. However, the Üpanishads did so poetically express the nature and beauty of the undying Seer within us. Such a description was really meant for the select student who could understand. The Buddha believed that if he taught a concept, an idea, that we have an Ätman, or Self, then he would be teaching just an idea or thought, and it would take away from the student's ability to attain inner understanding. On the other hand, there is a Seer within us that sees the impermanence of all else. The Buddha occasionally did point out to his disciples that there *is something that is beyond impermanence.* Robert Allen Mitchell reveals the Buddha saying in *The Buddha His Life Retold*: "O monks, there exists a condition in which the four great elements are not, in which boundless space is not, in which infinite consciousness is not, in which nothingness is not, in which neither-perception-nor-non-perception is not. There is neither this world nor a world beyond, nor both together; nor do sun and moon exist there. There, monks, I declare, is no being born and no dying, there is no falling and no arising. It is not something fixed, yet it does not change; it is, in fact, not based on anything that can be grasped by the mind. Verily, monks, it is Nirvana, the end of turmoil. There is, O monks, an unborn, an un-become, a not-made, an incomposite. If this was not so, monks, there could not be any escape from that which is born, become, made, composite. But since the phenomenal world—this Samsära—is of qualities converse to those of Nirvana, such an escape is possible."

Hindus call this "unborn, un-become, not-made, incomposite" the Ätman, a fragment of Brahman, the Supreme One God/Energy/Mind of the universe. In Hinduism, Brahman is both immanent and transcendent. Rather than being nothingness, it is a 'Whole in None.' The ultimate goal of all life is to attain Brahman, just as attaining Nirvana is the goal of Buddhism. The Îsha Üpanishad states: "At the heart of this phenomenal world, within all its changing forms, dwells the unchanging Lord." The Mandükya Üpanishad states, in the "nĕti, nĕti" or "not this, not that" approach: *It is neither outer awareness nor inner awareness or even a lack of awareness. Neither is it is not knowing nor unknowing; it is not even knowingness itself. It can neither be seen nor understood; it has no boundaries. It is beyond expression and beyond thought. It is indefinable. It is known only through becoming one with it. It is the end of all activity, silent and unchanging, the supreme good, one without a second. It is the Ätman, the real Self. It, above all, should all itself to be known.*

Truly, the goal of any human being should be the same; it *must* be the same. There are no separate laws for Hindus and Buddhists. Therefore, we need to identify our goals as being the same. Apart from the paragraph above, the Buddha seldom liked to describe Nirvana in detail, except to state that it is the state of cessation of suffering, where all desire has come to an end. The supreme consciousness of the universe, which pervades all beings and things, is the inner mind on which our thinking mind rests. When the incessant activity of the thinking mind comes to a standstill in meditation, the inner consciousness, referred to as the Ätman in Hindu thought, reveals itself in all its serenity and splendor. It is a state of tranquil awareness, the very same state as the Buddhist Nirvana.

The Four Noble Truths

These are 1: 'Dukkha,' or suffering, exists. 2: desire, or craving, leads to suffering. 3: there is a way out of suffering, which consists of an end to desire and craving, and 4: that way is the Noble Eightfold Path.

The first Noble Truth is often written in books as "Life is suffering,' which is a very pessimistic way of interpreting the teaching. It appears to me that what the Buddha really meant, was this: *until we attain a state*

*of understanding, intuition and insight into human nature, and until
we become enlightened from within, despite all the available pleasures
of life, our lives will be characterized by 'dukkha': unsatisfactory,
unfulfilled, unhappy, and miserable.* The second and third Noble Truths
are written as a kind of question and answer sequence, really, so indeed
the Four Noble Truths could be said really to be two Noble Truths: 1.
We live unsatisfactory lives of suffering because of our craving, limited
minds, and 2. The way out of suffering is the Noble Eightfold Path.

The Noble Eightfold Path

If the energy that is the heart of the universe were the hub of a wheel,
and all of existence the wheel itself, then it could be that there are eight
or even eight thousand spokes that hold it together. The truth cannot be
limited to a fixed number of "truths." Therefore, the Noble Eightfold
Path does not have to be an eightfold one, it could be just a single one:
the understanding that our lives are full of misery and lack lasting
satisfaction, and that there is a way out of this predicament: to attain a
higher level of consciousness, a more lofty perch from which we see all
the turmoil of the world. Anyhow, here are the elements of the eightfold
path:

1. Right view (often called right understanding) is to see life the way
most of us live it, realizing that it is unsatisfactory, unfulfilled.
2. Right resolve (often called right thought) is to resolve to live a life free
of obsession with sensuality, ill will, and cruelty. It is to be determined to
live a satisfactory and good life free from misery and suffering.
3. Right speech. The third element is where the actual intervention into
an unsatisfactory state of life begins. Right speech is to develop speech
free from idle or vain talk, deceit, malice, abuse, and silliness. Words
of anger are among the most destructive of words, as this poem of mine
illustrates:

Words to regret

*Harsh words, unwittingly said in haste
Spewing out of a troubled soul.
Fiery, destructive as volcanic lava,
They burn and destroy, leave ashes behind.
They cause regret, dismay and sorrow.
Then come the apologies,*

A mammoth task to rebuild from the waste.
So hard to rethink, to rearrange and redo.

If only, if only, they had not been said.

A moment of turmoil, and such are the consequences.
Strain, sadness and solitude.

The ensuing regret wrenches the heart
With considerable despair
Too late, however;
The firearm of words had already exploded
The destruction done.

To heal and repair takes forever.
We are then driven to words of conciliation
If only the tape could be rewound, and erased.

We apologize to our heartfelt utmost, and hope
That all is forgiven.
We pray that the river of wisdom will forever
Extinguish the glowing embers, the remnants of carnage
Of the unmeant, unintended, words of fire.

4. Right action is that which is gentle and non-violent, and free from killing, stealing, adultery, lying, and the use of intoxicants.

5. Right livelihood is the avoidance of an evil trade such as soothsaying, trickery, usury, trading in weapons, in living beings (slavery), in meat, in intoxicants, and in poison; and in converse, leading a livelihood of right and honorable means.

6. Right effort consists of four efforts: To prevent the arising of bad thoughts; to dispel bad thoughts; to develop good thoughts; and to maintain good thoughts.

7. Right mindfulness, or attentiveness, is where the practitioner abides balanced in a greater awareness and presence of mind; attentive and contemplating, according to reality, the body, feelings, the mind, and thoughts, seeing all as composite, ever-becoming, impermanent, and subject to decay.

8. Right concentration, is the development of one-pointedness of mind. This attainment leads to the development of the various levels of absorption, or Jhanas, discussed below.

The Buddha taught that there are eight levels of Jhanas. These are usually translated as 'absorptions.' Since the word Jhana is likely derived from the Sanskrit word Jnana, or consciousness, it could be said that they are levels of consciousness. Meditation can lead a practitioner to any of four levels of what are called "fine material absorptions":

In the first level, he becomes detached from sensual desires and unwholesome thoughts, accompanied by reasoning and discursive thought, born of detachment, and filled with rapture and happiness.

In the second level, with the fading away of reasoning and discursive thought, by gaining inward tranquility and one-pointedness of mind, he enters into a state free from reasoning and discursive thought, born of concentration and filled with rapture and happiness.

In the third level, rapture fades away, and he abides in equanimity--clearly conscious, attentive, experiencing that feeling which equates to equanimity and attentive mind.

In the fourth level, pain and pleasure are rejected, and through the cessation of previous joy and grief, he enters into a state beyond pleasure and pain, which is purified by equanimity and attentiveness.

Going even beyond the fine-material absorptions, the practitioner enters states of what are called "Immaterial absorptions."

The fifth level is the sphere of boundless space. At the sixth level, transcending the sphere of boundless space, one attains and abides in the sphere of infinite consciousness. At the seventh level having transcended the sphere of infinite consciousness, at the idea that 'nothing really exists' he attains and abides in the sphere of no-thingness. At the eighth level, having completely transcended the sphere of no-thingness, he attains and abides in the sphere of neither-perception-nor-non-perception.

I see the various levels of the absorptions to be innately present within each of us, to be unveiled rather than actually attained. Also, going from one layer of the absorptions to another consists of simply revealing layers of bliss inherent within us, and only has to be revealed by the removal what is *not* bliss, namely, ceaseless thought born of desire. The method of actually attaining these levels of consciousness is what is taught in the last two of the Noble Eightfold Path, namely proper mindfulness, called "Samma Sati," and proper meditative concentration, called "Samma Samādhi."

Books on Buddhism devote themselves in great detail to discussions on these two items of the Eightfold Path. Concentration practices are very similar to those taught in Yoga schools. Mindfulness practices, which are very essential pre-requisites to concentration practices, are unique to Buddhism, and indeed its crowning jewel. There is no better approach to making life rich in the joy of awareness than learning mindfulness practice.

Mindfulness of the breath is a superb technique that builds both mindfulness and concentration. If one is on a train, mindfulness would compare with simply watching all the scenery go by in an endless sequence, and concentration would be where one focuses on any particular object to the exclusion of all others. This is of course a very simplistic definition. The "simply sitting" practice of Soto Zen, in my view, consists of both mindfulness and concentration practice. Really, they both reinforce each other. If one is caught up in a reverie, a daydream, or stream of thought, then one has lost mindfulness. To pick an object of concentration, such as the movement of the breath, and focus on it unceasingly to bring the mind to a state of quietness, is concentration practice. An even greater concentration practice is that of unceasing attention to the endless flow of thought.

The Buddha taught mindfulness of the breath as follows: First he taught us to be mindful of the nature of the breath, whether long or short, and mindfulness of the actual passage of the breath itself. He next taught us to calm the breath while maintaining awareness, and to develop a feeling of serenity and happiness as we breathe. He then proceeded to teach even greater achievements:
With every breath we breathe in and out, he taught us to, in sequence:
Become conscious of the sequence of thoughts.
Calm the sequence of thoughts.
Perceive the mind.
Elevate the mind.
Concentrate the mind.
Liberate the mind.
Discern the impermanence of al composite things.
Become conscious of the absence of passion.
Become conscious of the extinction of craving and desires.
Become conscious of the otherness of craving and desires.

185

The Buddha said: "In this way, O monks, must mindful respiration be practiced and cultivated--peaceful, sublime, pure, bestowing happiness--that it suppress all ill and every immoral state which is apt to arise. In this way, O monks, must a monk train himself."

'Train himself' is the key word; all these are valuable during training. As the Buddha said, perceiving, elevating, concentrating, and liberating the mind is an important goal. Discerning impermanence, becoming conscious of the absence of passion, and the extinction of craving desires, are all-important. However, there comes a point when constant attention to these various steps can be self-defeating. As the mind becomes quiet during the practice of mindfulness of the breath, from the inner consciousness comes either quiet serenity or various revelations. Consider this analogy of a pole-vaulter: The person concentrates all his energy on the tip of the pole in its pit, but the actual focus is the movement of the athlete with the rest of the pole to various heights beyond the bar. Or for instance, during rowing a boat, the focus of energy is on pulling the oar over the water in a certain direction, but the goal is not to move the water but to move the boat in the opposite direction. Both these analogies point to the real nature of concentration practices such as mindfulness of the breath. The focus of energy is to concentrate the mind on the breath, but the result is releasing the inner/greater consciousness into view. It is like holding open the gate to allow the cattle or crowds through. The effort is to hold the gate open, but the actual goal is to allow crowds or cattle through! In meditation, the effort is to one-point the mind, but the actual result is the release of our inner/greater consciousness into full awareness; to wipe away the dirt that obscured the light of the lamp.

Mahamudra and Zen

Tibetan Tantric Buddhism is a collection of very powerful methods, but one of its practices, Mahāmudra, emphasizes essential Buddhist belief: we already possess all the potential needed to attain enlightenment. Mahāmudra appears to be a practice very similar to Soto Zen. One sits in meditation, strong as a mountain yet as relaxed as flowing water. This is the practice of meditation that I describe in the chapter "A Way Inward." The practice and the goal eventually turn out to be the same. In his book *Teachings of Tibetan Yoga* in the chapter entitled "The Essentials of Mahāmudra Practice as given by the Venerable Lama Kong Ka," Garma C.C. Chang writes: "There are three essentials in Mahāmudra practice:

equilibrium, relaxation, and naturalness. 'Equilibrium' means to balance body, mouth, and mind. The Mahämudra way of balancing the body is to loosen it, the way of balancing the mouth is to slow down the breathing, and the way of balancing the mind is not to cling to and rely on anything. This is the supreme way to tame the body, breath (präna), and mind. 'Relaxation' means to loosen the mind, to let everything go, to strip off all ideas and thoughts. When one's whole body and mind become loose, one can, without effort, remain in the natural state, which is intrinsically non-discriminative and yet without distractions. 'Naturalness' means not taking or leaving anything: in other words the yogi does not make the slightest effort of any kind. He lets the senses and mind stop or flow by themselves without assisting or restricting them. To practice naturalness is to make no effort and be spontaneous. The above can be summarized thus:

The essence of equilibrium is not to cling,
The essence of relaxation is not to hold,
The essence of naturalness is to make no effort."

Garma C.C. Chang quotes *The Song of Mahämudra by Tilopa,* a tenth century Tibetan sage:

"Mahämudra is beyond all words
And symbols, but for you, Naropa,
Earnest and loyal, must this be said.

The Void needs no reliance,
Mahämudra rests on naught.
Without making an effort,
But remaining loose and natural,
One can break the yoke
Thus gaining liberation....
Do naught with the body but relax,
Shut firm the mouth and silent remain,
Empty your mind and think of naught.
Like a hollow bamboo,
Rest at ease your body.
Giving not nor taking,
Put your mind at rest.
Mahamudra is like a mind that clings to naught.
Thus practicing, in time you will reach Buddhahood."

187

Therefore, Mahamudra refers to a tremendous state of being, which is achieved with the utmost simplicity and relaxed state. At the same moment, we are both our simple selves and also all that there is. Mahamudra is the goal, yet is also the beginning. In the instant of complete letting go of all clinging with body and mind, what results is the profound state of Mahamudra where the practitioner merges with all that there is. Yet an instant earlier, he was just simply himself. So the dramatic change emphasizes that samsāra is not different from nirvana, as the Buddha taught. We are fragments of the infinite consciousness; we can either be limited to our own ego, or we can relax and let go and become part of the universal consciousness. It is as easy as just switching a light on or off; yet unless that ability to do so is attained, it seems like a mountain cliff that cannot be climbed. Once we learn the ease of attainment, then we learn the truth of Mahamudra and that of Shikantäza in Zen.

Soto Zen consists of very much the same practice; indeed, the description of the state of Mahāmudra is identical to a state of Zen. They really cannot essentially be different. Mahāmudra can be loosely translated as "The great posture." It refers to a meditative state of being. It is the ultimate, the very goal of all human achievement. In theistic terms it could be described as being one with God at all times; in Yogic terms, it means to bind our life energy to God's energy, and in Buddhist terms, being in, and displaying, our essential Buddha nature. To rest in a state of Mahāmudra is to just be, and open up ourselves to the Cosmic Intelligence/Energy. Not just open ourselves up, but to allow ourselves to be completely overcome by It. A state of deep relaxation is a most essential pre-requisite. Similarly, the essence of Zen is to let go. In Sufism, it is a process of complete surrender to God. I've always said that there are not different laws for people from different religions. We are all subject to the same law. Therefore, once you understand Mahāmudra, then you understand the process of Zen, Yoga, Islamic Sufism and mystical Christianity. It is an achievement of the greatest of human achievements, without striving to achieve anything.

A Zen master once said that to know Zen is to imagine a snake in a bamboo. Our minds are like the snake, constantly slithering around, never at ease. Can it completely let go and be entirely at home in the hollow bamboo? If it does, it would be just the same as a mind that has attained a state of Zen. The snake needs to relax, let go, and completely surrender. Then it will become the hollow in the bamboo, become as part of it. In the same way, if we surrender our ego, then we become part of the whole. We become part of the void, the infinite, the everything....we become part of God.... as our most inner nature is nothing but part of a continuum which is God.

CHAPTER NINE:
PRAYER AND MEDITATION

Prayer consists of kind, caring, considerate and compassionate thoughts and intentions expressed in the presence of the Greater Being. Meditation, on the other hand, is *being* in the presence of the Greater Being, and transcends all thought, including kind, caring, considerate and compassionate ones, and yet including them all.

Prayer is talking to God; meditation is listening back.
Prayer is "my will be done"; meditation is "Thy will be done."
Prayer is asking; meditation is receiving.
Prayer is "asking God to let"; meditation is "letting go to God."
Prayer is supplication; meditation is application.

Anticipating a statement that the phrase "Thy will be done" is part of the Lord's Prayer, an important part of the Christian heritage, let me clarify that the boundaries between prayer and meditation are not clearly drawn. The word meditation itself has meant many things to many people. Prayer, on the other hand, is much easier to talk about. Prayer has been part of virtually all civilizations from time immemorial. It is a very intuitive thing. Even little children seem to accept prayer so naturally without any questioning whatsoever. The questions come later, as they grow up!

Does prayer work? There are many scientific studies now that prove it does, particularly to help the healing process of those who are sick. I'm not sure about prayers offered to help a group of people win battles over their enemies, however; God has no enemies, there is only one uniform Power of the earth and Universe, and I believe that God is an equal opportunity supporter!

Regarding the exact mechanics of prayer, there probably needs little to be said about it, except that it is probably intuitive, or more likely something that has been taught to most of us since childhood, as part of our religious heritage. There is in my experience, however, a deeper aspect to prayer that is supremely important. With deeper contemplative and meditative practice, we start feeling a certain power within us, which grows stronger and stronger with continued practice. It is a tremendous feeling of inner peace and power. Yet this is not a power that is self-serving. It is a power that wants to radiate itself outward. It is an embodiment of an incredible Universal energy, it is Love with a capital L; it is radiant goodwill. It is the essence of the teaching of the Buddha, Jesus, and other saintly beings that have taught us this. Once this energy is felt within us, prayer ceases to be a matter of "asking someone out there" to help us or help someone we care for. It becomes a matter of prayerfully directing best wishes and good will toward someone else. This practice is very powerful indeed. The mechanics of a pair of bellows comes to mind; just as the bellows draw in air, and direct it toward a point that needs its directed flow of air, in the same way this "directed prayer" comes from within our beings. Consider this situation: A child has just broken his arm and is tearful, upset and in pain. Which of these two people's efforts will be more effective: the child's father praying to God at then foot of the bed, or the mother, holding the child full of love, nurturing and comforting the child, touching, feeling the injured arm, transmitting her love and healing to the child?

It is very difficult to explain this phenomenon of Self-directed prayer; it must be personally experienced. Like other mystical experiences, it truly is beyond explanation. However, I submit that each one of us is capable of this phenomenon, which can be called "Self-directed prayer", 'Self' referring to God within, and the mind focuses on the object to be healed, transmitting the greater wisdom and energy of God to it. It is the result of deep spiritual practice. It does not matter what kind of spiritual practice, although an attitude of compassion and goodwill toward all is an absolute must. Hate and dislike of others is an emotion that will surely erase the ability to maintain this power, the reason being that this ability is a power, is a gift that comes with dedicated spirituality. Yes, it is an unconditional gift, but you will be sure to find that the power disappears if the frame of our mind changes from one that consists of genuine love, to that of hate or dislike!

Can one successfully pray for the destruction of someone else? I believe the human mind is an incredibly powerful thing. Over the thousands of years of human civilization (sometimes I wonder whether that word is appropriate!) it is clear that evil warmongers have often successfully destroyed good people, good civilizations, and good societies. Many religions attribute this success to Satan, the archenemy of God, and the one that incites evil. I personally don't see the need to postulate the presence of such a great evil power. To me, it is somewhat a myth to state that God, one who is all-powerful, can't successfully wipe out this so-called Satan. The human mind, caught up in extremes of either craving or aversion, is perfectly capable of all kinds of evil intent and destructive force. Paul Brunton, in his book *A Search in Secret India,* described a man who was apparently able to communicate with the spirit of his late brother and perform all kinds of supernatural psychic feats. It is quite possible that practitioners of voodoo-like arts "pray," or appeal to, spirit-like entities for help with their nefarious deeds. It is therefore important that we explore spirituality for our own safety and that of others dear to us.

As we explore spirituality deeper, the borders between prayer and meditation start disappearing. You stop needing to be convinced that God's power is ever present, all present, in us, all around us, and with us. It can be felt; it must be felt. Once experienced, prayer blends into meditation, and meditation blends into prayer. A wonderful form of prayer is simply to communicate with the greater power that is within and around us. The Kĕna Üpanishad said in so sublime a manner three thousand years ago, "May I never deny the Supreme God, and may the Supreme God never deny me!" Indeed, the Vĕdas, the ancient Scriptures of ancient India, are one huge collection of hymns largely consisting of prayers. The Vĕdas consistently maintain that there is only one Supreme Being, but they direct prayers to various entities that they maintain as communicating links, primarily Agni, the "God of fire." Vedic ritual consists of pouring offerings into a fire, usually clarified butter and articles of food, usually grains. Fire is the medium that "accepts" the offerings, which are made in acknowledgement of the supreme sacrifice: that which resulted in the Supreme Being transforming Itself into all that is visible and known.

An attitude of deep thankfulness is also a wonderful form of prayer. It is easy to say a prayer of thanks when all is well. In times of adversity, however, thankfulness does not come easy; we tend to resort to prayer for relief. How can one be thankful, we may ask, when we are suffering in pain or some such misery? A state of spirituality that results in the ability to achieve directed, "greater prayer" as I have mentioned above, also results in the ability to have deep down satisfaction in "just being," just living in the presence of the wonderful energy that constantly floods our being, whether or not we are conscious of Its presence. More commonly we are oblivious of this presence. It is extremely easy to become so oblivious. In the Buddhist tradition, the teaching is the development of greater mindfulness, during every moment of our life. It is such a practice that will make us realize that if we feel forsaken, it is because we have allowed ourselves to drift off, away from this greater awareness. It is a state of awareness where every breath, every thought, is in a state of prayerfulness, awareness, indeed where every thought is a prayer. The Buddha's teachings have been interpreted to be atheistic or agnostic, but I have discovered over the years that very few people in the history of humankind have had a greater understanding of the very pulse of energy that this universe is made of, namely God. The Buddha consistently avoided metaphysical or other discussions pertaining to God, but he insisted on practical methods of attaining God-realization. No one can possibly prove that the "God" they have discovered with prayer or meditation is any different than the state of Nirvana that the Buddha taught us to achieve; indeed, when we explore this realm of our existence, we discover that the goal of these various practices is really the same.

If we were to explore thoroughly the teachings of Yoga and Buddhism, we would discover that each one of us is capable of concentrating, storing, and directing this inner power. Advanced practitioners find that they are able to heal the sick, by touch and even by sight, as well as develop supernatural abilities, called "Siddhis." It is this power that leads many Masters of these arts to be considered as manifestations of God by those who do not understand the mechanics of this process. It is only a self-serving Guru who will not teach that each one of us is born with this innate ability to achieve the highest states of spirituality.

Greater prayer turns by its very nature, to "directed prayer." There is enough spiritual energy in such a practitioner, that thoughts of good will, or intention, gather energy around them, and are able to radiate outward towards those in need of it. The Buddha called it "Metta (Mĩthra in Sanskrit) Bhavana," which I translate as the "practice of radiant friendliness." Anyone who has developed an inner understanding of this process can very easily resonate with it, but it is so difficult to describe it to anyone who has not known it. It takes Gnosis, or Jnana, to "know" it. All I can say is that with the determined practice of any genuine form of spirituality, each one of us can, and indeed must, discover it. The practice of this art is of great value. Radiant goodwill can have a positive good influence on those around us, in direct opposition to the rage and anger that is rampant in so many situations of human interaction.

Eric Butterworth, in his book *The Universe is Calling,* takes an extremely in-depth look at prayer. Butterworth reveals great understanding of the spirituality innate within each one of us. However, he reveals some misunderstanding of the wonderful spiritual traditions of the East. He states: "Jesus was the one who discovered the divine depth as a potential within all persons. And he demonstrated the full potential in manifest form." The truth, that which is the theme of the Üpanishads of ancient India, written around a thousand years before Jesus, is that the Supreme God of the Universe, the One, whom they referred to as "Brahman," pervades the universe and resides as the crucial part of each one of us. In another section, he states, "I prefer the term silence over meditation, for it tends to distinguish the process from the Eastern practice." It is a strange statement, because, after all, the practice of meditation as taught in the East is to attain silence of the chattering mind. It appears that Butterworth has discovered the mystic truth of the wonderful inner power within us, the power that is nothing but the greater power of the supreme. However, he seems to feel that this is something only to be discovered by Christian religious practice, even though he quotes extensively from Eastern teachings. What a pity; he seems to be unaware that the teachings of the sages who created the mythical Jesus are no different than that of the sages who created the mythical Buddha, hundreds of years earlier. Indeed, as discussed in the chapter on Christianity, literalist Christianity has spent hundreds of years trying to destroy the original mystic teachings of the Gnostics. It would be interesting to know how many Christians accustomed to an orthodox Christian practice even understand the depth of mystic understanding that Butterworth speaks with. His delightful phrase "relax, let go, let God," for instance, is the essence of the Zen meditative process of "letting go." There is a subtle difference, in that Buddhists don't say, "Let God," they just let go, and find that they eventually, in enlightenment, are overcome with tremendous insight, understanding, and supreme inner peace. This inner peace can only come from one source, no matter what our religion. And that source is God. Overall, I consider the book to be worthwhile reading, something that we can resonate with after we have started radiating our own Inner Light. Once we discover our innate spirituality, our prayer usually radiates from within our center outward, rather than being an appeal to God at a point in the vague and far distance.

Butterworth has us imagine being deep in outer space. He writes: "We are within a canopy of stars around us on all sides, and they appear to be sending their shafts of lights specifically to us, like supporting hands of the Universe. Rest for a while in this image, and feel the universe rushing, streaming, and pouring into you from all sides while you sit quietly. Now you may be wondering, "Is this praying?" Certainly not as the world prays. For you are the center of the Universe, or of God. (Is there a difference?) God is a presence who is totally present. So there is nowhere to bow down and worship Him, even within yourself. Can you sense the awakening to a new insight into God and yourself? Not someone to pray to, but the "focus of an infinite idea" being projected into visibility as you, that you pray from." It takes someone awakened by prayer and meditation to be able to assert such a statement; for others, it may seem something beyond grasp, something difficult to comprehend. Interestingly, though he tries to emphasize Christianity in the book, he actually reveals the essence of Eastern Spirituality as well as Gnosticism.

As I have mentioned elsewhere, if God and his essential nature as described in Holy Scriptures such as the Üpanishads, the Tao, and the Bible, is a treasure, the Buddhist practice of mindfulness is the very best tool that I have ever known, to dig and unearth that treasure. It is then that we discover that the treasure was not buried far beneath us; it is indeed the very essence of our nature. As Krishna teaches Arjuna in the Bhagavad-Gîta, there is not a moment that God does not act in the universe. There is a fraction of a second in which God does not act in our personal lives, yet we are blissfully (or not so blissfully) ignorant of this truth. Meditation uncovers the treasure; prayer allows this treasure to enrich our everyday lives. After all, of what use is any treasure unless it is actually used? Praying for the well being of others and even of ourselves, is an effective use of the treasure. Greater prayer, the prayer that arises as a flow from the depth of our beings, is an unconditional gift. It seems to come from "us," but in truth it is the unconditional flow of energy from the incredible power in which and upon which our existence is built. It is God's energy; we only seem to think that it is ours. The saints, sages and Buddhas know it to be a fact; it is easy for the rest of us to discover that to be so as well.

There are significant differences between prayer and meditation as detected by physiological measurements. Jeff Levin, Ph.D., writes in his book *God, Faith and Healing,* (page 167): "Do brain wave data suggest that praying to God elicits an altered state of consciousness? A provocative study by scientists at the University Of Louisville School Of Medicine examined EEG patterns among male and female adults engaging in prayer. Subjects were evangelical Christians, members of the Church of God, a Protestant denomination based in Indiana. They were asked to pray silently in their usual fashion, concentrating on the adoration and praise of God. EEG readings were taken while at rest before praying, during prayer, and again at rest post-prayer. Investigators had hypothesized that electro-cortical rhythms would slow during prayer, as research had shown them to do in practitioners of yoga and TM. But they found just the opposite. According to investigators, "There is no evidence of EEG slowing during prayer. On the contrary, prayer appears to be accompanied by a shift in the direction of shorter duration half-waves, or faster EEGs." The pray-ers had actually shifted away from the alpha range and more toward the beta range of brain wave activity—in the direction of normal waking consciousness and hyper-alertness. In other words, the state of consciousness of evangelical Christians was "altered," to be sure, but in a direction quite the opposite of what had been found for practitioners of meditation.

The investigators were perplexed by these findings, but made an interesting observation. They referred to anecdotal evidence that some very highly experienced meditators—people thought of as spiritual "masters"—often "show acceleration in the frequency of electro cortical activity, particularly during deep meditation." The shifts in consciousness among evangelicals at prayer appear to mimic those occurring in the most advanced Eastern adepts who have spent years refining their meditative practices.

The implications of this last study are clear. If there are beneficial physiological consequences of spiritually altered states of consciousness, they are not just reserved for mystics and adepts. They are available to prayerful Christians, and by extension, perhaps any sincere spiritual seeker who desires to worship or connect with God."

It is my view, however, that this subject requires more study. It is very possible that the "most advanced Eastern adepts" had been practicing the equivalent of directed prayer: one of the cardinal principles of Bodhisattva (the highest state achieved by Buddhist meditators) practice is to pray and work toward the salvation of others.

Even before discovering this inner wellspring of goodwill, peace and power through the practice of meditation, it is essential that the mind as we know it start being cultivated into an attitude of good-will. This is the essence of the practice of Metta, or radiant friendliness, as taught by the Buddha. The Hebrew Bible taught us to love our neighbor, but Jesus went one huge step further, and taught us to love our enemies. To "love our enemies" is actually a bit of an oxymoron, is it not, because one who loves has no enemies…but if practiced diligently, it makes us discover that who we call "our enemies" are just simply people, people whose behavior or attitude makes us resentful or angry. It is then that we discover that it is our reaction that makes them enemies. So "Love" simply equates to developing awareness of this fact. It is always possible to try and correct the differences without that inner rage. Indeed, the less the rage, the more the inner greater power can guide and help the situation. My young cousin, who was a dental student, was killed by a man, who in a fit of jealousy, ran over her with is car. It would be natural for me to hate the man who viciously drove his car into the motor scooter on which my little cousin was riding, knocked her off it, ran over her and killed her. My family must see to it that he is brought to justice, simply because there would be anarchy if we did not have such a system of justice. But I believe in praying for the man's entire being to achieve a state of peace, because otherwise he will continue to exhibit rage and bring chaos and suffering to all those around him. Even death will not silence that raging mind, as he will be reborn both to suffer and continue to cause suffering to others. General understanding within the Hindu religion is that we suffer in this birth because of evil that we did in a previous birth, but this is impossible to state to be a fact. Such knowledge or belief is a deterrent, however. And it does open up a wide range of "karmic" possibilities. In any case, there is always a "karmic reaction" to everything we do. Evil only brings back evil, and love inevitably will reap its rich rewards. The Buddha, as quoted in the book *Dhammapada, translated by Thomas Byrom,* said: "In this world, hate never yet dispelled hate. Only love dispels hate. This is the law, ancient and inexhaustible. You too shall pass away. Knowing this, how can you quarrel?" Or in the wonderful words of the Îsha Üpanishad, "He who sees everything as nothing but the Supreme Being, and the Supreme Being in everything he sees, such a seer can not have aversion for anyone."

Among Jewish people, the practice of prayer, as we commonly understand it, becomes an integral part of daily life; there is a blessing for every activity. The celebration of life and its activities, all becomes activity accompanied by a prayer and a blessing. To "bless something" is to ask God to bless it. Offering blessings, as I see it, is a tremendous expression of the radiant power of good will from the depth of our being.

Hindus are taught to pray at twilight both at daybreak and sunset, as well as offer prayers and blessings at meal times. Those that practice deeper practices such as yoga, spend anywhere from a half-hour to three hours at dawn involved in prayer, meditation and yoga practice. Chanting of a mantra links the practitioner's being with that of the Supreme, and helps quiet the mind. Muslims practice Namaaz five times a day, in a posture that is the epitome of submission to the great Power around us. The Buddhists chant in prayer, as well as meditate, sometimes for hours on end. The aim of all these practices is to achieve an inner state of deep understanding and connection with the One that pervades us all.

CHAPTER TEN:
A WAY INWARD

I was a teenager when an uncle suggested I try meditation. I still remember the time--it was at a park on a hilltop overlooking lush green tropical vegetation. Looking out, I responded: "There is nothing to be found within us; everything is out there!" I was actively interacting with the world, where everything could be seen, heard, and touched. What was there to be found inside us?

There are countless people who react the way I did then. Mention the word meditation, and they recoil with suspicion. They have heard all kinds of things about meditation, that it makes the mind go blank; that it is a form of witchcraft, and so on. Or they have heard of this cult or that, and feel that meditation is what goes with cults. Or most importantly, their religion does not permit meditation. Scholars have written that the early Church made meditation a forbidden art, and limited people to supplication to God with prayer. In the chapter on Christianity I have discussed the Hesychast (meditative practice) of the early Church Fathers. It is known that countless gospels were destroyed by the early Church, and the entire Gnostic Christian tradition was wiped out, so it is impossible to know to what extent meditation was part of the early Christian tradition.

Fortunately, there is more and more scientific data being accumulated on the value of meditation. Awareness meditation is being shown to be of great value in stress related disorders. Meditation is an active part of Dr. Ornish's Heart Disease Reversal program, and Dr. Jon Kabat-Zinn has helped introduce awareness meditation into mainstream American medicine.

My initial learning about meditation was part of yoga practice. There are numerous books on Yoga, and most of them include chapters on meditation. Physical exercise Yoga, called Hatha Yoga, is considered a stepping-stone to the practice of meditation. Union with God, no less, is the ultimate goal of yoga practice. The Yoga Sutras (aphorisms) of Pathanjali, a sage who lived in the second century BCE, are considered to be the core teaching regarding meditative practice.

The meditation practice of Yoga utilizes the concentration method. We find an object to concentrate on, and start with pratyähära, separating the mind from distractions. Ähära means food, and pratya-ähära is to remove that which feeds the senses. The actual process of concentration begins. A flame is often used, or a rose, or various holy objects. Dhärana is the actual process of concentration, which deepens into Dhyäna, deeper concentration, and culminates in Samadhi, or absolute concentration. You are one with the object, there is no separation; energy blends with energy. Sounds wonderful, no?

But it did not work for me. Yogic concentration techniques use candle flames, flowers and religious icons such as the symbol Aum to concentrate on, but I found that concentrating using the sense of vision was extremely difficult to do. The natural phenomenon of blinking was a distraction as well. I recall lying on my bed and meditating on the ceiling fan above. After a few minutes, the blades of the fan disappeared, blending into the ceiling, and most of the motor too. It was quite a dizzying experience. Perhaps it was an optical illusion, but on the other hand perhaps it did reveal the truth of matter being just condensed energy, but I did realize that there was indeed something quite powerful in meditation. However, when the experience ended, there was no joy, no relief, no understanding, nothing worthwhile. That ended my foray into yogic meditation. I was 'back to the drawing board.'

At that point, I had been reading about other approaches to meditation: TM, Zen, Vipassana and such practices. Mindfulness of breathing without counting was recommended as a very valuable technique in meditation. So I sat and sat. While it was quite relaxing, and on one occasion I felt that I had been catapulted into a black void, it was still not quite a satisfactory experience. There was still a separation between the black void and me.

And then one day while sitting meditating, I decided to, well, just drop it, let go, quit trying, just- *be*. At which point an incredible, wonderful feeling of unbelievable lightness and airiness came over me. My body seemed to mostly vaporize, there was nothing but lightness. Added to it was a feeling of relief, immense relief; a feeling of a huge burden being lifted away. There were no waves of movement, just lightness and stillness. And there were no thoughts. I tried to cling to this remarkable feeling, and that was when it started fading away. It was not something that could be reached by any "active" processes of mind. Still, the feeling of relief was so immense that I laughed and laughed for a couple of minutes. I later realized that the thinking mind cannot meditate; it needs to be 'meditated upon' by the Inner/Greater Mind; that is true meditation. Subsequently, the experience helped inspire this poem:

The Seeker and the Sought

We see, but who is the seer?
We dance, but who is the dancer?
We think, but who is the thinker?

Greater, grander, and mightier,
Than the seer, thinker or dancer,
Is the Self, the Consciousness.
Still, silent, deep, yet suffused
With light, beauty and wonder.
Seek thou this light, this Source.

To seek, however, is not to find.
For It finds you, and you do not find It.
As you dwell in peace, at rest,
With the trust that It is not far--
Indeed a hairsbreadth away,
It overcomes, overpowers and enlightens.

With the power of a million candles
It burns away our ignorance, our ego,
Our craving, unrest and turmoil.
To infuse joy, restfulness, and peace.
With it comes wisdom, love, and understanding.

Centered, we are then, to dwell forever,
In That, the elusive goal,
The final frontier.

It was my first insight into the way of being. A way of total and absolute trust in our state as is, nothing more to be desired. This is probably the core of Zen without all its explanatory language including such words as Buddha Nature and so on. I had discovered a deep inner zone and dwelt there briefly. From there out to our superficial consciousness, everything is just an incredible rainbow display of energy, and power. From seeming stillness arises every action, movement, our thoughts, inspiration, everything. From there also arises desire, craving, wanting, reaching, needing, and hating, even violent anger. Good and evil, both arise from the same source. It is for us to encourage the manifestation of one more than the other.

Discovery of this deep inner peace, however, is only the beginning of the process of living the everyday Way of Being, to be discussed in the next chapter. I have summarized this approach to meditation by four "A's'":

Attitude
Awareness
Awakening
Ascension

Attitude

This is the knowledge base, the foundation, of this meditative practice; it is the finger that points to the moon. It is the theory that gives direction to the actual practice. The Buddha's teaching spoke of Samma Dhrishti, or right view, and Samma Sankalpa, or right resolve. These could be combined as right attitude. However, the attitude that I am writing about is more based on Hindu and Taoist teachings than those of the Buddha; indeed I have always believed that we can and should pick out gems of ideas from various religious traditions, and put them all together to create jewelry that suits us.

By attitude, I refer to a deep understanding or knowledge. In a way this understanding for me was the end result of meditation, but I am presenting it as the starting point to make it easier. This deep understanding is called jnäna in Hinduism. The word jnäna is similar in meaning to the word gnosis. It is Sanskrit in origin, and is not easy to pronounce! It is probably best learned by saying nyaana and then adding a J just before it. That changes the "n" to a somewhat nasal sound. Hindi speaking people take the easy way out and pronounce it gyäna, or gyaan for short. The massive body of literature that comprises jnäna includes the Üpanishads, part of the Vĕdas. Jnäna is a somewhat esoteric term, meaning "true knowledge." It is mystically derived knowledge rather than knowledge obtained by observing the visible world.

Pretend that your entire being is a sponge, lying soaking in water. Try to imagine the water penetrating every little nook and cranny of the sponge. Now equate this to the wondrous energy that surrounds us and pervades us. Unseen, unheard, unfelt. Yet this energy is there. Not for a microsecond is it not with us. As Krishna says in the Gita, "there is not a moment in which I do not act, for the worlds cannot be sustained without My action." Another analogy is that of you in a boat on water. Your mind and its energy is the rider, the body the boat. When the boat sinks, as the body eventually dies at the time of death, you are in the water. Now imagining that the water is this energy that surrounds us, what is there to fear? Whether living or dead, we are essentially floating in an ocean of energy. The name "God" is universally accepted, and could be used. God, Creator, Brahman, Ätman, Yahweh, Allah, Tao or Buddha-nature: call it what you will! There is but One. Guru Nanak, the founder of Sikhism, called It Sat-Näm, or the Name that is the Truth. Every molecule of our being is sustained by this wonderful Being. Our mind is a more dense form of this intelligence. I think of it as the ice cube in water. It is water, though it looks different. Our mind is something that many philosophers have argued about for a long time. To me mind is just crystallization of energy. Some translators of the Yoga-Sutras have used the word "mind-stuff" to translate the Sanskrit word Chittha. Just imagine you're preoccupied with something, and someone says something. Have you noticed that you can sort of "scan" your mind like looking over the surface of a lake, and "see" what the person said, still in the mind? This perhaps is why the writers used the word mind-stuff, referring to a rather gel like state where impressions of received or conceived thoughts stay for a brief spell before they sink deeper into it. If mind is the flower, the branch that it arises from is the greater consciousness. When the flower falls, another one takes it place. Thoughts in the mind are the same. As soon as a thought goes away, another takes its place. We never can, nor need be, free of thoughts, but there is a way to transcend them. Mind is the flowering of consciousness. Just as the flower appears different from the tree, yet they are integrally one; mind and thoughts are part of an ego process, which appears to have an identity of its own, but this so called identity is not an enduring, permanent thing. I keep thinking "I," or "me," but from second to second this "I" is changing!

The right attitude is this knowing and understanding. It gives the serenity and faith to relax and start meditation. The faith to know that with relaxation of mind, allowing it to let go of its usual habits, will come

203

the deep peace that is the essential nature of the greater consciousness beneath.

The Üpanishads taught us that "Tat Tvam Asi," or "That Thou Art." A literal translation would mean, "You are God." Such a statement would make many people bristle. Thinking of the flower and tree is an analogy to be remembered. Everything that we see is yet another of the varied manifestation of the Infinite Being. This is why I find the arguments of creation against evolution childish. All of creation is transformed energy. Yes, it took billions of years of our time, but Hindu sages thousands of years ago answered that when they stated that the many years of our life amount to just a moment in the life of Brahma the creator! So since "we are That," although in varied form, there never need be anxiety about our identity and essential nature. There need be no struggle to "achieve God." Wipe the dust off, and easily see the polished surface beneath! A Zen master once appropriately said, however, that our essential nature is empty of consistent form so there is no place for dust to settle! But the analogy that I refer to is the dust that our mind appears to be in comparison to the pristine consciousness that is our essential nature.

Within the center of each one of us, is a place of infinite peace, love and healing. This center is our connection to God; indeed it is a fragment of God. It is something we are seldom aware of. However, it can be discovered quite easily by meditation. Every great religious tradition speaks of this center. In the Christian tradition, it is spoken of by Jesus in the Gospel of Luke, 17-20: "The kingdom of God does not come with your careful observation, nor will people say, "Here it is," or "There it is," because the kingdom of God is within you." Similarly, in the Gospel of Thomas Logion 113, "His disciples said to him, "When is the kingdom going to come?" Jesus said, "It is not by being waited for that it is going to come. They are not going to say, 'here it is,' or 'there it is.' Rather, the kingdom of the Father is spread out over the earth, and people do not see it." In Logion 3 of the same Gospel of Thomas, Jesus says: "But the kingdom is inside of you. And it is outside of you. When you become acquainted with yourselves, then you will be recognized. And you will understand that it is you who are children of the living Father. But if you do not become acquainted with yourselves, then you are in poverty, and it is you who are the poverty." In the Hindu sacred scriptures called the Üpanishads this peaceful center is called the Ätman, (pronounced Aathmun) which is a fragment of God. But as we may well imagine, God is not fragmented!! If we imagine a pearl on a string of several pearls, the piece of string within each pearl could be claimed by the pearl as "belonging to it," but the truth is that the pearls can be slipped over any part of the string. Therefore, there is no fixed entity within us which could really and truly be defined as an Ätman. Which is why the Buddha, when asked about the Ätman, refused to describe it, but instead offered ways to let it radiate. In the Qur'an, Islam's holy book, God says that He is closer to us than our jugular vein. Dr. Wayne Dyer, author of several books and a recent Public Television program, calls it "Our Sacred Self," and the "Power of Intention."

Surrendering to the God within and around us is also the essential core of Islamic practice. In the best-selling book *Abraham—A Journey to the Heart of Three Faiths* author Bruce Feiler quotes Sheikh Feisal Abdul Rauf, the imam of the Al-Farah Mosque of New York City as saying: "The prime objective of religion is to know God, but the only way to do that is to discover God within our own consciousness. This happened to Abraham, and it can happen to us. And anybody that happens to will choose to live a life in accordance with God's practice."

To summarize, therefore, the attitude to take while practicing meditation is that our mind has a more turbulent surface, while just a little deeper is the stillness and peace of a wisdom mind. It ought not to be, and is not, an almighty effort to allow that inner peace to prevail. The right attitude is one of complete trust—in ourselves and in God.

Awareness

Once we achieve the serene understanding that I have described above, we can then proceed to meditate. Extending the boat analogy above, look at this way: while being content that our body and mind are like a boat floating in an ocean of water, not until we take a plunge into the cool refreshing waters will we experience the water firsthand! While meditation is usually done sitting, eventually every moment in life must be in a state of awareness. It is only then that we have achieved the goal. The goal sometimes becomes elusive, but it is always here and now. The goal is to be achieved now, maintained to the next moment, at which time the moment is born fresh, so the goal is to maintain the goal moment to moment.

Posture

When we sit to meditate, we must make sure that we are comfortable enough to be free from pain or discomfort, but yet with relaxed alertness. Sitting on a chair is perhaps the best for those unaccustomed to sitting on the floor. If we sit on the floor, we need to sit on a cushion 4-6 inches above the floor level, in order to help the knees rest comfortably on the ground. This will ease the strain on the lower back. Lying supine also works well and indeed is the Yogic meditation method called "Yoga Nidra," but it also makes it easy to fall asleep, which is not meditation. In many schools of meditation, pain in the knees, legs and feet is something to be put up with, to be ignored. I submit that every part of our anatomy is precious, and every cell and tissue of the back and lower extremities is an integral part of the activity of meditation. There is no need to struggle with pain; we must not struggle with pain. If discomfort begins in the legs, we need to stop and take a break; after all, with weeks and months of practice, our ability to sustain more prolonged sitting is greatly enhanced. There are students of Zen who have destroyed their knee cartilages by forcing themselves into prolonged periods of meditation, ignoring the pain. Relaxation is very important in maintaining good circulation in our low back and lower extremities while meditating. I have found that deep diaphragmatic breathing, along with deeper relaxation, helps the blood flow into the lower extremities. Also, micro movements of the toes and feet are helpful in keeping the circulation going. Roshi Shunryu Suzuki, in his book *Zen Mind, Beginner's Mind* writes: "Also to gain strength in your posture, press your diaphragm down towards your hara, or lower abdomen. This will help you maintain your physical and mental balance." Now, the only way to 'press the diaphragm downward' is with the in-breath. Deep diaphragmatic breathing associated with progressive relaxation of the body, allows vital energy (Chi in Chinese, Präna in Sanskrit) to flow from the lower abdomen where it is generated, into the parts of the body that need it, which in the case of sitting meditation, are the legs and feet. With practice, this process will become automatic and will not require frequent mental activity to maintain it.

Perhaps five to ten minute sessions to begin with, will slowly allow us to become familiar with sitting. Relaxed awareness of our posture will allow us to be adequately straight without strain. The lower back will have a gentle curve, with the convexity forwards. The head will rest equitably on the shoulders, ears in line with the rest of the body, thereby avoiding the head tilting forwards. The reader is referred to explore various books on Zen to learn more about proper posture. However, the Zen approach can be quite rigid and unyielding. Discomfort and pain have to be tolerated. It has been taught in Zen that with the onset of Kensho, or flashes of insight and enlightenment, pain and discomfort automatically go away, but I imagine that many practitioners will give up before this stage is reached.

Once comfortable, we then enter the meditative process. Having learned about the essential nature of our being, we will realize that rather than meditation being "something to do," it is a process of "not-doing." As I had mentioned in the poem, to seek is not to find. Mind cannot see Spirit. Spirit sees all. The idea, then, is to let mind go, relax, and allow Spirit to supersede mind. What we do is to relax and develop awareness. I have found that with every in-breath, if I let go and relax more and more, it very quickly helps the inner/greater mind to be more and more engaged. Developing awareness is best done by awareness in turn, of three areas:

Awareness of body
Awareness of breath
Awareness of mind.

Practicing awareness of body is to practice a "body scan." With practice, this does not take more than a few seconds, or a minute at most. Bringing attention to the neck, chest, upper extremities, and lower extremities, and developing awareness of the amount of tension in the muscles, being aware of feelings and sensations in them, and so on. We must not judge, or think about what we find, just observe. Actively using the mind to observe is also counter-productive, indeed the biggest hindrance to developing awareness. It is useful in the training process, but must be dropped. During training in mindfulness, we are taught: "lifting up a foot, I observe that I am lifting up a foot." The crucial thing is that the thinking mind must not keep actively repeating to itself, 'I am doing this, I am doing that.' We just do, and are aware from the deepest part of our consciousness that we are doing. It is so hard to explain, but an analogy would help. When we learn to ride a bicycle, we pay close attention to everything we are doing to balance and ride, but once learned, such close attention is a hindrance to the riding and enjoyment of the bicycle! Bringing awareness to the body is very valuable in maintaining proper posture, and awareness also ensures the right balance of effort and relaxation to minimize fatigue and discomfort. With every breath, a relaxed awareness of the entire body can (and should) be developed. This instantly helps correct sloth and poor posture. Body awareness is also a form of acknowledging that the body is not separate from the mind in this entire process of meditation. The body is not just a chunk of tissue that is in the way of the mind!

We then bring awareness to the breath. There are numerous books on mindfulness and Buddhist meditation practices that involve mindfulness of the breath. Some of them teach counting the breath from one to ten and then back to one, some teach to just observe the breath, and yet others advise that we observe the sensation of the breath as it flows through the nostrils. I believe that they are all valuable. The key is to *pay attention, be mindful of, the breath.* Zen practice consists of counting the breaths, focusing on the counting as a concentration method. Whether done with counting or simple awareness, the method is incredibly useful to help us keep attention to the moment. Joseph Goldstein writes in his book *One Dharma*, page 20: "Traditionally, mindfulness of breathing entailed the awareness of the breath moving in and out at the nostrils. A well-known discourse of the Buddha, the Änapänasati Sütta, explains the method in detail. Yet the Venerable Mahasi Sayadaw found that people sometimes became attached to the concentration and stillness produced by this method. He then taught another way of practicing, that is, watching the rise and fall of the abdomen as the breath goes in an out of the body. For many, this created a better balance in the mind, leading onward to deeper thoughts. It would seem that this was a harmless enough change. Yet when 'rise and fall' was first introduced, it created a firestorm of dispute among some of the traditional monks."

I have found that bringing awareness to the abdomen as it rises and falls with the breath, is a very intuitive way to practice awareness. Zen tends to use the lower abdomen as the focus of attention, and the Theravada tradition tends to focus on the nostrils as described above. I have often thought of the mechanics of pole-vaulting as an analogy to the meditative process. The focus of effort in pole-vaulting is to push down on the pole, but the goal is to fly over the bar. In the same way, the focus of effort in meditation is to either count or watch the breaths, but the goal is to limit the thinking mind so that the inner mind can expand wide open. It is possible to sense a wide openness like a great void, and see stray thoughts, the breathing process, and other sensations etc. as being just a small part of this great consciousness.

Awareness of the breath helps us be aware of whether our breaths are rapid and shallow, or whether they are slow and calm. I doubt that we will make any progress in meditation unless the respiratory rate is slow, and very calm. The respiratory rate is governed by the balance of the sympathetic and parasympathetic autonomic nervous system. Rapid and shallow breathing indicates a hyperactive sympathetic nervous system, and is not conducive to a good meditative state. It is essential that the parasympathetic nervous system be dominant, indicating a restful state. We can "hit the brakes" on the sympathetic nervous system by gently "forcing" a few slow, deep breaths, at a rate of about five seconds for an in-breath and the same duration for an out-breath. This may well become a strain to sustain, however. About 3 seconds for the in-breath and the same for an out-breath add up to six seconds a breath, which equals ten breaths a minute. This is an excellent start. It is quite proper to sit with a watch that has a second-hand, and actually measure our respiratory rate before starting meditation, and observe it for a little bit during meditation. As the inner/greater mind becomes more aware, the parasympathetic nervous system will become predominant, and the respiratory rate will diminish. Except for the first few gently forced slow breaths, the slowing down should come on its own, and if forcefully slowed down, will cause strain and be a distraction. Every now and then, however, it is useful to bring the watch out and see what our respiration rate is. I've been quite surprised by how shallow and fast my breathing has been even though I thought I was relaxed. My breathing rate has been an excellent source of bio-feedback for me. The subconscious mind, which governs the autonomic nervous system, has a "mind of its own!"

Once the breath is calm and settled, we then can bring our awareness to the mind itself. Despite practicing concentration on the breath, we get caught up in our thoughts and the mind wanders off thinking of this or that. It is possible, indeed most desirable, to be able to *watch the thoughts* as they drift by. We do not control them, concentrate them or focus the thoughts. The yoga sutras teach us to use concentration on an object as the means to Samadhi, and in description it sounds wonderfully effective: to blend our consciousness into the subject, so that the object and we become one. The problem is that seconds after we 'think' we are concentrating, the mind has wandered off somewhere. All we are clinging to is the resolve, the desire, to keep concentrating. So we think we still are. The key is that we *think we are concentrating.* It becomes a stream of thoughts, all of them focused on the "idea" that the mind is concentrated. There is a tremendous strain that develops in this state.

True concentration is attention that flows from the depth of our being. Pathanjali, the author of the Yoga Sutras, must have been a great Yogi, but his terse Yoga Sutras do not in any way explain the manner in which true Samadhi is attained. The truth is that unless we can consistently observe the thoughts, there is no way we can truly know whether we are concentrating or not!

The approach that I speak of can be looked at this way: Imagine you are above the clouds, and can see the clouds floating below. Farther below is the earth. In the same way we can observe the thoughts and the body. The space above the clouds is the pristine awareness. Dwelling here is to dwell in our true center. To dwell there is to be awakened. Once we develop the ability to observe thoughts as they fly past, it is even possible to eliminate thoughts as they arise. It is even possible to create thoughts and then eliminate them as they arise. These are more advanced techniques called Yoga Nidra, or Yogic sleep, taught by Swami Satyänanda Saraswathi, as part of the teachings of the Bihar School of Yoga.

I must reiterate that any effort at awareness or concentration must be accompanied by an equal effort at relaxation. This is what leads to a state of "not-doing" which is so essential for meditation.

Zen masters like to use the word concentration also. A proper understanding of the word is crucial. It means an unwavering attention to whatever task is at hand. Sometimes it comes easily, for instance when we are totally engrossed in something interesting. Even such an absorbed state may not quite be adequate for meditation. There are excellent books on meditation, which discuss the difficulties involved, and the difference between such absorption and meditation, etc. Some books that I have found useful are:

The Meditative Mind by Daniel Goleman; *The Meditator's Handbook* by Dr. David Fontana; *Teach Yourself Meditation* by James Hewitt (now out of print); *Breath Sweeps Mind: A First Guide to Meditation Practice* Essays, edited by Jean Smith; *Minding Mind—A Course in Basic Meditation* by Thomas Cleary; *Meditation for Dummies* by Stephan Bodian; *The Complete Idiot's Guide to Meditation* by Joan Budilovsky and Eve Adamson, and *Seven Masters, One Path* by John Selby.

John Selby writes in his superb book *Seven Masters, One Path:* "I was lucky enough to be at the right place and the right time to participate in seminal meditation research being conducted y Humphrey Osmond at the New Jersey Neuro-Psychiatric Research Institute....For our purposes here, the key insight drawn from this research is this: when a person is thinking actively (as documented with EEG equipment) and then focuses on one perceptual happening such as a sound, a tactile sensation, or an image, the brain waves remain basically the same and thoughts continue to flow through the mind. We can expand our mind's attention to include one perceptual input and still keep thinking actively without losing our concentration on our thoughts." Selby then goes on to describe a most exciting finding: "However, researchers have discovered that when the human mind focuses on two distinct sensory inputs at the same time, all thoughts almost immediately stop flowing through the mind. The thinking machine can be purposefully short-circuited simply by focusing on two distinct perceptual inputs at the same time...as soon as you focus on both the sensation of air flowing in and out of your nose and, at the same time, the movements in your chest and belly as you breathe, you've shifted into this expanded state where chronic thoughts tend to stop." So it appears that we need to combine the traditional Buddhist approach and that of Mahasi Sayadaw to obtain the best results! Selby recommends starting with two inputs at the same time, and then proceeding to using three inputs.

An even more fulfilling practice during meditation, in my view, goes even beyond the awareness of two, or even three sensory inputs, using body, breath, and mind. It consists of a greater awareness of everything happening at the moment, as well as a process of melting, deep relaxing, letting go of "trying to be aware," and to just - be. Zen calls it *Shikantäza.* It involves being 'mindful of everything,' even though there are Zen teachers who insist that Zen is not the same as mindfulness. The inner/greater mind then prevails, and is then in command. The mind needs to have complete trust in its mentor within. To return to the section on attitude, we need have great faith that there is a level of consciousness that knows what we need, what really ought to be done. Also, as described above, progressive development of deeper and deeper relaxation with each breath, as well as a very slow calm breathing pattern, is every essential to help develop total awareness. The inner consciousness is an ocean of knowing, understanding, and universal consciousness. It is really part of God's consciousness, or at least the part of God's consciousness that is within us. It is called Atman in

Hinduism. The Buddha declined to comment on Atman, and Buddhism has replaced the word Atman with 'Buddha Nature'; it is such irony that one term has simply replaced another, and Buddhism revels in the concept of "anätman,' or "no-soul." The greatest barrier between mind and God is—mind. The only way to truly succeed in meditation is first of all, quit trying with mind, and secondly, to maintain an attitude of deep relaxation, trust, and dissolution of repeated attempts of mind to take over. Very often at this time we get insight and understanding of various problems that we are dealing with, and then we are likely to get caught up in reverie or daydream again, get caught up in thought stream again. 'Just sitting' means to observe everything that goes on in the process of meditation. Watching that little numbness in the foot as it arises, watching the mind daydream, watching the breath speed up and then slow down, this awareness transcends it all. There is really nothing wrong with the mind's workings as such; after all, living life is our primary purpose. The thing to do is to acknowledge this insight with gratitude and a smile, and gently return to the process of letting go. It then becomes a process of just being with what happens. John Selby reminds us that when we are in a state of rapture looking at a beautiful sunset, we don't keep shifting our focus from one point of the sunset scene and then another, and so on; we just take in the entire scene and become one with it.

This is the meditative process which must accompany any physical yoga practice as well, whether it is Indian style hatha yoga or Chinese Chi Kung or Tai Chi. In my experience, Chinese masters have been better at teaching the art of deep relaxation than Indian teachers. One insight that came to me, for instance, is this: the day we quit trying to make great mental and physical effort to get into a pose, is the day we start achieving success in that pose. The reason being, the inner/greater consciousness can govern or control our yoga far better than the thinking mind can. In Kripalu Yoga this is taught to advanced practitioners as 'meditation in motion', but I feel that this ought to be the very foundation, the fundamental, of practice, and not an "advanced" practice: it is not likely we'll get "advanced" unless we learn the method! Wong Kiew Kit, a great author and teacher of Chi Kung, believes that unless we attain a one-pointed state, we will not have mastery over the yogic arts. It is very difficult to explain a "one-pointed" state; and indeed, in my experience, it can't be described as a "point" at all: it is a no-point state, really. Neither the mind nor body achieves a point focus; it is more an extremely wide "focus," where the thinking mind has disappeared, and there is only just consciousness and the body working in absolute harmony.

The meditative process is that of opening the floodgates and allowing this inner wisdom and consciousness to pour forth. All the mind can effectively do is to let go trying, to let go thinking itself into a false state of mesmerizing itself. Even the process of mantra meditation must take this attitude. The mind chanting the mantra, on analyzing deeper, is simply chanting a name of God taught by a guru. Our inner/greater mind makes for the meditative achievement, the thinking mind and mantra does not. Realizing this fact and putting it into practice, determines whether mantra meditation succeeds or not. The more the mind clamors over "persistence of its chanting," the less it is really meditating. We must use the mantra to help get the mind in order, in the right direction, and then make the mantra less intense or frequent. I can just imagine God a.k.a. our Inner/Greater consciousness, saying, OK, OK, I heard you the first time!

Some authors suggest visualization techniques. In his wonderful book *The Instinct to Heal* Dr. David Servan-Schreiber writes: "Eastern meditation practices would suggest concentrating on the breath as long as possible and keeping the mind empty. But to maximize cardiac coherence, it works better to actually center your attention on the region of your heart 10 to 15 seconds after your breathing stabilizes." It is very interesting to note that Sufis use a heart-centered concentration method, the details of which are to be found in a book called *Living from the Heart : Heart Rhythm Meditation for Energy, Clarity, Peace, Joy, and Inner Power* by Puran Bair. Dr. Servan-Schreiber goes on to describe what he calls the second stage, visualize the air nourishing the body, especially the heart. He describes a third stage of becoming aware of the sensation of warmth or expansiveness that is developing in the chest. He describes a heart-centered meditation, and encourages feelings of gratitude and love, and also to visualize peaceful and happy memories. He quotes a study in the *American College of Cardiology* by Dr. Watkins of the HeartMath Institute. Those authors demonstrated that the act of recollecting a positive emotion or imagining a pleasurable scene rapidly provokes a transition of heart rate variability toward a phase of coherence. The HeartMath Institute offers a software program called *Freeze Framer,* which uses a finger sensor to detect the rhythms of the heart, and helps generate bio-feedback to settle the heart rhythm into a state of what they call coherence, where the variability in heart rate is minimized. As instruction in the program, the authors write: "Many people have found that when they experience positive feelings like care, love or appreciation while breathing through the heart area, they feel regenerated, both physically and emotionally. This provides a far wider range of benefits than simple breathing techniques alone can create." They recommend recollecting a pleasant experience and allow that to help develop coherence. The program does start with an emphasis on lengthening the breath to about 5-6 counts, which in itself helps develop coherence. Though, taking 5-6 counts for an in-breath might be a strained effort; it seems best to observe the breath, and gently allow it to slow down, to about 10 breaths per minute. Following that, the focus is on the heart, visualizing the breath as flowing in and out of the heart area, after which the emphasis is on "heart feeling," which involves the recollection of pleasant memories, as well as the reinforcement of the emotions of care, appreciation and compassion. I cannot help but recall that this approach is an important part of the Buddhist tradition called *Mītra Bhavana* or "the arising of friendliness." Further information can be obtained at www.heartmath.com. Perhaps in future they will investigate the effects of various meditation techniques on cardiac coherence. The program does not mention diaphragmatic breathing, but I found it quite easy to do diaphragmatic breathing and imagine the air bathing and surrounding the heart. The program has been proven effective in thousands of people, and is to be considered yet another valuable addition to the list of effective meditation methods. I have explored the program to some extent, and have found myself achieving excellent cardiac coherence by changing the breathing pattern to a slower and deeper pattern, along with relaxed awareness and letting go of body tension. I plan to work with it further and see whether the "heart feeling" methods described above have an impact beyond the awareness method in which I feel most at home; awareness meditation releases the wisdom mind within us, and the radiance of care, concern and compassion are an inherent part of it. So perhaps there ought not to be much of a difference. Biofeedback methods and instruments may well be an important part of the future of meditation. Dr. Servan-Schreiber mentions a study by Dr. Frederick Luskin, Ph.D. in his book *Instinct to Heal* comparing patients with severe heart failure who took the cardiac coherence course and those who did not. The control group worsened, but the patients who underwent heart coherence improved their symptoms, as well as lowered their stress and anxiety level. He also writes that the HeartMath institute has tested thousands of people, among them staff at Motorola, and helped them counteract stress from a physical, emotional and social standpoint.

In London, 6000 executives from major corporations followed a training course in cardiac coherence. With all these participants, they had a significant drop in blood pressure, and significant improvement in DHEA (the "youth" hormone) levels, and a significant decrease in cortisol levels (excessive levels of which cause high blood pressure, skin aging, loss of memory and concentration).

Awakening

Roger Housden, writing in his book *Sacred Journeys in a Modern World,* describes a most wonderful moment of awakening that he experienced:

"Soon after that my last day in Benäres dawned. I had already decided to spend the day walking the path of the Buddha to Sarnath, where he gave his first sermon. Within an hour or two I was leaving the city behind and making my way up and down paths that wound their way through woodland from one small village to the next. I had been aware on waking that a heaviness, by now quite familiar, was weighing on my chest. Even here, in this magical landscape, following the very paths that the Buddha had taken, I was heavy with the absence of my beloved. This time, I let myself feel without restriction the burden I was carrying. And suddenly it struck me: I was actually choosing to carry this weight around me, like some kind of identity—the suffering lover. It was like walking round all day with a heavy stone in my rib cage, though it had become so familiar I had come to see it as normal.

In a flash I saw how I was doing this to myself, like some martyr. In that instant, all the leaves of the trees began to glisten with light; the air felt electric, the ground full of vibration. I saw beyond any doubt that the true goddess, the one true Beloved, was everywhere, in every living particle. The weight slipped from my body. I was filled with light, the leaves shot out colors like crystal prisms, and I was filled with the most unutterable joy. I opened my arms out wide and began turning, turning, like some made dervish drunk with life. This dance was my own true dance, and I was dancing it now."

An awakening consists of flashes of insight into the ultimate state of being. The most difficult problem of all is that there have been numerous people who have achieved super normal states of consciousness, and their descriptions are dramatically different from each other. One actually "sees" Jesus, another "sees" Krishna, others see demons or angels, others see white light, and others see a black void. Zen masters dismiss these as Makyo, or illusion. Mind is vast, like space. While traveling in space, one could see asteroids, or comets; others could see planets and stars. Yet, as the story of the blind men and the elephant teaches, each one of us tries to state that what we have seen is what the rest of us ought to see. Therefore, as the Taoist sage Lao-Tzu stated, the one who knows does not speak. A well-known Buddhist teaching is that if you see the Buddha during meditation, kill him!

What counts is that we allow this greater awareness to direct our lives. Let the reaction of the rest of humanity be the judge as to whether it has been worthwhile or not. Are we more centered, more full of equanimity, free of anger and hate, and radiating friendliness in our interactions? There have been yogis who have radiated light of various colors while deep in meditative practice, yet later on have been as egotistical as most of us. Therefore, achieving temporary states of super normal consciousness never was, and never will be, an end point. The most essential thing is to carry this state into everyday life, every waking minute of it. Perhaps even into sleep; it can, and perhaps should be done. Meditation performed just before sleep is highly valuable to help settle our minds.

It is extremely easy to switch back and forth, from a mind guided by its inner power, to a mind that operates on a more superficial level of its ego. Such a change is what causes a 'fall from Grace.' A Guru provides advice when s/he just returns from being in a higher state of consciousness, and later on in 'normal mind,' s/he behaves differently! In other words, do not create a rule unless you have practicing following that rule over a lifetime and know from the depth of your being that the rule is worthwhile following!

There are numerous terms for this transcended state, including Kensho, Satori, Samadhi, Kaivalya, Enlightenment, and others such as 'Christ Consciousness' or 'Krishna Consciousness'. It is characterized by an incredible feeling of lightness and the sensation of a huge burden being lifted. It is a state of deep understanding. Some state that objects seem to have a shimmer around them when observed from this state, as described in detail by Roger Housden above. Perhaps it is partly illusion, as a Zen master stated:

216

In the beginning, mountains are mountains
In the middle, mountains are no longer mountains
In the end, mountains are still mountains.

By 'in the middle' he referred to as the transitional state where
meditation leads to a state where the mind is starting to dissect the nature
of things for itself, and a variety of illusory effects could be seen. But
after obtaining understanding, we realize what an Üpanishad teaches:
'Pürnam ĕvävashishyathĕ,' which means 'perfection is all that remains'.
Whether it is a tiger that we see tearing a deer apart, or a fanatic
destroying others to bits with his bomb, the hard fact is that this is the
way things are. It is far from perfect to the mind's eye, but that is only
the mind's eye. To transcend the mind's eye is to see things with a greater
vision. And then we see things differently.

Prevention Magazine, April 2003, published an article by Dr. Herbert
Benson, MD, that is an excerpt from his book *The Breakout Principle:
Activate the Natural Trigger that Maximizes Creativity, Productivity,
and Personal Well-Being.* He writes about a lady called Rachel who had
a chronic weight problem and was unsuccessful with several diets. She
blamed it on lack of self-discipline, but Dr. Benson felt that she needed
to break the negative mental patterns that had been holding her back.
He felt she needed to have what he calls a "breakout: "something that
severs prior mental patterns and opens an inner door to a host of personal
benefits, including a sharper mind, enhanced creativity, increased job
productivity, maximal athletic performance, spiritual development, and
better health." This is referred to as Kensho in the Zen tradition.

Dr. Benson feels that an activity that triggers nitric oxide to flood
the brain is what is required to overcome negative mental patterns.
However, if indeed nitric oxide induces the actual effect, surely there is
some mental or spiritual process which helps produce the nitric oxide.
Anyhow, such an activity is what triggers the "breakout," and could be
one of different kinds: for instance a faith related activity, music, liturgy,
etc. Or it could involve repetitive activity, such as walking and jogging.
Repeating a phrase, which is the same as mantra meditation, could
induce the state. Activities which combines different ones, often work
very well, such as chanting a phrase while walking.

These activities trigger what Dr. Benson calls "peak experiences,"
characterized by "great insight, freedom from fear and anxiety, and a

sense of being unified with an infinite or eternal dimension of reality."
He further writes: "These peak experiences transform our lives,
overcoming mental roadblocks. They provide an infusion of personal
energy that will increase stamina, endurance, and strength. You may
rejuvenate your body by overcoming old patterns that have harmed
your health. You may even experience a deeper, more satisfying
spirituality." However, as Dr. Benson describes in his book, the term
'peak experiences' was actually used earlier by American psychologist
and philosopher Abraham H. Maslow (1908-1970) who, according to the
web site www.themystica.com "coined this term to describe nonreligious
quasi-mystical and mystical experiences. Peak experiences are sudden
feelings of intense happiness and well-being, and possibly the awareness
of "ultimate truth" and the unity of all things. Accompanying these
experiences is a heightened sense of control over the body and emotions,
and a wider sense of awareness, as though one was standing upon a
mountaintop. The experience fills the individual with wonder and awe.
He feels at one with the world and is pleased with it; he or she has seen
the ultimate truth or the essence of all things."

The "Awakening" that I describe in this section is very much the same
as the "peak experiences" described by Dr. Benson. It is very much the
same experience called Kensho in Zen, Samadhi in Yoga, and being 'One
with Christ' in Christianity, and so on. They are flashes of insight and
enlightenment, and are the end result of a combined physical, mental,
and spiritual effort. They transform our lives. They transform us into
individuals who live in an entirely new dimension, with significantly
less stress and significantly more joy. *It is the greatest experience
leading to Self-Healing.* Such an experience, in my view, is when the
outer 'busybody' consciousness is made quiet and the Inner/Greater
Consciousness prevails. Actually, the word "awakening" of this greater
Consciousness is a misnomer, because the Greater consciousness within
us is always awake, always aware. It is our thinking minds that are
oblivious of this awareness.

Episodes of awakening are wonderful, but bringing these peak
experiences into our everyday life is the greatest challenge. As the
most delightful title of the book *After the Ecstasy, the Laundry* by Jack
Kornfield suggests, if we keep craving the ecstatic experiences during
meditation, we might lose track of the reality of life. So this brings us
to the process of integrating meditative awareness with everyday life, a
process I call *ascension.*

Ascension

By this I mean a state of living in a higher state of awareness, which
is the goal of meditation. Perhaps we could call it "transcendental
awareness" for lack of another term. Whatever was learned by flashes of
insight during meditation is to be carried into every moment of our lives.
In other words, it must become *A Way of Being.*

Not until we attain a state of transcendental awareness, can we
understand the concept of 'Not doing in the midst of doing' as taught in
the Tao Te Ching, and that of 'Freedom from attachment to the fruits of
action' as taught in the Bhagavad-Gîta. These two concepts are, in my
view, the same concept, expressed in different words; quite difficult to
understand by the thinking mind, and yet very easy to understand by
transcendental awareness. The 'fruits of action' derives from the Sanskrit
term 'karma-phala;' phala means fruit. The term could also be translated
as either 'fruit of action,' or 'action or its fruit.' The latter translation
would be in keeping with what is taught in the Tao: the sage mind
watches it all, the wanting, the chasing, the finding, the clinging, and
so on. The greater mind is not disturbed by the infinite goings-on of the
ordinary mind. A master charioteer is now controlling the chariot.

This state of awareness leads us to easily understand why Hindu mystics
refer to life as "the play of God." Just as children play just for the sake
of play, we then learn to live "just living," moment to moment. This does
not mean that we abandon plans, hopes and fear, but we learn to live in
a state of awareness that transcends such limited thought. We spend a
year or two of life striving to attain a financial end, such as the purchase
of a particular fine object. Only to find later that it was just not worth
the effort. A state of awareness would have made us realize the possible
consequences, and learn to accept such a consequence with a smile.

In the gospel of St. Matthew 5:3 it is taught: "Blessed are the poor in
spirit; for theirs is the kingdom of heaven." 'Poor in spirit' refers to a
lack of clinging to things to the point that our lives revolve around them.
Further, the gospel asks: "Which of you by taking thought can add one
cubit unto his stature?" which means that satisfaction of craving leads
to no lasting satisfaction. The gospel continues in 6:31: "Therefore do
not think 'what shall we eat?' Or, 'what shall we drink?' Or, 'how shall
we be clothed?' For your heavenly father knows that you need all these

things. But first seek the kingdom of God, and God's righteousness, and all these things will be given to you. Therefore do not think about tomorrow, which will take care of itself. There is more than enough evil for us to deal with today." The 'evil', as I see it, is the clinging, to things, places and people. We need to let greater awareness prevail; we need to "let go to God," as Eric Butterworth put it.

The next chapter, "A Way of Being" explores the state of "ascension" in much more detail.

CHAPTER ELEVEN:
A WAY OF BEING

In some of the previous chapters we explored the grandeur of the Üpanishads and the Tao, and considered how the teachings of the Buddha can be used as the most effective tool in unearthing these treasures on a personal voyage of rediscovery. It is a voyage, indeed. It is therefore not surprising that the Buddha made frequent references to the word raft, from which the Mahäyäna, or greater raft, arises. The chapter "A Way Inward" explored a simple method of meditation that is not only easy, but extremely reliable. But having attained one or more flashes of insight into our true nature, the greatest challenge is to incorporate this understanding into a "Way of Being"—a way of living.

We must never forget one of the most important teachings of the Buddha, which is that once we reach the shore, we need to leave the raft behind and not carry it on our back! And once enlightened, we are no longer Buddhists; once we "know Christ" in the most profound sense, we are no longer limited Christians. Hindus who have explored the mystical revelations of their ancestors can easily achieve this deep peace, but much of the present generation educated in the secular modern world are unaware of the mystical teachings of Hinduism and are unaware of the real meaning of the profound truths taught in the Üpanishads and the Bhagavad-Gita.

The raft that we have brought ashore has brought with it the teachings of ancient sages, including the authors of the Üpanishads, Lao Tzu, the Buddha, Jesus, Mohammed, Guru Nanak, Kabir, Ramana Maharshi, and countless others. We are, or at least ought to be, on that raft!

But the shore has been reached. It is time to humbly bow to all these seers and acknowledge their wisdom and knowledge. It is time, also, to take leave of them and set out on our journey. The destination is the same for every being that has been born or yet to be born. The problem is that we have created false destinations. The Buddha had to deal with brähmins who were fixated with reaching the "abode of Brahma;" Jesus of the Gospels tried to point the right way to the priests of the temple, but now Christians have made Jesus the destination. When Jesus said in the gospel of John that "I and the Father are one," he was using inner knowledge similar to that taught in the Üpanishads, and we can see that each one of us is already floating in an ocean which is the "destination." Dissolve your ego, and find that "Tat Tvam Asi—Thou Art That."

A wise Zen master stated that heaven and earth are just a tenth of an inch apart. So close, yet so far! The distance of separation is created by our minds.

Zen has inspired this book, but if what I say is boxed into another version of Zen it negates or limits everything that I say, and gives it a label. So call it what you will...an off-label Zen if you like! Of the various books on Zen, I have found many which are excellent. They include *On Zen Practice—Body, Breath and Mind* by Hakuyu Taizan Maezumi; *An Introduction to Zen Buddhism* by D.T.Suzuki; *Minding Mind—A Course in Basic Meditation* by Thomas Cleary; *The Elements of Zen* by David Scott and Tony Doubleday, and *Zen Mind, Beginner's Mind* by Shunryu Suzuki, among others.

Everything that I have said could also be categorized as a synthesis of the various forms of Yoga. Let us not forget the true meaning of Yoga, and that is the union of our limited beings with that of the Unlimited Infinite Being. Yoga would state Christianity to be a form of bhakti, or devotion to Christ, a god-form. It would also state Islam to be a form of devotion consisting of submission to the god Allah.

All the knowledge and understanding that we have discussed so far are easily summarized as the Yoga of knowledge, or Jnäna Yoga. Jnäna and Gnosis not only have the same root, but their goal is the same: to contemplate the approach to immortality.

Karma Yoga is the path of action. All the teachings of the Buddha could easily be embraced into this path. Samma Dhrishti, or View, is the development of right attitude. Samma Sankalpa is right resolve: the determination to do the right thing in keeping with the Dharma. There is no separate Buddha Dharma or Hindu Dharma, by the way; there is only one Way, one Dharma. Samma Vächa is to be gentle and proper in speech. Samma Kammanta is the path of right action, Karma Yoga. Samma Ajiva, or proper livelihood, refers to livelihood that takes the greater good into consideration. Samma Väyäma is right effort. Sila, or proper conduct, is an essential part of Karma Yoga.

Anyone who has truly understood the various paths of yoga would unhesitatingly admit that the different branches are artificially created, but in fact they are but facets of the same uniform path. This then is the Way of Being, where we aim to obtain a synthesis that works.

So here I am, a partly solidified mass of energy surrounded by countless living things, also comprised of the same essential nature. Just the knowledge of that unity gives a feeling of rest and ease, and that is Jnäna, Gnosis. What do I do with that knowledge, which became clear in meditation? How does this bundle of energy behave in order to do the right thing?

The answer is mindfulness. There are numerous books on mindfulness. If you have found your peace through them, then there is no more to be gained from this book! But if you have read them and not quite grasped what they say, then what I write may be of use. The problem with explaining mindfulness is that the authors look around to see what else the great Buddha taught, in order to try and explain the concept. But that does not quite work.

I once asked a Buddhist Monk what mindfulness is, and I got the usual answer: "when you eat, eat; when you walk, walk." I came away disappointed. Anyhow, I tried to practice that. Starting with mindfully chewing a raisin, as taught by Jon Kabat-Zinn, I tried practicing other similar mindfulness exercises. But something was not quite right. I could not see that getting me anywhere.

It then dawned on me that I was being mindful with a closed mind; I was mistaking practice methods for the end-result. I was using a limited egotistical thinking mind to "practice mindfulness," causing mind constraint. A better approach was needed. So I took the lesson that I had learned during meditation with me during activity. The chapter "A way inward" explores this. The idea was to open up the mind, wide open, transparent, so that a deeply relaxed attitude was brought into the practice. I was doing "thinking mindfulness" and not true mindfulness. I can just see a mindfulness master saying, "Aha, I could have told you so!" To which my reply would be, well then why didn't you say so!!! Ven. Henepola Gunaratna's delightful book, *Mindfulness in plain English*, is one I recommend highly. Buddhism has always taught that there are three primordial ways of error: attachment, aversion and delusion. The first two are easy enough to figure out, but delusion, that

223

was another matter altogether. While reading the book, I thought: "How could you say I go through life deluded?" Gunaratna helped clear my mind: by delusion is meant the fact that we are constantly looking out with tinted glasses. The tinting is conditioning. Get rid of the tinting and we finally "see things as they are," as they say. But my response was, unless I know by conditioning that a snake is deadly, I may not have been around to write all this! So how can we speak disparagingly about our conditioning? So what does 'seeing things as they really are' really mean?

This is where 'getting the mind wide open' comes in. Erich Schiffman, author of a superb book *Yoga—The Spirit And Practice Of Moving Into Stillness*, teaches the analogy of a helicopter patrol that can see a traffic block ahead that you cannot. If we are operating out of our helicopter mind, then we can easily see that our vision is tinted. This vision is the pristine vision, one that can see and understand the tinting and yet act accordingly. This vision arises from the deeper layers of consciousness, which in the Indian tradition is called the Vijnanamaya kosha, or layer of intelligence. It is the art of bringing the wide-open mind developed in awareness meditation, into action every minute of our lives. Even the analogy of using wide angled lenses falls into disuse at this point. There is no analogy; there is just the matter of discovering it.

This therefore is it—the process of becoming a transparent wide-open human being in all actions. Such a being sees anger developing and instantly channels it into effective use. Such a being chooses gentle speech over offensive speech. Such a being eats, works, loves, and sleeps like everyone else. Yet, just a minute's interaction with such a person would cause an impression on us that would last forever. To know such a one, is to love such a one. A Buddha, a Jesus, and countless other wonderful beings, have made sufficient impact on others to have survived in our minds for thousands of years. It is our duty to evolve in this way. Good heavens, I thought to myself one day, the Buddha lived twenty five hundred years ago, and I have evolved to only a fraction of that level of achievement and enlightenment! The problem is humanity's response to such beings. They were signposts pointing the way, and we took the signpost down, took it home, adored it and adorned it, and worshipped it. We never did see in which direction the signpost pointed, and neither did we head out on the path it pointed to!

If mindfulness is hard enough to explain, trying to explain this business of being a wide-open being is probably even harder!! But the results become clear to the practitioner. Even cutting vegetables and fruits becomes more serene, methodical, proper, and orderly. There are students who became enlightened just by seeing their Zen master drinking tea! One can never open a door except in the direction it was designed to open; no matter how hard one tries, it will not open in the opposite direction. So it is with mindfulness. However hard your mind tries to "concentrate" on being mindful, if your understanding of mindfulness is incorrect, even years of effort will fail. Which is perhaps why some of us have an element of mindfulness that we are born with, some do not. I do believe that there is a large element of joy inherent in each of us. This, I believe, is the reason the Buddha's message of suffering was not well received by many. Suffering happens in ignorance, but there is plenty of sunshine: it is not all clouds. But admittedly there is an enormous amount of haze!

Hatha Yoga, when practiced with a closed mind, becomes indeed a Hah!ta yoga of forceful practice. I cannot help but feel that the Buddha was exposed to ascetics practicing in the forest, who were somewhat deluded in the kind of ascetic practice they were doing. Someone doing Hatha yoga in the right manner radiates a presence of a special kind. There is no force exhibited, just tremendous power and energy. It is an art, something that must be developed, just as the right understanding of mindfulness must be developed. Improper hatha yoga leads to weakness, disease, even death. Improper mindfulness could accentuate delusion and cause an obsessive disorder of some kind, fatigue and loss of ability to properly do what we are supposed to do.

Wide-open mindfulness leads to an incredible ease with which life can be lived. The Buddha was truly not telling a story when he talked of leaving the raft behind. All those Sutras are delightful or a burden to go through depending on one's frame of mind, but it is such a relief to leave them behind. Even the Gita said it so delightfully: 'To one who is enlightened and has understood the Infinite Brahman, all the Vĕdas (sacred scriptures) are just about as useful as a well when everywhere there is a flood!' And practice makes perfect. Discovery alone is inadequate. Learning to practice this awareness at all times is important. It is an effort at first, but should become automatic as time goes by.

The result leads to an exalted state where pleasure and pain are the same, wealth or poverty, hot or cold; in other words, there are no extremes to either cling to or have an aversion to. Clearing of delusion we talked about above. Again, this last one, delusion, is the most difficult. I can imagine the greater mind trying to tell the lesser mind, "I know what you know, but what you know is something I know that you do not quite know…" or something to that effect!!!

Anger

One of the most difficult things for us humans to do is to control our anger. Anger is a very deep-seated emotional expression; in some people it is like a coiled snake ready to spring and strike at any time. There are many books dealing with anger, but the exact mechanisms of anger are probably a mystery. Like fear, it is a primordial reaction. Buddhism speaks of the two extreme states of mind, attachment and aversion. I have often wondered whether anger belongs in one extreme or the other, or whether it has its roots in either. Seems to me that extreme aversion leads to hate; perhaps a frustrated state of attachment causes anger. In other words, anger is a response reaction to either extreme, or indeed an inappropriate response to even minimal attachment or aversion. Animals reveal rage as well. Anger is an incendiary reaction to situations which we find wrong, unsatisfactory, or unacceptable. It can manifest either in a slow burn or in an explosive reaction. Just as a snake hisses when challenged, or animals bare their teeth, anger was likely programmed into us as a defensive reaction.

Anger was well known among the mythical gods and ancient rishis of India, and mythical stories speak of rishis getting so angry that they burn people in front of them down to ashes. Interestingly, the Yoga Sutras do not say anything about anger, though they go into great detail about other desirable states of mind such as truthfulness, non-covetousness, and so on. I have often wondered whether that was an intentional omission rather than an accidental one. Perhaps the sage who wrote the Yoga Sutras felt that an appropriate reaction of anger was an integral part of human behavior. Ahimsa, or non-violence, is one of the five virtues mentioned in the Yoga Sutras, but Akhrōdha, or avoidance of anger, is not; it is mentioned, however, in the Bhagavad-Gîta. The Buddha, however, spoke strongly against anger. It is a destructive emotion unless controlled.

Like pouring water on the fuse of a stick of dynamite, anger can only be combated at its very root. A state of mindfulness can see anger arise, in an extremely early stage, and let it dissipate. Physician Andrew Weil states in his book *Spontaneous Healing* that he has seen a person develop improvement in cell counts and state of health after an outburst of anger. Perhaps the great outpouring of hormones and chemicals which occur when we are angry, and cause damage in the long run, just happen to be beneficial at times. There are exceptions to the rule that people who get frequently angry develop heart disease; they are, however, exceptions. Anger is quite likely to be an important cause of heart disease and cancer; hostility is equally important. It used to be thought that a Type-A person is always hurried and rushed, but it is more likely that the true pathogen, or cause of disease, is hostility. It arises from a deep down sense of insecurity and distrust. Once someone asked a prisoner as to why he had shot someone, and the answer was that he had "looked at me wrong." What a pitiful excuse to shoot a man dead, you think, but that is the way it is: that is the way anger destroys. Such people have extremely short fuses.

The inner/greater mind is calm and serene. It constantly guides us in our reactions to our environment, to others. Regular practice of mindfulness can be so soothing to the mind that indeed, the fuse is extinguished and stays extinguished. Or in any case, even if the fuse ignites, an initial anger reaction develops, and we can channel it in such a way that we can have full control over it. There are many times I've seen anger arise within me, and knowing full well knowing that I'm on top of it, allowed it to manifest, in order to express upset over something that was wrong. It is kind of like using nuclear power for generating electricity rather than in a bomb. Let's face it…anger does get a response. I've seen on many occasions that while uncontrolled anger or rage is destructive, rightful wrath can accomplish things. The line between the two is thinly drawn, however; the practitioner must beware!

Forgiveness

Forgiveness is a very important part of a way of being, so it would be appropriate to discuss it here. It has become fashionable lately for people to "forgive" others who have committed even the most heinous of crimes, such as high school kids who have murdered several of their classmates. On many occasions such students show no remorse whatsoever, some arrive in jail, behave like frightened children, some demand pizza, and yet others break down afterwards.

The victims and their families are always totally devastated by these attacks, and the rest of us have no right whatsoever to take on the role of God and declare that the criminals are "forgiven." Every country has its own system of justice, systems that have evolved over hundreds of years with methods of punishment for crimes. Such punishment is a major deterrent. If forgiveness is automatic, we would not have to bother with having police, or a criminal court system. Crime would be rampant. Having devised a system of punishment, randomly abandoning it in a misguided sense of 'forgiveness fervor' is quite senseless.

There was an occasion when my wife and I were discussing an incident of an acquaintance hurting someone's feeling by making offensive statements. My wife stunned me by asking "what is there to forgive?" Ordinarily I would have wondered what on earth she meant, but on that day I was perfectly in tune with her line of thought. A flash of insight came to me, and I knew exactly what she meant. It was as if a Zen student had a flash of understanding from a Zen Koan. Koans are questions, seemingly strange questions, and coming up with an answer has led to a state of enlightenment for many students. In this case, it was to do with realizing that each one of us reacts differently to a given insult or provocation. "Forgiveness" simply involves washing away that feeling of aversion or anger over what happened. The death of an evil person, who tortured and raped several women, is not anywhere as likely to evoke sympathy in the minds of most people as the death of a minister. Yet both are human beings. Our perception of the situation determines our attitude toward the crime. It is mind that "judged" an action to have been wrong, and it is essential that we meditatively understand that it is the mind that so judges. The mind can just "unjudge" the situation or action, and that becomes "forgiveness."

The Buddha not only strongly favored forgiveness but taught it as a firm requirement of leading the life of a Buddha. In the *Dhammapäda*, (the path of Dharma) he taught:

"Look how he abused me and beat me,
How he threw me down and robbed me,
Live with such thoughts and you live in hate.
Abandon such thoughts, and live in love.

In this world, hate never yet dispelled hate.
This is the law, ancient and eternal.
You too shall pass away,
Knowing this, how can you quarrel?"

Christianity has taught that it was the victim of the crime who has the privilege of forgiving the perpetrator, and not someone else. Since the legal system must carry out its duty, we must try and understand what forgiveness means and its mechanics. Suppose someone mugged me. Ramana Maharshi taught us to think "who is the 'I' that is speaking." Using Ramana Mahärshi's system of teaching, I must question "who is the 'me' that was mugged?" My body was beaten, certainly, and my mind reacted with upset, anger, and a deep sense of being 'wronged.' In meditation we discover a deeper, wider consciousness that can easily "watch the mind so reacting, and watch the body that was injured." This greater consciousness was neither hurt nor offended. As the Gita teaches, this greater consciousness 'slays not, nor is it slain.' The perpetrator is ignorant of his greater consciousness, and his deluded mind, driven by craving, perpetrates the crime. Understanding this state of affairs is the beginning of the process of forgiveness.

Forgiveness must, of essence, comprise two parts. For the first part, the person committing an offense must realize his or her folly, and the anguish that it has caused. S/he must understand, or made to understand, the extent of suffering that was caused by the action, and based on the understanding, deep remorse or repentance must be felt. Such remorse could be 'put on' or acted out, but usually such an act can easily be recognized. Then, the person who was subjected to the crime has the privilege of "forgiving" the one who committed the crime.

It is my sincere belief that there is a universal law of karma that is always active. Every action has a consequence. Our actions are recorded on a "videotape" that is our consciousness. Judeo-Christian and Islamic cultures believe in a judgment day, which is the day of reckoning. Hindu and Buddhist thought believes that our actions cumulatively affect our karma which powerfully influences what happens after death, affecting the destination of the mind after death, into one of heavenly or hellish realms, or as a third possibility, being recycled into earthly rebirth. For them, 'judgment' happens at the time of death and the forces of Karma come into play. They do not believe that they will lie in graves waiting until judgment day. There may indeed be numerous factors influencing karmic consequence, such as prior good deeds, the influence of heavenly beings, the influence of the spirits of those affected by the actions of the person, such as someone murdered, and so on. These can argued or debated, but the fact remains that karma is real. Those who believe in judgment day should accept that there is a "record" of our deeds- such a "record" constitutes part of what is called karma. Either we can forgive the assailant who attacked us, or stew in our own anger and resentment against the person. Harboring such resentment impairs judgment, and affects our health adversely. It is up to us to decide on a course of action. Those who wronged us have made an imprint on their karma. They will most certainly pay for the karmic consequence for their deeds. That is their problem, not ours.

It is possible, indeed likely, that a wave of extreme liberalism could develop if "forgiveness" is indiscriminately carried on. To avoid this happening, the laws of the land must be constantly evaluated and re-evaluated to make sure that they are meaningful. Prison duration must be appropriate. Indiscriminate "early parole" makes a mockery of the justice system.

I believe in the reincarnation of evil. That, to me, is a logical explanation for the severity of evil behavior in young children. There are reports of eight year olds shooting their parents to death. Capital punishment, then, does not truly rid the earth of the evil that it wishes to destroy. Good riddance, we mutter, after we have just executed a death row inmate. But putting such a person to death without offering a chance for redemption with prayer and meditation perpetuates the evil in that person's mind during its next incarnation. Death sentences, then, are meaningless, but so are lifelong jail terms without the offering of spiritual support. The criminal's own religious preference must be honored. However, there are numerous instances where awareness meditation has made dramatically positive impact on prison inmates. Spiritual awareness cannot be enforced on anyone, but I believe that spiritual leaders ought to be allowed to speak to inmates, allowing them to make a choice of the path they wish to follow.

To summarize, therefore, implementation of justice for criminals must not be based on either hate or revenge, but done in acts of carrying out the laws of the land. We who live in the United States must be so thankful that the founding fathers chose to make cruel and inhuman punishment such as cutting off of hands totally unacceptable and wrote it into the Constitution. Along with firm implementation of justice, the rest of us would be well advised to pray for the minds of criminals to obtain divine healing and for our own minds to use prayer and meditation to develop deep understanding as discussed above. Metta, a Buddhist term which I like to call 'radiant friendliness,' which Buddhist writers like to call 'loving kindness,' is an important state of mind to develop. An effective system of dealing with crime would therefore involve:

1. Constant re-evaluation of our laws providing not just fair prison terms but spiritual and psychological support and guidance.
2. Prayer for criminals that the Greater Power may help them understand their erring ways.
3. Prayer and meditation to be learned by criminals to help them redeem themselves.
3. Prayer and meditation for those of us, or surviving friends and relatives, who have been subjected to crime of any kind, to learn to release the accumulated hate and aversion for the perpetrators.

Transcending Sensuality

Ode to an Angel

Wilt thou allow, sweet lady, this poet's adoration to flow as a river,
Celebrating thy celestial beauty and charm?
Or paint a picture, perhaps, a portrait so perfect,
Of a living Mona Lisa?

Or wilt thou perhaps allow him to hold thy hands to his eyes
In gratitude to providence for the fortune
Of thy presence, thy grace, and friendship?

For above so slender and tender a vine like waist does arise,
The supreme blossom that is your heart.
A fresh camellia more rare, than all the blossoms of the
Gardens of Babylon.

Thy swan like neck does hold, thy face so precious to behold.
Not even a warm harvest moon comes even close in radiance,
Enveloped by tresses of lovely raven hues.

A WAY OF BEING

The moon fades to shadow beneath your eyes like stars,
Stars like diamonds from which yet shine
Rainbow hues dark and bright, the deepest blues of despair,
Crimson red passion, and peace, green like leaves,
Fluttering in the breeze.

Ah, the poet could lie basking in this sunshine for ever,
But is drawn to those lovely lips that are rubies set in pearls.
But nay, no rubies could compare to sweet cherries supreme
Whose essence is the sweetness of nectar, of ambrosia of the gods.

Wouldst thou not grant this poet a touch, a kiss, of thy sweet essence,
That would awaken the sleeping prince, to bring him to life, to
awakening,
To know joy that knows no bounds, forever in your sweet presence?

Written April 28, 1998

It is love that inspires poetry. Lust does not. It is not easy, however, to differentiate between the two, and it is more than possible that love and lust can and do blend together. However, love is giving; lust tries to take. Love flows outward; lust just wants and desires. Love enriches; lust depletes and drains.

Love between man and woman is the ultimate in human interaction. It is a blissful, joyful state. Purists and others that follow ancient biblical or similar directives have forced upon themselves an attitude of guilt about this part of our existence. And sooner or later, the dam breaks loose, and the ensuing action leaves them even more in a state of guilt and confusion. It is a sad state of affairs, because opening ourselves up to love can cleanse us of lust, which is the result of pent-up desire.

Lust never inspired anyone. Or did it? I understand what poets must have felt when their hearts were moved by someone. The result is an outpouring of emotion that becomes translated into beautiful words. Poets did not necessarily have any intimate relationships with people who inspired them; who knows, perhaps it is the unconsummated desire that gives rise to poetry…there may sometimes be only a hazy difference between love and lust.

232

Every once in a while our hearts are touched by someone, who could be either someone close to us or a relative stranger. Such are the ones that inspire us to poetry. It is not just their words; it is the manner, the radiance, and the warmth, which leads you to a high level of comfort near and with them. One cannot help but remember that the human aura radiates outward from the physical body, and this radiance from a loving human being must have such comforting warmth that it is almost magnetic.

When such a person is a stunningly beautiful person, I cannot help but wonder whether this positive response is simply biological, but it is much more than that. There are so many stunningly beautiful people that come by us in life and they often do not elicit any greater response than a mental murmur of "mmm, nice!" and little else. No further thoughts. Not to the extent of the poet who "just saw her passing by and love her till the day I die."

Is it that the aura of such a person just happens to fill a void in ours? Perhaps; not to fill a total void, but little or even large niches here and there, such as the pieces of a puzzle that uniquely fit. Sometimes the pieces of the puzzle only complete part of it; still, our lives are often enriched by others. If we depend on just one person for total fulfillment, there is eventually nothing but severe disappointment, and later-divorce.

It takes quite some knowledge and understanding of the nature of our beings, our composition, to realize our inner nature. In ancient Indian Tantra, the teaching is that the body is composed of five layers or sheaths, referred to as the koshas. Four, really, the fifth being the universal cosmic energy, that really is – God, that wonderful, infinite source of power and comfort, the energy that pervades our every cell and thought. Every living thing on earth actually floats in an ocean of this Spirit. In Tantra it is called the layer of bliss, Änandamaya kosha. In Vedänta, another school of thought, it is called Brahman, or That from which all creation originates. From this deep hidden spirit arises the rest of our being. The next layer, really the layer that actually connects to the Infinite Spirit, is the layer of Intelligence. Enveloping that is the mind layer. Around the mind is the Energy Body layer, the one that radiates the aura. The aura is profoundly influenced by the states of mind. A random reading of the aura, therefore, is as futile as judging a person by the clothes that they happened to wear that day! The energy body is visible to psychics and those who have learned to 'see' it. We sense it, actually,

233

though it is said that the eye can see it as well. Finally, visibly, is the physical body. Saying that there are "layers," however, is in a way an artificial separation. If you place ice chips in a glass of water, they form a "layer" on top, but the ice really does not compose a truly distinct layer. In the same way, these various layers taught in Tantra are really blended without borders into one being.

It is said that it is the energy body that gives out the aura radiating its influence around the person. Upon physical death, the aura remains, along with the other layers, particularly the mind energy layer. It is perhaps the "ghost" that is visible, particularly at night because daylight is overpoweringly bright and hides the energy body from view. Not only is this energy body translucent, but as easily as you can mix clear water and colored water, this energy body can very easily blend into and influence others. Such a blending of mind/energy bodies is likely to be the mechanism of "reincarnation" "possession," and other phenomena. The energy and mind body of the person whose physical body passed away, has no physical means of expression, has not discovered its true inner self. It could have, but has not, discovered either greater celestial beings, or that infinite one power, that it can be with, and therefore chooses to continue its human expression. It finds a growing child, an embryo.

The growing embryo did not need this "rider on the horse," it could have done quite well with the intelligence that it inherited from its parents, and from heaven and earth, but the reincarnating mind energy body has made itself a guest for life! Such understanding so easily allows us to understand such phenomena as past-life recall, child prodigies, and even sexual preference. Mind energy bodies of males don't necessarily reincarnate themselves in male bodies in their "next life." The sexual preference of the reincarnating energy has a powerful influence on the behavioral characteristics of the being in the next life. It appears to me that this "reincarnating" mind only has glimmers of memory and skills of its previous life. Which is why Tibetans have to teach a reincarnating Lama their religion all over again; if not, the child would be born with the full wisdom of the Lama and would not have to be taught anything. The reincarnating mind, it seems to me, is rather like a digital photograph with quite some file corruption, leaving only parts of it visible.

Ah, but I digress! Let's come back to the interaction of the aura between people. We are complex beings. The factors which attract us to each other, and also repel us from each other, can now be understood better. I personally don't believe in the idea of a "soul mate." We have probably had countless loves and hates in our countless lifetimes.

Men can receive soothing, invigorating and healing energy from women, and vice versa. I have been truly blessed with the good friendship of women over the years. I am so thankful that here in the United States, men and women interact in a much more free and natural manner than in the cloistered, sequestered societies of the East. The Old World abides by ancient law. Such law often even prohibits even looking at someone of the opposite sex. It is such a pity because we are all human beings, and can so enrich the lives of others. Restricted society in the east has led to evils such as "eve-teasing," which cost the life of one of my young cousins. And as I have said above, the opposite sex very often has the most positive influence on us. Think of how brothers or sisters, cousins, aunts or uncles, have been such a wonderful part of our lives. When we make friends, it is often with couples, not necessarily with just the man or woman. The spouse then becomes a friend too, and can and will become a delightful part of the friendship.

There can be a state of relationship between a married man and another woman, which is neither a platonic friendship nor an affair. It is a loving, intimate relationship, but without being sexual. I dislike the word "flirtation;" it is just too flighty a word, does not indicate that there is any genuine emotion in the relationship. There are authors who feel that flirtation is a good thing, and is harmless; I am not sure at all. The word loving friendship seems more appropriate.

What if a sexual interest then develops? There are religious books that state dogmatically that you have committed adultery if in your mind you had any lustful ideas. My, oh my, most of us would be in penitentiaries if judges could read minds. The religious texts admonish that we not be lustful, and strongly advise against what they call "sexual misconduct." I imagine that they simply mean that we "shall not either look or behave lustfully with anyone aside from our spouse." The spouse, being, of course, the one whom, legally and lawfully, in the view of God and man, we have chosen to marry. But aside from such stern admonition, these religious texts just don't go far in teaching us the way to get to the root of such "misconduct" and the way to be purified from the heart out. It is like setting food down in front of a person and say, "don't eat." Adultery is perhaps as ancient as the institution of marriage itself. It has been considered a sin in most societies, and yet is very prevalent. I submit that all ideas of "sin" have generated by humans in order to have a peaceful orderly society. Western missionaries arriving in the South Pacific had been stunned with the extent of sexual permissiveness in those islands, and yet people there had been free of strife. This strongly suggests that our customary concepts pertaining to pre-marital and extra-marital sex have been generated by religious traditions simply to fit existing ideas of an eternal bond between a man and a woman. Such a bond is ideally required for the proper raising of children. Adultery committed by a married person is a sin in the mind of society, particularly in the mind of the spouse who feels betrayed. There is no 'punishment in hell' for adultery, but there surely is a hell on earth to be obtained by it. This is why the inclination for adultery must be transcended.

One of the teachings of what was called left-hand Tantra, an esoteric practice from India dating back a thousand years, is that sexuality does not rule out spirituality. A ritual practice of Tantric practitioners would involve five elements, or "sacraments:" fish, meat, intoxicating drink, food grain, and sexual intercourse. A man choosing to be initiated would be so initiated sexually by an adept. The sexual aspect is but one aspect of Tantra, however. And there is absolutely no need to venture into Tantra as an initiate to attain transcendence from addiction to sensuality. It is adequate to know the essence of Tantric teaching. The practice is one of *awareness and transcendence of craving.*

We need to find a way out of this sensual senselessness. There was once a documentary on public television about a species of monkey that is very sexually promiscuous. For these monkeys, sex is the way out of anger, irritability, boredom, or whatever mentally ailed them! The link to human behavior was unmistakable. What is "adultery," after all? Simply this: we humans have created a rule that we shall never be sexually involved with anyone aside from the one that we have publicly, legally, chosen in the eyes of our society. Yet our biological nature is primate-like. And temptation walks by us every day. Down the street, or down the runway on modeling shows, display of sexuality is commercially rampant. And we are supposed to get more and more layers of some kind of veil around our eyes to deal with it, but that does not work. Besides, I see woman adorned as one of the supreme creations of nature. It is ridiculous to deem display of female attractiveness as sinful on the one hand, and allow exploitation of it commercially on the other. Commercial dogma using sensuality in TV and magazines appears to be: "Reveal thy cleavage, girl, and they shall cleave unto your product." The Islamic veil is the extreme opposite reaction.

The way out is to practice "awareness of sensuality." This can only effectively be learned *after we understand* the meditative practice of awareness meditation. In this practice, called by different names such as mindfulness, one starts developing an intuitive awareness of all the fleeting phenomena that we are. It is an awareness of our bodily states, awareness of our breath, awareness of our thoughts, feelings and emotions, *as they happen.* It is an art to be learned, cultivated. And if you think it is against your religion to learn meditative practice, you can continue being controlled by the ignorant that make rules for you that cry out to be broken. Besides, I can't see a single sentence in religious books that teach against it. It's just that we've been taught to avoid any practice that was not written in our "holy books."

Awareness practice is the antithesis of fantasy. We need to readily admit that our magazines and movies keep us in fantasy land most of the time. And commercialism of sensuality accentuates this fantasy beyond all apprehension. Seldom do we realize how freedom of speech has got us to become slaves of sensuality. But freedom of speech is here to stay in the west, thank goodness. But that still does not get us out of the mess. Only awareness practice does. It might help avoid the fantasy expressed in this poem of mine:

For we dream of forever

He did but see a fleeting shadow and glance of her.
A wondrous sight she was, to see.
Lovely as the blooms of the garden around.
A fantasy did flower in his imagination,
Of a delightful, dreamy nymph.
Delicate, fragile, yet lively and joyful.
With the best of all human qualities.
Soft, and yielding, yet of character and charm.
Gentle of temperament, soft in speech.
Considerate, graceful, and witty.

But she had only just passed by in a haze
Not to return for what seemed a millennium.
Great expectations, yet to be fulfilled.

Would she be the same, or
Was it just an illusion?
Will the yielding branch harden with eventual intolerance?
Or stay forever in a state of tranquil flexibility?
Would those sweet lips of gentle surrender
Harden in resolute non-compliance?
Would those beautiful eyes, open in love
Show the strain of distrust, of despair?

Wonder not, whispered the trees of the forest,
For with every spring we turn green anew
To again bring the blessed awareness that
Love, forbearance and tranquility
Will forever blossom anew.

Raja Bhat, written July 11, 1992

It is very difficult to describe the transcended state of awareness. It is one that has created all those rapturous songs and poems about God that mystics have written based on what they experienced and described. The rest of us admire such work if we share those religious beliefs, or look at it with contempt if it does not. Ramakrishna the mystic used to wax lyrical about the goddess Kali, whom some adore; and yet others are repulsed by the image of her tongue dripping blood. We may not achieve the rapturous states of mystics, but awareness practice is something that each and every one of us can learn. It leads to such deep peace of mind, which once explored and discovered, there is no living without it.

The next time you see an object that appeals to you as sensual, particularly a magazine photograph, set it aside for the practice later. And it does not have to be a magazine devoted to sensuality, either! These days, the amount of raw sensuality used in advertising of perfumes in most women's magazines is amazing. For the practice, you need a few minutes of privacy, just you and the object of sensuality. Gaze in a relaxed, attentive manner at it. Start developing awareness of your breath as you so sit. Typically the breathing is fast in an aroused state. As you deepen the practice, you soon become aware of the ability to let the breath calm down despite being steeped in the practice. Watch your entire body and mental state. If the body is aroused, just let it be so. But you must not physically stimulate yourself in any way, as the practice is ruined if you so do. Just keep awareness. Let the mind just flow with all its attachment, its intense desire and attraction to the object. Keep watching the breathing and you may just find that it speeded up again. No matter; just watching it alone will allow it to settle. And just simply watching your whole being in its state of interest, or arousal, will allow your whole being to settle down along with the breath. There are no judgments to be made during this practice, no self-criticism, because that would defeat the purpose. The idea is to just start becoming aware of just how deep our attraction is, to what we find to be sexually attractive. Such awareness practice allows us to transcend such attraction. Not eliminate, but to transcend.

The next step is to start practicing such awareness in the intimate life. Meditation is not to be learned by sitting in a forest and hiding from life. If we practice a meditatively aware state during romantic times with our spouse or loved one, we will discover our inner depths, and realize what attracts and repels us. This is crucial to help us maintain the monogamous state that not only society demands but also what we personally require. It is a state of continuous flow of energy into the loved one. We will discover sooner or later that sexual interaction must be considered the most intimate and deep connection between man and woman. And we then will discover the real meaning of Chinese Taoist and Indian Tantric teachings. That total union, of mind, emotion and body, between man and woman is an ecstatic state. To say that such a state is divine would be heresy to anyone but Taoists and Tantrics. But it can only become divine if it is consistently between the same two people life long. Promiscuity breaks away from the sanctity of such a state. In any case, a deepening state of such awareness makes even the idea of promiscuity something you just laugh at, as something arising from a state of ignorance. There are various views about celibacy; I see such views as simply just ideas generated in someone's mind. I really cannot see anyone becoming wise in the ways of the world unless they have been through it themselves. In the Indian scheme of things, Käma is one of four states of being. Käma simply means love but usually refers to all the sensual activities in life. The other three are Artha, pertaining to right interaction with wealth and possessions; Dharma, the right manner of religious and lawful life; and Moksha, the state of attaining immortality and freedom from death and rebirth. All are integrally connected factors of life. Immortality is not something that is fervently hoped and prayed for, but something that is to be achieved as a state of deep peace and understanding that only the right practice can help one attain. And that practice, in my understanding, is awareness practice, which as it deepens and bears fruit, will also help develop deep states of bliss.

There are so many yogis and spiritual guides who have fallen from grace, because they broke rules of either celibacy or monogamy—rules they created themselves. In other words, they created a trap, and then fell into it themselves. Roman Catholic priests are not allowed to marry, and that is well known. There are also cults within Hinduism where the monks do not only marry, but are not allowed to even interact with women. Sadly, in such cults women are required to serve and yet have to sit in the back of halls or even away from the sight of the monks if they preside over a meeting. Those who did make such rules obviously did not discover the inner meaning of the rules themselves and fell prey to temptation out of ignorance. They may have attained yogic powers, manifested Siddhis (supernatural achievements such as the ability to levitate, radiate light, have a healing touch, etc.), but biological craving goes to the root of our being, and such gurus never did truly reconcile themselves to that reality. In other words, the *idea* that 'celibacy is essential for the attainment of spirituality' is simply that- just an *idea*. It has no basis in reality. A guru should teach that if we allow our greater consciousness to guide us, we will find the right way. 'Sexual misconduct' is entirely in our conceptual minds: this becomes evident when we see that some societies consider polygamy to be perfectly acceptable.

It is my view that a way of being is being true to what we are biologically. Yet, we are not under the guidance of the dictates of holy books, but under the guidance of the greatest guide of all, our inner wisdom. So we must start exploring awareness practice, or mindfulness. I assure you with the deepest sense of sincerity that you will richly reap the reward, which is a state of total involvement with all that life offers, a wonderful state of being in it but yet above it. It is a state of total and complete freedom; a state where we personally rediscover the laws of nature, and blend it into the laws of man. Premarital attraction to the opposite sex is very natural, and yet there are countless Islamic societies which abhor the phenomenon, and have killed young innocent girls who simply for just talking to boys, calling it an act of dishonor. Crimes of honor are often condoned in such societies, and the world needs to speak up against such abomination. Extra-marital attraction is equally natural, but is destructive to society, so dealing with it requires awareness and mindfulness. I love a situational comedy where a husband and wife are on the beach, and an attractive girl in a bikini goes by. The husband gazes admiringly at the girl, and the wife pours a bucketful of water on his head; not in anger, but in good humor. Awareness helps us realize the arising of desire, and the need to play with it in our minds, but not become steeped in it. Just as long as there has been a socially organized institution of marriage, there probably have been times when men or women have broken their vows and sought out other relationships. Typically the reason people do so is to find elsewhere what they have come to miss within marriage, intimacy, friendship, that close loving feeling. Arguments and disagreements often cause lasting spells of aversion, which can lead to other relationships.

If anyone is to say that it is either right or wrong for a married person to become sexually involved with someone else, such an opinion would be just opinion. The matter is extremely complex. It is probably a deep biological instinct, but is socially unacceptable. An intimate relationship with someone else will, in all likelihood, be destructive to the marriage. People involved in an affair would typically spend their lives with their minds elsewhere, and that would not be compatible with a mindful life. The human mind being what it is, possessive and egotistical, the spouse who discovers the affair is bound to feel betrayed, enough to cause life-long hurt. Divorce is very painful to children and friends. The turmoil that subsequently develops ought to make us stop and think whether it is truly that essential that we seek out and establish another relationship. I have known married women who felt severely emotionally deprived because of an alcoholic and abusive husband, and did find comfort elsewhere. Having been "unfaithful" for awhile, they wind up marrying the other person after obtaining a divorce from the abusive husband. Who are we to judge the woman in any way? Our limited minds just cannot seem to allow for a full spectrum of human activity.

The aversion that develops following arguments and disagreements can be meditatively recognized to be just that, persistent aversion. Realizing and stating that one is in such a state may just be the beginning of a corrective process. It is far less painful than the state of marital breakdown. I have seen just too many people leave a spouse who everyone else thinks is a wonderful person, find someone else, be happy for a couple of years, and then wind up in the same state as before. The grass that appeared greener turns out to be scorched earth, all over again.

For a married person, a valuable method of dealing with and transcending attraction to another person is *attitude:* that of neither

241

being obsessed with desiring nor a constant dwelling in the fear of consequences. Perhaps a neutral state could be called 'non-desiring.' This would be roughly similar to the 'middle way' as taught by the Buddha. Until understood, it is a seemingly strange approach. 'Desire' is easily understood; by 'non-desiring' I refer to a balanced awareness of both the desire as well as the fear of consequences. There is an inherent conflict involved, that goes deeper and deeper into a conditioned state of being that is the trap keeping us from a joyful state. So if desire arises, the mind should quickly jump to the state of 'non-desiring.' And in-between state would seemingly be a lifeless, passive state of just existing, taking no interest in anyone for fear of consequences. It is not, and it need not be. It is a state of pure, guileless love. It flows, it gives, it does not want or take. The object of desire now turns into a receptacle of flowing energy. There is indeed a state of connection between a man and a woman where such mutual flow of energy occurs. It could be called a non-physical Tantra. Tantric practitioners involve themselves with a partner who is not necessarily the spouse. For most of us, however, venturing to "connect" physically with someone else is fraught with social and marital disaster. Therefore, cultivation of spiritual intimacy between man and woman in marriage is the ideal way to avoid attraction developing elsewhere. The ultimate in marriage therefore is spiritual union. The flow of such a river of spiritual energy helps wash away the stains of desire elsewhere.

Therefore, in my view, friendship between men and women is to be encouraged. However, for those of us who are married, it would be essential to pretend that our spouse is present when for instance having tea or a meal with a friend of the opposite sex. The sanctity of the relationship with the spouse must be maintained in mind. Yes it is easy for such a friendship to deepen further into a deeper physical connection. The best way to deal with that is to remember the hurt that the spouse would feel when s/he comes to know of what occurred. The act would probably be unacceptable, or 'sinful' to the other person. In an Islamic society which approves of a man having three wives, it is taken as a matter of course when a man finds attraction to a second woman and brings her into the home. In most societies today, however, such behavior is not only illegal but just totally unacceptable to anyone's mind. An act that causes social turmoil and upset is just not worth doing. The principle of 'ahimsa' is that of not-hurting. This principle requires that we not hurt the feeling of someone else, particularly our spouse, by an extra-marital affair.

A Way of Being, then, is for us to understand ourselves more fully. A way for us to understand our attractions and aversions; a way for us to transcend them. All that glitters is not gold; wisdom is to not let aversion for the man or woman we have married to sow the seed for desire and attraction to someone else. And once settled in that state of understanding, to allow our spiritual nature to develop, and thus deepen the bond between man and woman, husband and wife, lover and beloved.

Mindful Eating

Many of us are quite frustrated with the "diet du jour," meaning whatever is in dietary fashion. One time its low fat, another time its low carbohydrate. So we go with one, then the other, lose some, gain it back, lose some more, gain much more back, and so on. There is but one way to attain and maintain weight loss, and that is to consistently burn off with activity and exercise, as much or more than we consume as calories. Having studied and explored various diets, I have found that the best diet is what I call a "straight from nature" diet. Most of what we eat needs to be unprocessed or only minimally processed. Such a diet is low in bad fat and bad carbohydrate, and rich in good carbohydrate and good fat. So it is neither low fat nor low carb. Fresh fruit for breakfast, balanced meals with veggies, beans, lentils, nuts and seeds, low-fat dairy products, and keeping animal sources such as meat or chicken, preferably fish, as only a small part of the meal. I am a lacto-vegetarian. The only supplements I take are a multi-vitamin and one or two flaxseed oil capsules a day as a good source of Omega-3 fatty acids. While exploring Yoga and meditation some years ago, my desire for meat (for me anything that moves is meat) suddenly dropped away, and I've been a vegetarian ever since. Harvey Diamond, author of the book *Fit For Life* preaches vegetarianism, or at least a "mini-meat" diet minimizing animal sources.

It would seem easy to follow this sort of diet, but actually it is not. The attraction for sugar and refined carbohydrate and saturated fat is enormously strong. Perhaps this is a cultivated thing, starting from childhood when we are rewarded with candy for being good. Or perhaps we do indeed have receptors in the brain which can only be appeased with sugar or saturated fat. Have you ever met anyone who has a craving for cucumber and carrots? No; we only crave the bad....the "good" stuff. Therefore, developing a state of awareness of this craving is essential to long term weight maintenance. Meditative awareness during eating will help us develop a deep appreciation for food and respect for the fact that food is life, gives life, and is derived from life. Overeating is an act of aggression. In between eating, if we get an attack of craving, mindful awareness that we are craving will significantly help the craving to go away. Or, we can mindfully sip on water or some other non caloric beverage, or even pieces of fruit or vegetable along with water, as part of a mindfulness practice. Tiruvalluvar, the ancient South Indian sage, wrote in the Tirukkural that the best way to maintain health is to wait until previously eaten food is fully digested before eating again. If we allow genuine hunger, and not craving, to direct our eating, we will have begun a lifelong program of weight maintenance.

It is important to remember that eating is the most primordial act of aggression in ensuring our survival. Life must feed on life. That being the case, we need to minimize this aggression to the level of maintaining our lives, and not to the level of indulgence. Perhaps this poem will be a reminder of this fact:

May we be ever thankful, dear God,
For our food, our life and all your blessings.
Bountiful is the earth your creation;
You have given in abundance
And ask nothing in return.

From the elements did you create us;
With the elements do you sustain us;
To the elements will you return us.

We therefore ask, dear God,
That you now nourish us with that
True nourishment that is your Spirit.
Raise us beyond the elements, to your sphere.
Nourish and enrich our souls
With your divine eternal presence.
Fill these empty vessels;
May they run over with your Love.

Raja Bhat, Jan 94.

In this section, I'd also like to mention my personal views regarding alcohol. Many people believe that one alcoholic drink a day is beneficial to their health, and believe that the medical profession believes that also. I don't. I believe that alcohol is harmful to health even in small amounts. I personally find that one-third of a glass of wine is acceptable on occasion, simply as a little occasional indulgence. Wine connoisseurs use their sense of smell and taste to appreciate a wine, and usually don't ingest much. Alcohol is metabolized in the liver, and a byproduct of metabolism is acetaldehyde. We know that formaldehyde is used to harden and preserve dead tissues and bodies for anatomical laboratories. Well, acetaldehyde is an aldehyde, too! It is this chemical that makes Asians, many of whom are poorly tolerant of alcohol, experience dizziness, nausea and flushing after an alcoholic drink. It is acetaldehyde that is toxic to the heart and liver. Therefore, alcohol is unhealthy. Alcohol killed Chogyam Trungpa, a Tibetan Buddhist teacher, who believed that he had transcended sensual indulgence, especially alcohol. However, he really did not; he consumed enough alcohol to succumb to it eventually.

A way of living, a way of being, a way of healing

Our inner center is our birthright. It is unborn, and will survive our death. However, it does not belong to us, we belong to it. The mind may think it owns a body, from which all ego-related problems arise. However, the mind fails to realize that it owns nothing; it takes nothing with it at the time of death. This realization is the beginning of freedom. A state of mind-quietness is the origin of healing. We do return to this state when we are in dreamless sleep, but it is important to allow this peaceful state to prevail in as much of our waking state as possible. With practice, we will find that we can allow it to prevail right in the middle of activity. This is the practice of mindfulness. Unfortunately, obsession with the very concept of mindfulness can itself be a distraction. We can become simply "full of mindfulness," at which point we "stink of Zen," as a Zen master once said. Perhaps the practice could be called Inner Self Radiance, or Transcendental Awareness, or whatever. As long as it is not misunderstood, the phrase mindfulness is, in my view, the best, particularly because it gives credit to its founder, the Buddha.

The inner/greater Mind is the healer; it is the Consciousness of God. It will always guide you in the right direction. It will not fail, if you allow it to prevail! We go through life in a state of high alert, with the mind extremely busy. This constant cascade of thoughts causes a constant cascade of destructive chemicals throughout the body, impairing immunity, and causing delayed or failure of healing. This leads to disease, which is a state of dis-ease, a lack of rest to the mind and body. Primary care doctors have come to notice that a majority of diseases in the West and in the urban East, originate with stress, and they call them psychosomatic disorders. Skin rashes, colonic disorders, hypertension, asthma, rheumatoid arthritis, back pain, the list is endless. Unfortunately, most people don't recognize that their mind and body are in this high-alert state, and often deny feeling stressed. It becomes the "normal" state of mind. Dr. Samuel Mann, author of the book *Healing Hypertension* found that many hypertensive patients, even when appearing obviously tense or stressed, denied that they were feeling any stress. When the mind is in a high-alert state, the entire body's musculature becomes taut and strained, with a significant increase in muscle tension. This state leads to elevated blood pressure, and eventually leads to destructive disease of the joints as well. Stretching of the muscles as part of a physical exercise program is valuable if are to prevent musculo-skeletal disease, but the muscles will quickly return to a state of high tension if we do not practice relaxation in action. Such a relaxation can only come if we allow our inner center to prevail, no matter what we do. It becomes a state of "spiritual coherence." As mentioned in the chapter *A Way Inward,* Dr. David Servan-Schreiber in his wonderful book *The Instinct to Heal* has revealed most dramatic improvements in the physical, emotional and social health of participants who undergo cardiac coherence bio-feedback methods. The core method is heart-centered meditation, with positive imagery and a sensation of air entering the heart and causing healing. The variation in heart rate is monitored, and the computer reveals a continuous display of cardiac coherence, which is a state where heart rate variation is minimal, and not chaotic. The meditation method which I have described is quite different, and does not encourage either recollection of pleasant memories, or any kind of visualization. However, a practitioner needs to find his or her preferred method. It's all meditation; whether it is heart-centered or breath-and-body centered, I am convinced that all these methods allow our "heart," which is our inner/greater mind to prevail, and when it does, we will see a dramatic improvement in our feeling of well-being, and in our physical, emotional and spiritual health. Dr. Servan-Schreiber gives impressive figures on such improvement: "In the psychological domain, the figures are equally striking. The proportion of employees who say they are "anxious" most of the time in large corporations declines from 33 percent to 5 percent. Those who say they are "dissatisfied," from 30 percent to 9 percent; those who declare they are "angry" from 20 percent to 8 percent." These are remarkable results indeed. It is time we devote an enormous effort at the start of this new millennium to methods of mind-body coherence and make dramatic improvements to our health and well-being.

I recall one day driving my car and I started sneezing because of an allergy. My mind was feeling quite stressed that morning, anticipating a great deal of work intensity. Then I had an insight about my allergy: could it not be that my mind had once been stressed, while my body was exposed to pollen, my immune system decided that the pollen was what was causing my stress?? It may well have been a reaction similar to that described by Pavlov and his dogs, decades ago. Most days if a fit of allergic sneezing comes over me, I just relax and breathe with calm diaphragmatic breaths, and I feel better. Indeed, I have a "sinus relaxation routine" that works. I hope it will for you, too. Here it is: Close or partially close your eyes. Let the eyeballs relax and look downwards gently. Relax the tension in the forehead muscles. Now in a combined effort, completely relax the muscles of the eyes, eyelids, and forehead, and let those tissues "just drop." Now focus inward a little, and imagine the sinus tissues beneath. Let the sinuses "drop" in a similar manner. Imagine the sinuses just dropping away with every breath as you breathe out. I really believe we tend to lock in tension into our sinuses, and in - such a state they don't have proper blood flow, thereby lowering their defenses against infection as well as increasing sensitivity to allergens. There is also a "head cleansing" technique that works very well. I have taught this to numerous people and they have found it beneficial. Every day, especially in the morning, either at the sink or in the shower, blow out your nose very briskly three to four times. Cleanse out the nostrils with warm water, using the fingers which of course must be washed with soap after. Then gargle the throat briskly three to four times with warm water. Peroxide could be mixed with the water in case of a sore throat, but not otherwise; normal mouth bacteria must not be killed unnecessarily. This head cleansing method really works, as long as it is done regularly, as regularly as brushing your teeth.

It is not just with allergies and sinus problems that deep relaxation helps with the healing process. I am convinced that a stressed hyperactive mind promotes inflammation throughout the body, which in turn generates aging, disease and death. It is known that inflammation plays a big role in the swelling of cholesterol-laden plaque in coronary arteries, which often leads to their rupture causing heart attacks. Stress impairs immunity while at the same time promoting inflammation. Destructive auto-immune diseases such as rheumatoid arthritis, lupus, inflammatory bowel disease, and possibly even cancer, could well have their origins in our "inflamed" minds. It has been shown that white blood cells, taken out of subjects and left in a test-tube and monitored electrically, show immediate responses with emotional distress in the subjects from whom the blood was taken. Such findings have enormous impact on our understanding of disease: until now it was felt that hormones released by the nervous system influence white blood cells, but how do they respond to stress while in a test tube outside the subject?? Obviously, the mind works as an electro-magnetic force like radio waves. The mind's processes, therefore, must be understood if we are to overcome these diseases whose causation is poorly understood. Visualization techniques have been employed extensively to boost immunity in the fight against cancer. I see such methods as playing with a hose while the energy of the inner mind which is as powerful as a waterfall lies untapped within us.

CHAPTER TWELVE:
EPILOGUE

As I look back at all that I have written, one thing becomes clear: I have only just begun on the spiritual path. Much yet needs to be done, and more important, much yet needs to be *undone.* My journey has never taken me to the Himalayas, or to any *teerthas,* places of pilgrimage. I have not practiced asceticism at any time; indeed, regretfully, there has been too much indulgence. However, I now find that the middle road is squarely in the middle of life itself. I find no need for ritual, asceticism, tedious journeys, and other similar preoccupations of the 'holy life.' There is nothing holier than being right where I am doing what I need to do in life. Better my life and karma properly done than a fruitless endeavor to perform what appears to me a more arduous and seemingly more spiritual practice that *appears* more appropriate. My family has expressed concern that I have sometimes looked strained and tension-ridden during my search, and I know that I sometimes carry all my thoughts with me like a backpack, dragging me down. Perhaps I should see that ever word written down is one rock less to carry around in my mind. As seemingly precious thoughts appear, perhaps once written, they could be forgotten. Like precious rain from the heavens, these thoughts cannot be something I cling to; like raindrops, they do some cleansing, and then they are gone, never to return. Others come in their place, but again, must be allowed to settle, perhaps do some good work, and then they in turn are gone. The mind is sometimes barren, and sometimes thought-filled, albeit wisdom laden. Like the legendary cornucopia, it is endless. Still, only from the empty silence of the mind will a never-ending stream of wisdom and insight keep pouring forth: keeping the baggage within eliminates the possibility of fresh renewal, faith and inspiration. Neale Donald Walsch writes in his book *The New Revelations—A Conversation With God*: "All the grandest qualities of God—love, compassion, caring, patience, acceptance, and understanding, the capacity to create and to inspire—are what humanity is all about. Living a life of goodness, rather than just "the good life," is perhaps our goal."

Stephen Mitchell, in his remarkable book *The Gospel according to Jesus* writes: "As a second and contrary example, perhaps the greatest example of patience and meticulousness in the history of religion, I would like to propose Chao-Chou, who lived during the golden age of Zen in the

T'ang dynasty China. He experienced enlightenment in 795, when he was seventeen years old, then remained with his teacher for forty years, refining his insight and gradually dissolving his opacities and character flaws. Zen Master Kuei-shan, his contemporary, describes this process: "Through meditation a student may gain thoughtless thought, become suddenly enlightened, and realized his original nature. But there is still a basic delusion. Therefore he should be taught to eliminate the manifestations of karma, which cause the remaining delusion to rise to the surface. There is no other way of cultivation."

Mitchell then describes how Chao-Chou remained in the monastery for three years after his teacher died, then set out on a twenty-year pilgrimage to hone himself against the greatest masters of his time. He writes: "He said, in words that must have shocked the hierarchical and age-venerating Confucian mind, "If I meet a hundred-year-old man and I have something to teach him, I will teach; if I meet an eight-year-old boy and he has something to teach me, I will learn." Only when he was eighty years old did he feel mature enough to set up shop as a teacher. He taught for the next forty years, and his sayings are a marvel of lucidity, compassion, and humor."

Heating iron up to red heat is not enough; it is only the beginning of the process of developing, of molding, and creation of a useful object from the metal. This process of transformation is vast. It may take a lifetime, several lifetimes. I believe that this process must apply to all of us; there is no separate law for those of different religions or beliefs. Sooner or later, we must all discover that we must start the process of self-transformation.

One important consequence of this discovery is the removal of the fear of death. When Ramana Mahärshi was on his deathbed, his followers implored him not to die. He said, "Where will I go?" That is exactly it; there is no far-away heaven to go to, it is a different realm of existence in and around us. But the mind that does not achieve full realization of the Greater Mind that envelopes it, will continue to suffer after death and can only find solace in continued expression of itself in a new birth. Or an enlightened mind will want to provide solace for those in suffering by continuing to express itself in a new birth. Oh yes, there are heavenly astral realms, but those realms are here and around us, and not separated from the suffering of those on earth. Call them what you will, angels, ancestral spirits, devas, whatever, but these beings are intimately linked with us in some way or other. Nobody is banished to some kind of hell forever.

I know by the deepest intuition that I have found the right path. It is a path that all of us are on, and yet either we do not know it or we have been deluded into thinking that it is somehow different for each of us. If you have waded past turbulent, muddy water, and then found yourself in serene crystal clear water, you don't have to be convinced of the difference between the two. The greatest teachers in the world have all taught, or tried to teach, this path. Yet their followers have consistently misinterpreted such teaching, and created new doctrine.

Although I have made a feeble attempt to reconcile followers of various religions into the understanding that every human being on earth ultimately comes under only one set of rules of law, it is likely that most people will reject this view and follow their own prerogatives as they were taught or indoctrinated into; religion truly takes a powerful hold of its believers. There is some sense of security in staying within the confines of what we are taught and believe. Indeed, aversion and hostility often develops in us when we are confronted with a view that seems quite alien to our beliefs. But unless we realize that all our religions, without a single exception, are based on myth and inspired writings, and not on the actual verbatim words of God, we will keep fighting each other. For me, it has been a tremendous source of relief and rest to ultimately achieve the understanding that it is all myth. This does not mean that I ridicule religion; most certainly not. This realization gives me the ultimate freedom, the ultimate liberation, to personally experience the wonder, mystery, grace and power of God in and around me, never hesitating to question whether some religion or other holds the truth. Indeed, without the deep-down understanding that all religion is based on myth, I could not have achieved a state of real liberation.

In the distant past, it took years of travel to find a good teacher, and further years of residence with the teacher to learn the teachings. In contrast, one can now, using books and the Internet, put in a few months of dedicated study, learn the teachings of various paths, and find one that feels right for us. But we must be wary. There is only one teaching, in my view, that will always stand the test of time: our own minds have all the ability to eventually understand Truth in all its glory. The greatest of teachers tell us that we ought to be our own teacher. But it takes effort. It takes patience. It takes time. And even after great flashes of insight, there is much to be done, honing, polishing, and shining. Even this process must be done correctly, with inner guidance. There is such a thing as too much effort, and that is contrary to the wisdom of the inner mind; as the Buddha taught, the strings on the musical instrument should neither be too lax nor too taut.

Modern journeys use radar and radio and other means of guidance. The guidance on our spiritual journey often seems absent, and we feel lost. But as long as we have deep trust in the inner guidance system that each one of us has built-in within us, we will never be lost. Besides, heaven is spread across the earth: where is there to go?

ABOUT THE AUTHOR

Dr. Raja Bhat, MD is a physician, Board Certified in Internal Medicine. He has been in private practice in Wilmington, North Carolina for over twenty years. Ever since he was a teenager, he has been interested in religion and spirituality, and has read extensively on these subjects, as well as about natural ways of healing. He has found personally that attaining spiritual enlightenment and awareness is extremely simple, and reveals the process in this book. The book helps us personally experience the tremendous wellspring of energy and wisdom within each one of us, and explains how to allow this inner consciousness to guide us in our everyday lives.

CPSIA information can be obtained
at www.ICGtesting.com
Printed in the USA
LVHW042042021219
639194LV00003B/381